Pervasive
Vulnerabilities

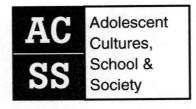

AC Adolescent Cultures,
SS School &
Society

Joseph L. DeVitis & Linda Irwin-DeVitis
GENERAL EDITORS

Vol. 54

This book is part of the Peter Lang Education list.
Every volume is peer reviewed and meets
the highest quality standards for content and production.

PETER LANG
New York • Washington, D.C./Baltimore • Bern
Frankfurt • Berlin • Brussels • Vienna • Oxford

Regina Rahimi & Delores D. Liston

Pervasive Vulnerabilities

Sexual Harassment in School

PETER LANG
New York • Washington, D.C./Baltimore • Bern
Frankfurt • Berlin • Brussels • Vienna • Oxford

Library of Congress Cataloging-in-Publication Data

Rahimi, Regina.
Pervasive vulnerabilities: sexual harassment in school /
Regina Rahimi, Delores D. Liston.
p. cm. — (Adolescent cultures, school and society; v. 54)
Includes bibliographical references.
1. Sexual harassment in education. 2. Girls—Violence against.
3. Bullying in schools. 4. Aggressiveness in children. I. Liston, Delores D.
II. Title.
LC212.8.R34   371.7'86—dc23   2011043825
ISBN 978-1-4331-1280-5 (hardcover)
ISBN 978-1-4331-1279-9 (paperback)
ISBN 978-1-4539-0258-5 (e-book)
ISSN 1091-1464

Bibliographic information published by **Die Deutsche Nationalbibliothek**
Die Deutsche Nationalbibliothek lists this publication in the "Deutsche
Nationalbibliografie"; detailed bibliographic data is available
on the Internet at http://dnb.d-nb.de/.

Cover art by Tasha Liston-Beck and D'Asia Lipsey

The paper in this book meets the guidelines for permanence and durability
of the Committee on Production Guidelines for Book Longevity
of the Council of Library Resources.

© 2012 Peter Lang Publishing, Inc., New York
29 Broadway, 18th floor, New York, NY 10006
www.peterlang.com

Printed in the United States of America

Table of Contents

Chapter 1: Learning Sex in Schools: Sites of Pervasive Vulnerabilities

"I think that if there was more of an opportunity for somebody to talk to, if I felt open enough to go to someone to say this is what is going on. That would have helped." Jocelyn

"Puberty which gives the man the knowledge of greater power, gives to woman the knowledge of her dependence." (Ussher, 1989, p.18)

This work represents a culmination of over ten years of research in which we have sought to examine sexual harassment within the context of young adolescent women's lives. We hope, through this work, to offer a contribution to the work of ending harassment and abuse of young women. Throughout this text we utilize the term 'sexual harassment,' it is deliberate and should serve to remind us of its existence within the lives of young women. However, it is perhaps necessary for the authors of this text to elaborate a bit on what we recognize as sexual harassment. We could use the 'textbook' definition of the sexual harassment provided by the EEOC and cited in this chapter of the book. However, for the purposes of what you will read from our participants, we view sexual harassment as any behavior directed at an individual that highlights sexual difference, gender inferiority or creates an uncomfortable, unsafe or hostile environment. As you will read in the proceeding chapters, there is a great deal of this that goes on in young women's lives. From name calling (daily), to ogling and cat calling in public spaces, to grabbing young women's buttocks in the middle of class, to more violent acts of sexual aggressions such as dating abuse, rape and molestation, sexual harassment is pervasive in the lives of young women. The voices you will hear in this book share very personal accounts of their experiences with sexual harassment in contemporary settings. In the proceeding chapters, stories of women who experienced labeling in school reflect on how those experiences shaped their adulthood, young women recently out of high school reflect on their experiences with harassment (and in some cases abuse), young men who share their perceptions of harassment, from both a heterosexual and homosexual context of experience, and finally, teachers who work with middle and high school students elaborate on their perceptions of their students' sexuality and harassment within their school. Our final chapter will elaborate on the ways in which harassment can be eradicated through a complex discussion of the sexist, gendered nature of harassment itself. Before we share our participants' stories, we feel it is imperative to provide some contextualization to our work. In this chapter, we provide an introduction to the history of sexual harassment, a review of literature on sexual harassment, discussion of prevalence of harassment both peer and teacher harassment. We also provide a brief discussion of media and youth culture, and a brief glimpse into the current discourse surrounding harassment and sexuality education, including cyberbullying, bullying, and sexual orientation. Of course, throughout the book interwoven in each chapter, we rely on other studies as well to highlight all of these pertinent issues and to examine the pervasive vulnerabilities of young women.

History of Treatment of Sexual Harassment in Schools: Policy and the Reality of Sexual Harassment in Schools

Although sexual harassment has existed in schools (just as elsewhere in society), it has not always been recognized by that name, or even recognized as a problem. Prior to the 1970s, when Johnny pulled Sally's hair, it was written off as "boys will be boys." After Title IX legislation passed, things changed. Title IX states: *"No person in the United States shall, on the basis of sex, be excluded from participation in, be denied the benefits of, or be subjected to discrimination under any education program or activity receiving Federal financial assistance..."* (U.S. Department of Labor, n.d., para. 1).

Of course, legislation must emerge from somewhere, and the same is true of Title IX. This legislation emerged as a result of pressure generated from the Women's Movement. The term "sexual harassment" was coined in the 1970s by feminist activists. Crouch (2001) cites Lin Farley as one of the earliest feminists to coin the term. In her work at Cornell University, in which she held discussions with groups of women concerning working conditions, she found emerging from these discussions a common theme involving harassment. This led to the formation of Working Women United in 1975 with the established goal of addressing 'sexual harassment.' In the first survey on sexual harassment distributed by Farley in 1975, sexual harassment was defined as "any repeated and unwanted sexual comments, looks, suggestions, or physical contact that you find objectionable or offensive and causes your discomfort on the job" (Crouch, 2001, p. 42). Crouch notes that this definition is very similar to the definition that is used today in common discourse and that is used by the EEOC (Equal Employment Opportunity Commission):

> Unwelcome sexual advances, requests for sexual favors, and other verbal or physical conduct of a sexual nature constitutes sexual harassment when submission to or rejection of this conduct explicitly or implicitly affects an individual's employment,

unreasonably interferes with an individual's work performance or creates an intimidating, hostile or offensive work environment.(para. 1)

Catherine MacKinnon went on to elaborate the earlier notions of sexual
harassment and in her work, "Sexual Harassment of Working Women"
(1979), she offered the distinction between "quid pro quo" harassment and
"hostile environment" harassment. The former involves a sexual exchange as
a condition of employment, while the latter involves a persistent presence of
harassment within the working environment. The earlier work of these feminist scholars and the expanding concept of sexual harassment have led to
legislation regarding sexual harassment. Although, according to Brandenburg
(1997), there is still debate present regarding how sexual harassment should
be regulated, with some arguing that it is purely an issue of a violation of
Title VII of the Civil Rights Act, and others arguing that it should be pursued
as tort law as invasion of privacy or assault. Nonetheless the feminist movement changed public attitudes. For example, the general public today shows
acceptance of the following, once deemed radical, feminist views: equal pay
for equal work, belief that women should be able to become educated to any
level they desire, and belief that no job is fundamentally a woman's job or a
man's job. Unfortunately, along with these changes came a belief that we
have achieved sex equality. Clearly, as this book will show, there still remain
large issues of sexual inequality as women continue to be victimized by harassment. You will see this in the stories of the young women, the middle
aged women, the teachers and the young men presented in this book. Clearly,
sexual equality has not been achieved, despite the strides that have been
made, and of course, it should be strongly noted that progress has been made.

Of course one extremely important piece of legislation for addressing
sexual harassment has been Title IX legislation. Title IX was put in place to
guarantee equal access to educational resources, and the early years of its
application (1970s and early 1980s) focused on equalizing funding of athletics, particularly in high schools and colleges. By the early 1980s, applications of Title IX were extending from athletics toward sexual harassment
complaints. In 1981 the Office of Civil Rights of the US Department of Education, established guidelines for addressing sexual harassment. According to
their established definition sexual harassment is: 1) sexual in nature; 2) unwelcome; and 3) denies or limits students' ability to participate in or benefit
from schools' education program. As this is the body responsible for enforc-
ing Title IX in the schools, it was mandated that all schools receiving federal
monies must have a sexual harassment policy (Yaffe, 1995). Clearly the tra-
jectory of the applications of Title IX legislation was toward expansion from
limitations in athletics to broader sexual discrimination in schools.

Thus, over time, the clauses related to discrimination began to be applied to the larger educational spectrum, and Title IX was utilized to fight sexual harassment in schools. In the case *Franklin v. Gwinnett County Public Schools*, the Supreme Court determined that students could seek damages under Title IX for gender based discrimination (Short, 2006). Short discusses the decade of the 1990s as a time in which the transformation of "boys will be boys" behaviors into *peer sexual harassment* occurred": "While courts took the better part of a decade to sort out who had what legal rights, schools took the lead in establishing and institutionalizing quasi-legal remedies for sexual harassment in the form of policies and grievance procedures" (Short, 2006, p. 32). As Brandenburg (1997) points out, the establishment of explicit sexual harassment policies and grievance procedures is a very necessary step to eliminating harassment; however, these procedures and policies "should involve all of school constituents and should address both the 'broad climate' within schools and provide specific strategies for addressing harassment" (p. 67). And, as we will unveil through the research in this book, simply having a sexual harassment policy does not adequately address harassment, particularly when the policy is grossly ignored within the schools.

While the studies presented throughout this book provide further support for implementing clear policies and establishing procedures for investigating and responding to sexual harassment complaints, we argue that merely viewing sexual harassment through policy fails to address the underlying constructs of gender and sexual inequality that permeate the culture of schools. We will elaborate on how schools can work to address these larger ideological assumptions as we discuss more specific policy and procedure suggestions in the concluding chapter. For now, it is important to understand the history of policy and the way it has shaped current notions of dealing with harassment in schools. For example, it should be noted that the decade of the 1990s was in many ways the zenith for the development of sexual harassment policies in schools (Marczely, 1993; Rowley, 1999). These policies were developed to provide punitive measures for those who were viewed as perpetrators of sexual harassment.

In 1993, Marczely provided a snapshot of the legal status of sexual harassment in schools. At that time, of the approximately 40 cases of sexual harassment being reviewed by the Supreme Court, just under half were related to incidences taking place in schools. Her review showed that the courts were applying the precedents of cases related to workplace sexual harassment directly to schools. This action held schools more accountable for all forms of harassment within their walls. And policy developers in schools became more aware of the various potential harassment scenarios including those of administrator-to-teacher, teacher-to-student and student-to-student incidents (Marczely, 1993).

By 1999 *Davis v. Monroe County* BOE firmly established Title IX as legal precedent holding schools accountable for incidents of sexual harassment (Chaves, 2000). Following this court decision, many scholars legal experts and administrators encouraged school districts to develop a sexual harassment policy and train staff on how to respond to complaints (Yell & Katsiyannis, 2000; Harrington, 2004). The studies presented in this text clearly show that while sexual harassment policies have been developed in most school districts, the training on how to respond to complaints has remained virtually non-existent, or ineffectual. Clearly, it was becoming transparent that the costs of sexual harassment were mounting and so was the awareness of the general public and school administrators that these costs were not only financial, but emotional and psychological and sometimes even life-threatening. Although the courts and schools established these policies in the decades of the 70s, 80s, and 90s, many of these policies remain on paper only. After the zenith of the nineties, the issue of sexual harassment seemed to become muted.

In 2004 Lisa Harrington published an article in the *Delta Kappa Gamma Bulletin* which exemplifies much of the current discourse on sexual harassment in schools. Most school districts have a policy in place. However, Harrington highlights the remaining need to "investigate *all* claims of sexual harassment, have a person at each school designated to investigate these incidences, and train *all* faculty and staff to recognize and respond to peer sexual harassment" (Harrington, 2004, p. 31). These goals have yet to be accomplished in many school districts. Without proper understanding, training and diligence, sexual harassment can not be eradicated.

So again, although most schools and districts have developed policies, there is still work to be done to eliminate sexual harassment in schools, and reemphasizing policy is but a part of the eradication. As Brandenburg (1997) points out, "sexual harassment is a manifestation of deeply held beliefs, attitudes, feelings, and cultural norms" (p. 39). Simply providing policy can not address all of the complex sociocultural issues surrounding harassment. The next stage following the establishment of policies is to make sure these policies are followed, that the policies address all aspects of the law, are accessible to all school personnel, students and parents, are adhered to consistently, and additionally that there is discussion and discourse surrounding the issues of power that frame sexual harassment. These essential follow up actions are neglected by most school districts.

Recently, Lichty (2008) conducted a study which assessed the sexual harassment policies at 784 primary and secondary schools. This study focused on three main elements: "accessibility to students (ie, via the Internet), consistency with federal guidelines regarding their content and the inclusion of 10 key components, and consistency of content across educational levels" (Lichty, 2008, p. 607). At the time of this study, very few (14%) policies were available online, and therefore not easily accessible by school personnel, students or parents. She also found that "the majority of policies incorporated only 5 of the 10 critical components" and the policies at the elementary schools contained fewer of the "key components" (Lichty, 2008, p. 607). Lichty recommended that schools publish policies online and conduct thorough reviews to make sure that all key components are addressed in sexual harassment policies. Currently, we argue, sexual harassment policies that were established in previous decades by school districts have *not* been revisited, reviewed, or discussed with school constituents. Many of the policies and grievance procedures exist on paper only, but have not made their way into the culture of the school, as can be seen by the frequency with which young women continue to experience name calling, abuse, assault, and an environment of hostility surrounding their sexuality. The revisiting of such policies is especially needed given the ways in which new 21st century modes of communication have provided additional forms of harassment and personal invasion for young women. The new century has ushered in new foci for sexual harassment initiatives: cyber-harassment, bullying and same sex harassment, most of the outdated sexual harassment policies fail to examine these contemporary contexts of harassment. Cyber-harassment, for example, has carried the potential of exponentially increasing the opportunities for and magnitude of trauma for young teens experiencing sexual harassment. With the ever-increasing ease of online publication, harassment has extended beyond the walls of the school. As Stein points out, computers have taken the 'slam book' used to denigrate young girls and provided opportunities for mass distribution of such slander (Stein, 1999). Barak (2005) found that much of the harassment that is found offline is impacting young women online such as gendered harassment, unwanted sexual attention, and sexual coercion. Not just through the social networking that young women are involved in, but even through the sexualized commercials provided through SPAM, and much of this is continued onto school grounds. Scott, Semmons, and Willoughby (2001) discuss how the practice of "flaming" or deliberately being derogatory or verbally assaulting online, creates a hostile environment for young women. Today, those who are victims frequently experience harassment invading their consciousness insidiously: online, on their phones and seemingly being distributed across the globe in record time, we question where school culture and/or policy address these concerns. Green and Adam (2001) found that the in the majority of cases involving cyberstalking the victims are women, making the inclusion of cyberbullying, cyberstalking, and online sexual harassment important for school policies on harassment. Concurrently, same sex harassment and harassment based on (presumed) sexual orientation emerged as a focus for sexual harassment scholars; however, these concerns are not adequately reflected in school policy either. Michaelis (2000) presents an overview of same sex harassment legal cases and precedents. Each of these foci will be discussed later in this chapter as part of the current discourse on sexual harassment.

The history of sexual harassment research clearly shows that what began in tentative steps in the 1970s and 1980s pushing the boundaries of Title IX away from exclusive applications in athletics has been transformed into a multifaceted approach to attacking the pervasive vulnerabilities related to sexual harassment in schools. With a critical examination of social justice issues, we have a great deal left to accomplish. Throughout this book we will be highlighting specific ways in which sexual harassment impacts the lives of students, teachers and others within contemporary middle and high schools.

Prevalence of Sexual Harassment

The prevalence of sexual harassment in schools is difficult to measure. One complicating factor is related to defining sexual harassment. The current, established definition of sexual harassment and one recognized by the courts bears repeating here:

> Unwelcome sexual advances, requests for sexual favors, and other verbal or physical conduct of a sexual nature constitutes sexual harassment when submission to or rejection of this conduct explicitly or implicitly affects an individual's employment, unreasonably interferes with an individual's work performance or creates an intimidating, hostile or offensive work environment. (EEOC, n.d., para. 1)

A related term, gendered harassment has recently entered the literature. Meyer proffers and defines gendered harassment:

> Gendered harassment is defined as any behaviour, verbal, physical, or psychological, that polices the boundaries of traditional heterosexual gender norms and includes (hetero) sexual harassment, homophobic harassment, and harassment for gender non-conformity. (Meyer, 2008, p. 556)

It is important to note, here that, for the purpose of our examination, we have chosen to use the terminology of 'sexual harassment' exclusively. As we mentioned earlier, we recognize the profound impact that same sex, homophobic harassment and harassment for challenging gendered 'norms' has on students. However, this is not the primary focus of our work in this book. We have chosen to most directly focus on the sexual harassment of young women, which is perpetrated primarily by young men. We recognize the gendered power dynamic within these relationships, and since our focus is narrowly defined by these heterosexual relations, we have chosen to primarily define our work in the context of sexual harassment.

> From the research that has been done on the sexual harassment of young women, it is clear that sexual harassment remains a pervasive reality of their lives. Estimates of the prevalence of sexual harassment range from approximately 75% of males and 85% of females to 83% of males and 93% of females. One study completed in North Dakota in 1997 found: High school seniors indicated that 88.1% of the students (83% of the males and 93.3% of the females) had experienced sexual harassment at school. These findings are slightly higher than those found on the national average in a study by the American Association of University Women (AAUW), which indicated an overall total of 81% of the students (76% of the males and 86% of the females) reported that they had experienced sexual harassment (American Association of University Women, 1993). (Stratton & Backes, 1997, p. 163)

Support for these staggering statistics can be observed in studies looking at the microcosm of a few weeks. Walsh (2007) found that about 15% of high school students reported a direct experience of sexual harassment at school during the two weeks prior to taking the survey. According to her participants, nearly half of the incidents reported were "of a physical nature" (Walsh, 2007). Ashbaugh and Cornell (2008) found that sexual harassment was a *common* experience among 6th graders.

Further examination of statistics on sexual harassment also provides evidence that African American and Hispanic girls are more likely than non-Hispanic white students to be victimized by sexual harassment. Miller (2008) in her work examining sexual harassment of young women in urban communities, points out that harassment is endemic with very little recourse available for young women. As we will examine at various junctures in this text, hegemonic notions of race and class continue to plague women of color and add an additional barrier to the eradication of their harassment. As we will note, in particular, as we examine teachers' perceptions, bias regarding the sexuality of women of color serves to veil the harassment they experience.

As we mentioned, the precise prevalence of harassment is difficult to determine. However, the pervasiveness of sexual harassment has led some researchers to abandon statistics in favor of more qualitative assessments. DeLara states, "Bullying or harassment are a part of the everyday experience of many school children in the U.S." (2008, p. 72). Many researchers use terms such as *everyday, common, constant, pervasive, prevalent, and continuous* to gauge the frequency of incidents of sexual harassment. Brown and L'Engle report: "Some surveys have found that sexual harassment such as touching, grabbing, or pinching in a sexual way; pulling clothing off or down; forcing a kiss; or other unwelcome sexual behavior has become *almost normative* in some high schools" (Brown & L'Engle, 2009, p. 134).

As revealed throughout this book, there are a number of ways in which young women are victimized by sexual harassment, both on school grounds and off. In the next sections of this chapter we will provide a general discussion of various forms of sexual harassment faced by young women. In the chapters that follow, we will provide insight into specific experiences and reflections of adult women reflecting on adolescence, young women, young men, and female teachers as they contribute their understandings of/experiences with sexual harassment in schools.

Abuse of Students by School Personnel

For young women, the potential for being harassed permeates their experiences, is a daily possibility, and can be experienced in almost every domain of their lives. While it may be difficult to comprehend, and certainly this is not the most prevalent form of sexual harassment, some incidents of sexual harassment include sexual abuse or harassment of students by school personnel (teachers, counselors, administrators or staff). One early study that explored adult to student harassment was conducted by Shakeshaft and Cohan (1995). This study is one of the *few* that explores abuse of students by school personnel. Their groundbreaking study looked at 225 cases of abuse, and found:

> In over half of the cases (58.8%) the superintendents in our study reported that the district gave no help to the victim. In the remainder of the cases, the victim was offered counseling, although the superintendents were unclear about exactly what services the victims received. In most cases the superintendents believed that, if the abuse had been stopped, the problem was over. Few superintendents seemed to have a clear understanding of the long-term effects of sexual abuse on children and the importance of intervention. (Shakeshaft & Cohan, 1995, para. 71)

This article shows that little is done to deter future incidents of sexual harassment of students by teachers. Of the teachers from Shakeshaft and Cohan's study:

> 38.7% resigned, left the district, or retired; 15% were terminated or not rehired; 8.1% were suspended and then resumed teaching; 11.3% received a verbal or written reprimand; 17.5% were spoken to informally; 7.5% of the accusations turned out

to be false; and 1.9% of the cases were unresolved at the time of this study. (Shakeshaft & Cohan, 1995, para. 59)

Adult to student sexual harassment is as difficult to measure as other forms of sexual harassment. One study, conducted in Canada found that "37.5% of participants… reported being sexually harassed by a teacher while in high school" (Winters, Clift, & Maloney, 2004, p. 249). Although not as prevalent as peer sexual harassment, studies show that adult to student harassment is generally more distressing to students than peer harassment, yet as the research points out, schools provide little help to those young women who experience this type of harassment. Presented in the following chapters, participants articulate examples of harassment from school personnel, indicating that this behavior may be more prevalent than the research literature documents. Presumably, since adults are authority figures, students experience more feelings of betrayal when the perpetrators are their teachers. Timmerman (2002) reported that "Students experience teacher harassment as more upsetting than unwanted sexual behavior by their peers" (p. 397). Teacher harassment may be nonverbal or physical and is more often directed at girls than boys. "Of the 2808 students 512 (18%) reported unwanted sexual experiences at school in the past 12 months: 370 girls (72%) and 142 boys (28%)" (p. 397). In our interviews with adult women and young women and young men, they provided some examples of the harassment of students by adult males in their school buildings, corroborating these earlier studies.

Coaches and Sports

Title IX, the legislation called upon to initiate claims against sexual harassment in schools, was originally focused on athletics. Therefore, it seems appropriate to have a separate discussion of sexual harassment in athletics. Ironically, there is not much research literature addressing this topic. One early study, reported by Lackey (1990) notes:

Although incidents of sexual harassment were reported, female athletes tended to accept the profanity, were concerned with the intrusive physical contacts and demeaning language, but subjectively reported on the questionnaire that they personally (and collectively) did not view sexual harassment as a major problem in women's sports. (Lackey, 1990, p. 22)

Lackey concludes that since these incidents are "accepted" there is not a problem of sexual harassment in sports. We disagree. The level of "acceptance" or expectation surrounding sexual harassment does not excuse the actions, and moreover, this harassment serves to create a demeaning and hostile climate for all young women in the schools.

Another, more recent study (Fasting and Brackingridge, 2009) noted that discussions of sexual harassment are nearly non-existent in education programs for coaches. Contrary to Lackey's conclusions from 20 years before, Fasting & Brackenridge find plenty of data indicating that sexual harassment is a problem in sports. In their study participants were female "elite athletes." The authors note: "Data from interviews with 19 female elite athletes who were sexually harassed by their coaches produced a sport typology that consists of three main types: (1) The Flirting-Charming Coach; (2) The Seductive Coach; and (3) The Authoritarian Coach" (Fasting and Brackinridge, 2009, p. 21). Fasting & Brackenridge go on to discuss this typology and recommend that curricula for coaches include information on the importance, pervasiveness and avoidance of sexual harassment in athletics.

Again, as is revealed through participant responses, the young women and men in our studies confirmed the literature on this topic. Coaches and athletes within the school buildings seem to "enjoy" a certain lack of accountability when it comes to sexual harassment. This is in large part due to the establishment and maintenance of hegemonic masculinity that seems to be protected within the school building (Pascoe, 2007).

Peer Behaviors and Harassment

Adolescence is a time of identity development and the emergence of romantic relationships. Along with these transitions, comes an increase in sexual harassment (Pellegrini, 2001, 2002). Studies show "an increase in sexual harassment from 5th to 9th grade, with boys more likely to report harassment than girls in each grade. An analysis of harassment type indicated no gender difference in 9th grade cross-gender harassment, but boys received more same-gender harassment than girls" (Petersen & Hyde, 2009, p. 1173). Given these findings, it is likely that the prevalence of sexual harassment is even higher than projected. Since girls are more likely to experience sexual harassment, but less likely to report it. Thus, it is important to explore interpersonal dynamics that are in place during these important years.

This section provides an overview of research on romantic relationships in early adolescence and identity development. As research supports, there is a great deal of abuse and harassment that surrounds the dating lives of young women as well. Much of that relational abuse gets carried into school settings. The American Bar Association found that 1 in 5 school girls has been abused by a boyfriend (Durham, 2008, p. 56). The prevalence of this abuse speaks to yet another way in which women find themselves victimized by a culture that seems to promote the sexual aggression of men. These romantic

Pervasive Vulnerabilities

relationships that have often been formulated based on the "romantic script" (Tolman, 1991), which serves to silence desires of young women. Young and Furman (2008) conducted a study of relationship styles, and found that:

> Of the three basic types of relationship styles (secure, preoccupied and dismissing), the dismissing type is more positively correlated with abuse. It is hypothesized that those who are "dismissive" tend to gravitate toward more risky behaviors because they tend to view sex as "an opportunity for exploration and self-gratification. (Young & Furman, 2008, p. 298)

These findings indicate that attachment "type" is better indicator of potential for being a victim of sexual aggression than being abused earlier in childhood. The preoccupied group is also more likely to be victim of sexual aggression than secure type.

In addition to studies of relationship styles, some studies have explored the contexts in which sexual harassment occurs. As Raspey and Murachver (2006) posit, much of adolescents' understanding of sexual behavior comes from the problem with how sex is conceptualized in the cultural imagery as something that girls give and boys experience. Welsh, Rostosky, and Kawaguchi remind us that "adolescent sexuality takes place in the context of institutionalized heterosexuality, gendered power relations, male sexual values" (p. 118). Livingston et al. (2007), for example,

> Identified four contexts in which adolescents were sexually victimized emerged: Within Intimate Relationships, At Parties/Social Gatherings, Abuse by Authority Figures, and While Alone With a Friend. Thematic analysis revealed that inexperience with sex and dating, lack of guardianship, substance use, social and relationship concerns, and powerlessness contributed to adolescent vulnerability within these contexts. (Livingston, Hequembourg, Testa, & VanZile-Tamsen, 2007, p. 136)

In addition to these four contexts identified by Livingston et al. it appears that poverty correlates positively with "fear of sexual harassment, coercion and rape" (Popkin, Leventhal, and Weismann, 2010, p. 715). Miller found that the "odds that a woman will experience intimate sexual violence is 1/3 higher for members of disadvantaged communities" (p. 7). Brandenburg (1997) has also written how members of marginalized groups are much more likely to experience harassment in schools. Even if the harassment is not more prevalent, according to our research, teachers seem to view the harassment of marginalized groups as less worthy of attention, and males in our study indicated that these young women were "fair game."

Poverty has also correlated positively with early entry into puberty and "problem behaviors." Goldstein found that "teens who associate with and engage in 'problem behaviors' are also at risk for sexual harassment. Also, girls who enter puberty early are at higher risk for sexual harassment than girls who mature later" (Goldstein, Malanchuk, Kean, & Eccles, 2007, p. 209). Early maturation can be problematic for young women. Duncan (1999) found that girls' early development of breasts is viewed as their sexual maturity and is viewed by some girls as a threat to their safety as there is an awareness of the potential for harassment and violence against their bodies. Girls are often plagued with reminders about the danger that exists in their lives through parental warnings, teachers' comments and reminders from peers and others. This too will be illuminated in the proceeding chapters.

Based on studies, adolescents face a range of risk factors from "inexperience with sex and dating" to "being sexually active"; from "being powerless" to "being a bully"; and from having a "preoccupied relationship style" to having a "dismissive relationship style" (Young & Furman, 2008). It seems, young women need to avoid the poles of these spectrums and attempt to walk the middle line. This requires opportunities to discuss relationships and discussion of pertinent issues related to their romantic involvement; opportunities not often available to them. Additionally, factors beyond their control such as living in poverty, and previously experiencing sexual aggression or abuse increase their continued risk for sexual harassment. Further, the stressors common to adolescence exacerbate their risk. As adolescents, developmentally struggling with identity concerns and at higher than average risk for depression, they also have an increased risk for alcohol and drug abuse. Their feelings of powerlessness or sensitivity regarding how others perceive them also increase their risks. With all of these stressors and factors increasing their risk for experiences of sexual harassment, the staggering statistics of 85-90% of teens reporting incidents of sexual harassment are validated, and further confirmed by the participant responses that will be presented in subsequent chapters.

Youth Culture and Popular Media

Since the advent of television and even radio, urban legend has held that media and popular culture spur adolescents on to aggressive and violent behaviors. Intuitively, teachers, preachers, news reporters and others point to the latest media as inciting negative attitudes and leading to destructive behaviors. Some forms of expression are considered more virulent than others – rock and roll was the culprit in the 1950s, and hip hop and BET are considered major culprits today. Video games (especially games like Grand Theft Auto) also get on the radar of corruptors of teens. However, we would be remiss to not mention the ways in which popular media has framed issues of sexuality for young women and the way in which the current youth culture mediates some of this imagery. Durham (2008) points to the for profit media which constructs girls' sexuality as commodity. Girls themselves, as revealed in this study are critical of the way in which media construct the scantily clad adolescent. Yet they also seem torn between the peer pressure to look sexy and the risk of being perceived as *sexual*.

While it is difficult, if not impossible, to establish direct connections between media and violent or destructive behaviors, some studies do show correlations. For example, Brown and L'Engle (2009) state: "Adolescents who used sexually explicit media also had more permissive sexual norms, had less progressive gender role attitudes, and perpetrated more sexual harassment activities compared to their peers at baseline" (Brown & L'Engle, 2009, p. 139). In their study of adult males, Dill Brown and Collins found:

> A significant interaction indicated that men exposed to stereotypical content made judgments that were more tolerant of a real-life instance of sexual harassment compared to controls. Long-term exposure to video game violence was correlated with greater tolerance of sexual harassment and greater rape myth acceptance. (2008, p. 1402)

These findings make Yaffe's observation all the more poignant:

> [Today] even the bumper stickers are obscene. Lyrics on MTV are X-rated but available for all to see and hear. Movies and television programs contain violence and exploitation unimaginable just a generation ago. Sports heroes are convicted of rape; others boast of sexual exploits with thousands of women. Even the President of the United States is not immune from seamy lawsuits. No expletives are deleted anywhere anymore. (1995, para. 122)

To further the examination of the potential influence of media on harassment and sexual aggression, Durham (2008) found that that girls that were engaged in profound amounts of viewing music videos, were more likely to be part of and not leave after sexual violence.

Thus, although we cannot make direct connections between violent video games, BET or hip-hop culture and incidents of sexual harassment, we also should not dismiss the overall impact of continual exposure to and adulation of violence, aggression and rape. As we will argue throughout this book, in the context of addressing harassment, it is important to discuss the sociocultural context in which violence exists. Giving students opportunity to engage in critical media literacy is one way, we argue, that educators can help students combat abuse and harassment.

Impact of Sexual harassment on Girls and Boys:

The impact of sexual harassment on girls and boys is pervasive. This impact is usually "directly and negatively" experienced for girls and "indirectly and negatively" experienced for boys (Ormerod, Collinsworth, & Perry, 2008). The list of negative impacts is long and telling. These negative impacts include: decreasing self-esteem (Polce-Lynch, Myers, Kliewer, & Kilmartin, 2001); "not wanting to go to school, talking less in class, having difficulty paying attention, feeling embarrassed, losing sleep and self-confidence, and changing behavior – classes, seats, routes home, even friends" (Yaffe, 1995, para. 53); avoiding spaces on school campuses where harassment typically occurs, limiting participation in extra-curricular activities, limiting enrollment in non-traditional courses (Larkin, 1994); undermining connections and commitment to school (Fineran & Gruber, 2009); "drop in grades, loss of appetite, nightmares, feelings of isolation from family and friends, and nervousness and anger" (Klusas, 2003, p. 91); and experiencing OBC (objectified body consciousness) in girls (Lindberg, Grabe, & Hyde, 2007). OBC is a manifestation of heightened awareness of being watched that results in a third person external observation of one's own body rather than an internal awareness of how one's own body feels or what one's own body can do.

The intersection between this list and the list of risk factors for sexual harassment is telling. As students experience sexual harassment their self-esteem drops, they feel isolated, nervous and angry. This often leads to feelings of "sensitivity," "fear of rejection" and "powerlessness" – items on the list of risk factors for sexual harassment. Thus, negative impacts on the girl or boy who experiences sexual harassment generates an exponential increase in risk factors for continued sexual harassment and a cycle is begun that can spin out of control for the victim of this abuse.

Yaffe notes, "Students of both sexes report the same debilitating impact of harassment, but the effect on girls seems to be more profound and longer lasting" (Yaffe, 1995, para. 53). Girls come to see the sexual harassment as "normal" (Larkin, 1994), and experience OBC (objectified body consciousness) as a result of self-surveillance and peer sexual harassment (Lindberg, Grabe, & Hyde, 2007). "Sexual harassment must be acknowledged as a negative psychosocial school environmental factor of importance for the high degree of psychological ill-health symptoms among girls compared with boys" (Gillander, Gådin, & Hammarström, 2005, p. 380).

Ormerod et al. (2008) underlines this point:

> Girls are particularly targeted with sexual harassment, appraise it as more distressing, and experience a wider array of negative outcomes directly associated with har-

assment. It is essential that policies and programs designed to intervene include an understanding of the gendered nature of harassment. (p. 123)

Ormerod et al. (2008) states that adolescents are at a stage of psychosocial development focusing on individual as well as group identity. Peers play a large role in this development and thus, "it is logical that a climate that tolerates the harassment of peers would have a negative impact on teenagers, regardless of whether they are direct victims" (p. 122). When students witness incidents of sexual harassment and see that the authority figures do not take action, thus giving tacit approval, the result is a hostile school environment. The hostile school environment has a negative effect on feelings of safety at school and increases withdrawal from school for both direct victims of sexual harassment and for those who witness these events.

Sexual harassment negatively impacts both girls and boys, as well as perpetrators, victims and bystanders. It creates a hostile school environment that is psychosocially negative for everyone at the school. Thus, sexual harassment is not just a problem for the victim, but is a problem for everyone. Its prevalence is undeniable. As Shute, Owens, and Slee (2008) write, there is a 'cultural acceptance of sexual harassment as normal" (p. 478).

Current Discourse on Sexual Harassment

As we mentioned previously, the zenith for sexual harassment policy seemed to exist in the 90s. We have been concerned by the current discourse that seems to center largely around bullying. Of course, we recognize how damaging bullying can be to the psychological and academic development of both its victims and perpetrators, however, the discussion surrounding bullying seems to mute the issue of sexual harassment and has in some ways silenced this very prevalent, and related phenomenon. Additionally, there seems to be, in some cases, an assault on feminist advancement, and much conversation and attention has turned to the victimization of young men, while the victimization of young women is sidelined. Keddie sums up the some of the contemporary views on sexual harassment in her article. She states that current popular discourse creates a "climate where boys are perceived as victims of gender discrimination and the 'feminization' of schools in which males have to abide" (p. 1). Although based in Australia, the discussion is pertinent to the U.S. in that similar anti-feminist attitudes are capturing headlines. Keddie goes onto show that "issues of sexual harassment are located within prevailing contemporary western educational contexts that position boys as 'victims' of feminism and 'girl-friendly' schooling" (p. 1). This article highlights the need to look more closely at the "power dynamics" in which males are still dominant, and look more closely at "boys' colonization of the gender equity agenda" (p. 3). Keddie describes:

> The disturbing reality is that, despite decades of feminist reform in schools, the widespread and long-term institution of school sexual harassment and bullying policies, and girls' apparent victory in the 'gender wars,' a discourse of entitlement prevails in terms of many boys' continued domination of classroom and playground space and resources; domination of teacher time and attention; and perpetration of sexual, misogynistic and homophobic harassment. (Keddie, 2009, p. 2)

We concur with Keddie's sentiments that the focus regarding sexual harassment has shifted considerably since the 1990s. In our assessment of the research literature, we find that three main topic areas have dominated the research agenda and taken center stage in the popular discourse regarding sexual harassment: cyber-harassment, bullying and sexual orientation. While we concur that these are important topics, we do not believe that they should dominate the discourse as they do, but rather they need to be incorporated into feminist analysis of the gendered power dynamics that promote sexual harassment in all forms. These topics hit "hot buttons" for sensationalizing media news-outlets, and obscure our view of the preponderance of sexual harassment victims who are female. We maintain that like other aspects of the sexual harassment research agenda, these topics need to be re-integrated into the larger feminist discourse that recognizes cyber-harassment, bullying and sexual orientation as factors of the continuing gender discrimination and sexism against which feminists (women and men) have been fighting for centuries.

Cyber-Harassment

Early on, the advent of the internet was touted as a "great equalizer," a space where race, social class, sex/gender, nationality, religious affiliation and all other aspects of discrimination would be non-existent. The internet promised to put people in closer touch with one another, carry news and information instantaneously across national and international borders, and improve our lives in numerous ways. Some of these promises have been fulfilled, while others have not. Further, the development of the internet has created "new spaces" for "old problems" as well as "new" problems.

Among the "new problems" has been an exponential increase in use of new and advancing technologies by youth, coupled with a "lack of keeping up" with new and advancing technologies by those older than 21 (a lack that increases exponentially with each decade of age). This has meant that kids are teaching adults (parents, teachers and others) how to use their computers, telephones and televisions and other emerging devices that we didn't even envision a decade ago.

Meanwhile, in the midst of this shift in power/knowledge away from adults (parents, teachers and others), parents are expected to protect their children from potential dangers on the internet. While some hazards are obvious (chatting online with people you don't know); other hazards are more subtle (chatting online with people you *think* you do know). The anonymity that was touted in the 1990s as liberating us from the "-isms" pervasive in the "real world" by moving us into "virtual worlds," has meant that when we are online, we cannot be absolutely certain that we are indeed corresponding with the person with whom we think we are corresponding. News reports have documented parents (and others, including predators and sex offenders) pretending to be "the good-looking boy next door" or "the popular girl" in charge of entry to the much coveted clique at the local high school, and using this to gain access to children and teens in order to abuse, harass and molest our youth. In response, news outlets have warned parents to closely supervise their children's internet use and restrict access to potentially harmful web sites. When parents, teachers and others discourage teens and girls, in particular, from using the internet, they are also perpetuating and exacerbating the "digital divide" and the fear discourse surrounding girls' entry into adolescence.

But, are these the best responses? Mitchell, Wolak, and Finkelhor (2008) finds that teens who post online journals (blogs) are not more likely to "interact with people they meet online" than their peers who do not post blogs (p. 277). Further, even "posting personal information did not add to risk" (p. 277). However, youth who *do* interact with people they meet online *are* at risk for sexual harassment and sexual solicitation (Mitchell et al., 2008). Thus, according to this study, the hazards of the internet are not in the content of what teens access or what they post, but rather in the acts of communicating with strangers, and we would add people they presume to know.

Again, we argue that cyber-harassment needs to be understood in context with gendered sexual harassment. The internet is, in many ways, merely another space (like hallways or bathrooms where predators hang out), and stopping this abuse and harassment hinges on addressing and eliminating sexism and enforcement of traditional gendered roles which lead to and sanction sexual harassment.

Bullying

Bullying has recently experienced its share of the spotlight, as perpetrators of massive school violence have been shown to be bullies or bully/victims. Bullies and bully/victims, as should be noted, are almost exclusively male. Therefore this discourse decidedly moves the agenda from victims and by-standers to perpetrators of sexual harassment. As we assert, as well as others including Stein (1999), Shute et al. (2008) and Miller (2008), the discourse on bullying has served to silence the gendered, sexual nature of sexual harassment. Shute et al. argue that the conversations on bullying have "over-looked the importance of sexualized elements, particularly in boys' victimization of girls" (p. 480). While bullying is undoubtedly a detrimental social phenomenon in schools, we must not fail to explicitly examine the sexual victimization of young women. This section is designed to provide a brief presentation of some of the ways in which bullying is contextualized in schools. However, we will quickly resume the conversation surrounding the sexual harassment of young women as not to veil the gendered, power differential faced by young women in schools.

Espelage and Holt's exploration of the bully-victim spectrum (from un-involved, victims, bully-victims to bully) found that "victims and bully-victims experienced the most negative consequences from sexual harassment, experienced more dating related violence, and experienced more anxiety/depression than the other groups" (Espelage & Holt, 2007, p. 799). Gruber and Fineran explored the boundaries between bullying and harassment and found that although bullying tends to be a more frequent occurrence, sexual harassment has "adverse effects on more health outcomes" (Gruber & Fineran, 2008, p. 13). Further, these authors document a spectrum of frequency whereby boys and girls in general are bullied very frequently, and girls are harassed more often than boys and sexual minorities (or presumed sexual minorities) experience higher levels of both bullying and sexual harassment. Further, girls and sexual minorities show more adverse health effects from bullying and sexual harassment than boys in general (Gruber & Fineran, 2008).

Also alarming are studies that show an increase in incidences of bullying and harassment as children move from elementary to middle school (Pellegrini, 2001, 2002). Especially troubling are Pellegrini's findings that the aggressive behaviors of bullies and harassers at this age are popular, or at least tolerated. The increase in aggressive and harassing behaviors coincides with the increase in interest in heterosexual relationships and harassing and aggressive behaviors mark the emergence of heterosexual relationships (Pellegrini, 2001, 2002). Dating in middle school appears to be associated with peer status and the dominance and popularity of the bullies enhances their peer status in middle school. Disturbingly, Pepler finds that bullies tend to be perceived as "more attractive" by their peers (Pepler, 2006). This finding is especially important since it highlights the connections between traditional gendered roles, male dominance and the emergence of heterosexual relationships. Jones (2006) points out that "methods used to research bullying make the processes supporting gendered bullying difficult to uncover" (p. 147). Thus, as Shute clarifies: "the term 'sexual bullying' appropriately captures the gendered power structure underlying these behaviors. As such, they need to be understood, and become visible, more broadly than in terms of individual pathology" (Shute et al., 2008, p. 477). As Robinson shows:

> Sexual harassment is integral to the construction of hegemonic heterosexual masculine identities; the importance of popularity, acceptance and young men's fears within male peer group cultures; and the utilization of sexual harassment as a means through which to maintain and regulate hierarchical power relationships, not just in relation to gender, but how it intersects with other sites of power such as 'race' and class. (Robinson, 2005, p. 19)

We conclude from this research that the bully experiences increases in popularity, is perceived as fitting in with traditional gender roles, and is generally supported in these behaviors, his actions then, become normative rather than problematic. In fact, according to Duncan (1999), boys' masculinity is often confirmed by 'cultural forms of bullying' (p. 39). Pascoe (2007) found that boys are 'never reprimanded' for bullying in the form of lewd comments (p.160). In fact, those lewd comments seem to be rewarded in school settings in which hegemonic masculinities are maintained. The young men in our study elaborate on how this maintenance occurs and it appears that degrading behavior towards young women plays a significant role in the establishment of perceived masculinity. As Miller (2008) posits, sexual bullying discourse is often conceptualized as gender neutral or couched in a discussion of a male phenomenon. Stopping this abuse and harassment hinges on addressing and eliminating sexism and enforcement of traditional gendered roles which lead to and sanction sexual harassment.

Sexual Orientation

The third focus of contemporary discourse regarding sexual harassment that emerged from our review of research literature is sexual orientation. While this is a hugely important area of focus, this discussion has tended to highlight harassment of males by other males, and shifts the agenda away from female victims. However, this form of sexual harassment simultaneously highlights the enforcement of traditional gendered roles and expectations which undergirds all sexual harassment. Among the recent research publications on sexual harassment stemming from (presumed) sexual orientation are Henning-Stout, James, & Macintosh, (2000); Ryan (2003); Hansen (2007);

and Rivers (2011). These publications make it clear that sexism and hetero-sexism contribute significantly to peer sexual harassment. Sexual orientation is now, and has always been a significant risk factor for sexual harassment. However, unless it is intended to be covered in "coded" language of "risky" and "problem" behaviors, this factor is commonly not listed among the risk factors. This erasure of such a significant risk factor in the majority of research literature is glaring. Stader (2007) documents the current context:

> Student-on-student harassment on the basis of real or perceived sexual orientation may be relatively common. Any student-on-student bullying or taunting is harmful. Homophobic bullying, however, may be even more harmful and significantly impact feelings of safety, grades, and future plans of the victims. At least some teachers and administrators seem reluctant to intervene and enforce district and campus sexual harassment policies when witnessing sexual orientation harassment. That reluctance may result from a variety of personal beliefs, a misunderstanding of school policy, or a misunderstanding of current law. However, there should be no doubt that public schools are again caught in the middle of the cultural wars. A failure to protect sexual minority students can be costly. Efforts to promote safety and tolerance can easily escalate into controversy. Although conservative groups protest, courts across the country are clear: school districts can be monetarily held liable for student-on-student sexual orientation harassment when school officials fail to adequately address known harassment. (p. 121)

International research in the U.S, the U.K., Australia, Canada and other nations support Stader's assessment. Homophobic and misogynistic discourse is used regularly to regulate sexual behaviors of teens (Chambers, Ticknell, & Van Loon, 2004). School personnel often fail to address name calling that is designed to marginalize particular students. Rivers (2011) notes that victimization based on sexual orientation may range from physical attacks such as hitting and kicking to sexual assault and assault with a lethal weapon. Further, he notes that some sexual harassment based on sexual orientation may be as "subtle as a look or stare" and therefore difficult to substantiate (p. 37).

Yaffee (1995) notes that words such as "homo" and "lesbo" are among the most offensive verbal taunts being heard on school campuses. Her work predates the emergence of the phrase "that's so gay" which is directed toward anything and everything teens wish to malign. Although the words used may have changed somewhat, the sentiment remains very much the same, and so has the impact on GLBTQ youth. Yaffe relates comments from a 1995 special Commission of Gay and Lesbian Youth convened by the Massachusetts Board of Education: Paul Reville, a board member, says, "Young people came forward to talk about how miserable their lives had been made.

They reported that often adults were standing by and participating, permitting other students to mock them" (Yaffe, 1995, para. 54).

When it comes to harassment stemming from sexual orientation, school personnel are likely to remain deaf, dumb and blind. Several of the male participants involved in our research discuss their personal experiences with being harassed for their sexual orientation. Their harassment was daily and pervasive and often was overlooked by the school personnel. This lack of response from school authorities reads as approval to the teens, and harassment increases. Sexual harassment needs to be understood in context with gendered sexual harassment. The interconnections between traditional gendered roles, heterosexism and sexual harassment must be underlined.

Teacher/School Response to Sexual Harassment

Of course, of great concern to us in this project was the ways in which the school responds to issues of sexual harassment. We provide data from a study conducted with middle and high school teachers in which they address their understandings of sexual harassment; those results are shared in a proceeding chapter. In another study in which a survey was given to nearly 200 teachers (both male and female) teachers responses indicated that they recognized peer sexual harassment and would take action to curb sexual harassment if they witnessed it. This survey (Stone, 2004) showed little difference between male and female teachers' responses on the survey questions. Only one difference emerged between male and female teachers – male teachers were less tolerant of statements indicating that sexual advances come with the territory of being an attractive female. The most common action teachers checked on the survey was "report the incident to campus authorities." This is consistent with most school policies. This study contrasts with earlier studies (e.g, AAUW, 1993) indicating that teacher awareness of peer sexual harassment has increased since the 1990s. It also contrasts with Yaffe's report:

> Homosexual students were not the only ones who talked of the unresponsiveness of teachers and administrators, however. One of the most demoralizing aspects of harassment, many students reported, was the lack of support from adults. Many described the agony of having teachers or administrators stand by while harassing behavior was occurring and do nothing to stop it. They said that, when they reported instances of harassment to adults, they often encountered disbelief or found themselves blamed for the harassment. (Yaffe, 1995, para. 54–55)

Perhaps there is a disparity between what teachers believe they would do when presented with a hypothetical scenario and what they actually do when they witness incidents of sexual harassment. As our research points out, teachers often say that harassment doesn't exist in their school, yet, within the same interview cite examples of harassment which they have witnessed. Additionally, while teachers seem to assert that they do an adequate job of addressing harassment, both young men and women suggest harassment occurs frequently and without interception from school personnel. This disparity of perception needs to be further explored.

One researcher who has taken this on is Elizabeth Meyer. Meyer's (2008) work highlights internal and external barriers to teacher intervention in sexual harassment. She states:

> This study shows that educators experience a combination of external and internal influences that act as either *barriers* or *motivators* for intervention. Some of the external barriers include: lack of institutional support from administrators; lack of formal education on the issue; inconsistent response from colleagues; fear of parent backlash; and negative community response. (Meyer, 2008, p. 34)

In general, teachers do not perceive bullying as a problem; therefore they do not directly discourage it. They tend to only address direct verbal or physical forms of bullying, and do not recognize, much less address indirect forms of bullying. Research indicated that teachers often are in the vicinity when sexual harassment is happening but they do nothing, they don't perceive there to be a problem (Stein, 1995). Bullying and teasing behaviors are ignored by teachers. Miller (2008) notes that teachers' lack of concern for girls' harassment sends a message to both male and female students that harassment is not a serious issue. Miller also argues that this disregard for harassment is compounded for young women in disadvantage areas where displays of masculinity are even greater. Stein (1995) also found that teachers fail to address issues of sexual harassment, sexual bullying and sometimes even actively participate in the harassment. In a study Preble conducted with adolescents in school, 1/3 of the students surveyed noted that teachers did little to intervene in slurs/name calling (Wessler & Preble, 2003). As we address in the final chapter of this book, it is imperative that teachers are adequately prepared to address the issues of sexual harassment. Much of this preparation begins in teacher education programs. It should be noted that we don't wish to be critical of teachers' responses entirely. Many teachers believe they work very hard to address the harassment of their students. However, we argue that there are a variety of reasons that school personnel don't adequately address the sexual harassment of their students; some of those reasons have been created by a culture of school that requires school personnel to focus on standardized testing rather than the affective needs of their students. In our concluding chapter, we attempt to address some of these reasons more fully.

Of course one of the arguments we will make is the need for school counselors to set the climate enabling students to report sexual harassment, and to be aware of the policies, and to protect students' confidentiality (Stone, 2000). School counselors are perhaps in the best position to revisit, interpret, and provide clarity for sexual harassment policy and issues. School counselors can report instances of abuse, console the victim, and observe the claimant in the social settings of the school (Linn & Fua, 1999). As many of our participants' reveal, there are very few counselors in the schools today who are given the task or readily embrace the task of dealing with issues of harassment. Many counselors are overwhelmed with tasks associated with standardized testing, and they have little time during their day to address all of the pressing affective needs of the student population. In the final chapter of this text we urge school districts to reexamine their assignments of school counselors and stress the importance of establishing safe climates and safe relationships with adolescents in school buildings.

Without access to school personnel who students view as interested and caring in matters of violence and harassment, many young women are forced to fend for themselves. Victims of sexual harassment are less likely to report incidents when they do not trust the investigative process or the organization – if they do not feel their complaints will be given a fair hearing (Vijayasiri, 2008). Miller (2008) argues that this is an even greater problem for girls in disadvantaged areas who have had to develop their own mechanisms for coping with their own victimization.

Given previous research that students perceive teachers and staff as ignoring harassment (AAUW, 1993; Dupper & Meyer-Adams, 2002; Hand & Sanchez, 2000; Lee et al., 1996) and our findings that when students perceive that teachers and administrators tolerate sexual harassment, there is a corresponding increase in peer harassment, this issue obviously needs to be addressed more thoroughly (Ormerod et al., 2008).

Student Response to Sexual Harassment

Students having received little support or action by school personnel for dealing with harassment have had to develop their own approaches for dealing with harassment. In our studies presented in this book, many of the participants discuss their reactions to harassment and the ways in which they and their peers have systematically dealt with the existence of harassment in their schools. While many of the female participants in our study suggest that they simply overlook blatant harassment, other studies have found that girls find other ways to deal with it: however, each response seems to come at a cost to the young women. Duncan (1999) notes how girls fear retaliation for confronting their harassers or reporting their harassment to school personnel. Miller (2008) in her work researching harassment of girls in urban communities found that "girls face a double bind, not standing up for themselves meant that sexual harassment was likely to continue and would be desired, while standing up for themselves prompted an angry response" (p. 52). She found girls' responses to harassment from boys ranged from avoidance, going to a 3rd party or standing up to harasser; however the latter two responses increased risk for escalation. She also found that girls that took no action in response faced social stigmatization. Our work also substantiates this as the participants in our study (young women, young men and teachers) all cited a girls' lack of response as acceptance of the harassment or even desire for the behavior to continue. In their work, Smith, Pepler & Rigby (2004) found that in response to witnessing those sexually harassed, over half of the participants would "object" to the boy's action, another, nearly 1/5 would tell a teacher, about 1/4 said they would ignore the event and one in 40 would support the boy. Projected action is not the same as real action – and most likely, fewer students would actually take action when witnessing an incident of sexual harassment. The main factor students expressed for determining their course of action when witnessing sexual harassment was their attitude or knowledge about the victim (Smith, Pepler and Rigby, 2004). This study found that when the peer-perpetrator was known to the victim, the degree of distress was less than when a peer-perpetrator was unknown or not in the same peer group as the victim (Lacasse & Mendelson, 2006). Also, students with high self-esteem had less severe negative response to sexual harassment.

Believing that they are "in the minority" may lessen the tendency for victims and bystanders of sexual harassment to identify negative behaviors. Such pluralistic ignorance makes victims feel that they may be the only one who views these behaviors negatively, and may be part of what encourages students to "play along" with the harassment rather than take action against it (Halbesleben, 2009).

Intersection of Sexuality Education and Sexual Harassment

Throughout these chapters we will interweave discussions of sexuality education within the context of school curriculum. We argue as do many other researchers (Carlson, 2011; Lamb, 2011; Giroux, 2011) that sexuality education does not take into account the sexual worlds of students. Also, while girls spend a great deal of time learning about male sexual proclivity, boys spend very little time learning about girls' sexuality. As Johansson (2007) points out, sexuality education provided to youth today is 'mediaized" and provide contradictions to adolescents. Johansson points out that "while boundaries, distinctions, and moral norms are disintegrating in the media world, we can see in everyday life a repressive normative sexuality has gained a foothold" (p.12).

Additionally, sexuality education in schools has served to perpetuate sexist notions of relationships. As many of our participants noted, sexuality education in middle and high schools is scarce, and is largely centered around an abstinence-only discourse which fails to take into account the realities of adolescents' lives. As Fine (1988) has noted:

> Inside the hegemony of what they call 'Law of the Father', female desire and pleasure can gain expression only in the terrain already charted by men. In the public school arena, this construction of what is called sexuality, allows girls one primary choice-say yes or no to a question not necessarily their own. (p. 34)

Fine also contends that the naming of female desire or pleasure rarely exists in sexuality education. If it does, she argues, it is "tagged with reminders and consequences-emotional, physical, moral, reproductive, and or financial" (Fine, 1988, p. 33). Girls seem to be faced with a fear and guilt discourse surrounding sexuality and this is maintained through the sexuality education provided them in schools. As we will point out, harassment is *rarely* discussed within any discussion of sexuality education and issues regarding dating violence, etc. even more rarely mentioned.

Sexual Harassment Outside of School

In our research, we discovered that in addition to frequent and pervasive harassment on school grounds, young women face violence, abuse, and ridicule in nearly every domain of their lives. As we report from our discussions with young women, girls do not escape harassment outside of school walls. Many of the young women we interviewed cited examples of harassment in their neighborhoods, at various public venues, at work and even in their homes. While our work is especially concerned with the ways in which girls experience harassment at school, it is important to contextualize school harassment as a part of the systematic harassment that young women face. Fineran's (2002) study also describes adolescents' experiences with sexual harassment while working part-time and attending high school. In a sample of 712 high school students, 35% of the 332 students who work part-time report experiencing sexual harassment (63% girls, 37% boys). Results revealed that there are differences in the experience of sexual harassment by gender, work relationship, and emotional reaction. Students experienced harassment from supervisors (19%), coworkers (61%), and unidentified others at work (18%). Girls reported being significantly more upset and threatened by the sexual harassment they experienced at work than boys reported (Fineran, 2002, p. 953). The women and girls in our study cite numerous instances where they were harassed and abused by various persons outside of school (friends, coworkers, family members, church members, etc.). As the participants share their accounts, it is evident that girls continue to be plagued with pervasive vulnerabilities.

Moving Forward

During the 1990s, schools developed policies, ahead of the development of legal mandates, and based their policies on "fair treatment and the maintenance of a hospitable learning environment" (Short, 2006, p. 53) rather than on principles of justice, equality and ending discrimination. Consequently, policies may have limited application, and the record shows that there has been little change in the quantity and/or quality of sexual harassment in schools. Chaves sums up the legal mandates:

> The Court says that schools must not clearly unreasonably respond to students' allegations. However, if schools only discipline, the problem of peer sexual harassment will never go away. Schools must do more than just respond to allegations – they must attack the source of the problem. They must educate the entire school community concerning sexual harassment in order to eliminate the myths, assumptions, biases, stereotypes, and misconduct. Through proper education, schools can effectively curb incidents of sexual harassment among students. This will allow them to effectuate their goal of providing an equal education to all of their students and help them truly produce socially responsible and productive members of society. (2000, para. 58)

Until we adjust the sexist system that values males over females and permits males perceived access to female's bodies, sexual harassment will continue (Chamberlain, 1997). The chapters in this book detail the perceptions of students and teachers as they reflect on sexual harassment in schools. In many cases, the participants were asked to provide demographic information and provide some contextualization of their definitions of sexual harassment. Many discussed roles of religion, popular media, family and educational experiences. Many shared very personal experiences with us and we are grateful for their courage and time. This book provides a strong understanding of the sexual harassment of students in school and highlights the prevalence of this harassment for young girls. In our concluding chapter, we offer some suggestions for eradicating sexual harassment in the schools. We recognize the severe complexity of this issue and would not suggest that a simple fix is possible. However, we will examine ways in which educators, in particular, can begin to address ideological underpinnings surrounding sexism and harassment existing in school culture.

References

Adam, A. (2001). Cyberstalking: Gender and computer ethics. In E. Green & A. Adam (Eds.), *Virtual gender: Technology, consumption and identity* (pp. 209–224). London: Routledge.

American Association of University Women. (1993). Hostile hallways: The AAUW survey on sexual harassment in America's schools. Washington D.C.

Ashbaugh, C., & Cornell, D. (2008). Sexual harassment and bullying behaviors in sixth graders. *Journal of School Violence*, 7(1), 21–38.

Barak, A. (2005). Deviance and the internet: New challenges for Social Sciences. *Social Sciences Computer Review*, 23(1), 77–92.

Brandenburg, J. (1997). *Confronting sexual harassment: What schools and colleges can do*. New York: Teachers College Press.

Brown, J. D., & L'Engle, K. L. (2009). X-rated: Sexual attitudes and behaviors associated with U.S. early adolescents' exposure to sexually explicit media. *Communication Research*, *36*(1), 129–151. Retrieved from http://search.ebscohost.com/login.aspx?direct=true&db=a9h&AN=36002133&site=ehost-live.

Carlson, D. (2011). Constructing the adolescent body: Cultural studies and Sexuality Education. In D. Carlson & D. Roseboro (Eds.) *The sexuality curriculum and youth culture*, pp. 3-28. New York: Peter Lang.

Chamberlain, E. (1997). Courtroom to classroom: There is more to sexual harassment. *NWSA Journal*, 9(2), 135–155.

Chambers, D., Ticknell, E, & Van Loon, J. (2004). Peer regulation of teenage sexual identities. *Gender and Education*, 16(3), 397–415.

Chaves, L. (2000). Responding to public school peer sexual harassment in the face of *Davis v. Monroe County Board of Education*. *Brigham Young University Education & Law Journal*, 2, 287. Retrieved from http://search.ebscohost.com/login.aspx?direct=true&db=a9h&AN=3310548&site=ehost-live.

Crouch, M. (2001). *Thinking about sexual harassment: A guide for the perplexed.* New York: Oxford University Press.

Cunningham, G. B., & Benavides-Espinoza, C. (2008). A trend analysis of sexual harassment claims: 1992-2006. *Psychological Reports, 103*(3), 779–782.

DeLara, E. (2008). Developing a philosophy about bullying and sexual harassment: Cognitive coping strategies among secondary school students. *Journal of School Violence, 7*(4), 72–96.

Dill, K. E., Brown, B. P., & Collins, M. A. (2008). Effects of exposure to sex-stereotyped video game characters on tolerance of sexual harassment. *Journal of Experimental Social Psychology, 44*(5), 1402–1408.

Duncan, N. (1999). *Sexual bullying: Gender conflict and pupil culture in secondary school.* London: Routledge.

Dupper, D. R., & Meyer-Adams, N. (2002). Low level violence: A neglected aspect of school culture. *Urban Education, 37,* 350–364.

Durham, M. G. (2008). *The Lolita effect: Media sexualization of young girls and what we can do about it.* New York: Overlook Hardcover.

Equal Employment Opportunity Commission. n.d. www.eeoc.gov/facts/fs-sex.html.

Espelage, D., & Holt, M. (2007). Dating violence & sexual harassment across the bully-victim continuum among middle and high school students. *Journal of Youth & Adolescence, 36*(6), 799–811.

Fasting, K., & Brackenridge, C. H. (2009). 'Coaches, sexual harassment and education' *Sport, Education and Society,* 14(1). 21–35.

Fine, M. (1988). Sexuality, school, and adolescent females: The missing discourse of desire. *Harvard Educational Review,* 51, 29–53.

Fineran, S. (2002). Adolescents at work: Gender issues and sexual harassment. *Violence Against Women,* 8 (8), 953–967.

Fineran, S., & Bennett, L. (1999). Gender and power issues of peer sexual harassment among teenagers. *Journal of Interpersonal Violence,* 14 (6), 626–641.

Fineran, S., & Gruber, J. E. (2009). Youth at work: Adolescent employment and sexual harassment. *Child Abuse & Neglect,* 33(8), 550–559.

Halbesleben, J. (2009). The role of pluralistic ignorance in the reporting of sexual harassment. *Basic & Applied Social Psychology,* 31(3), 210–217.

Hand, J. Z., & Sanchez, L. (2000). Badgering or bantering? Gender differences in experiences of, and reactions to, sexual harassment among U.S. high school students. *Gender and Society,* 14, 718–746.

Hansen, A. (2007). School-based support for GLBT students: A review of three levels of research. *Psychology in the Schools,* 44(8), 839–848.

Harrington, L. (2004). Peer sexual harassment: Protect your students and yourself. *Delta Kappa Gamma Bulletin,* 71(1), 31–35. Retrieved from http://search.ebscohost.com /login.aspx?direct=true&db=a9h&AN=15079962&site=ehost-live.

Henning-Stout, M., James, S., & Macintosh, S. (2000). Reducing harassment of lesbian, gay, bisexual, transgender, and questioning youth in schools. *School Psychology Review,* 29, 180–191.

Gillander Gådin, K., & Hammarström, A. (2005). A possible contributor to the higher degree of girls reporting psychological symptoms compared with boys in grade nine? *European Journal of Public Health,* 15(4), 380–385.

Giroux, H. (2011). Teenage sexuality, body politics, and the pedagogy of display. In D. Carslon & D. Roseboro (Eds.), *The sexuality curriculum and youth culture.* Peter Lang, New York.

Goldstein, S., Malanchuk, O., Kean, P., & Eccles, J. (2007). Risk factors of sexual harassment by peers: A longitudinal investigation of African American and European American adolescents. *Journal of Research on Adolescence* 17(2), 285–300.

Green, E., & Adam, A. (Eds.), *Virtual gender: Technology, consumption and identity.* New York: Routledge.

Gruber, J. E., & Fineran, S. (2008). Comparing the impact of bullying and sexual harassment victimization on the mental and physical health of adolescents. *Sex Roles,* 58, 13–14.

Johansson, T. (2007). *The transformation of sexuality: Gender and identity in youth culture.* Burlington, VT: Ashgate.

Jones, C. (2006). Drawing boundaries: Exploring the relationship between sexual harassment, gender and bullying. *Women's Studies International Forum,* 29(2), 147–158.

Keddie, A. (2009). 'Some of those girls can be real drama queens': Issues of gender, sexual harassment and schooling. *Sex Education: Sexuality, Society and Learning*, 9(1), 1–16.

Klusas, J. (2003). Providing students with protection they deserve: Amending the Office of Civil Rights' Guidance on Title IX to protect students from peer harassment in schools. *Texas Journal of Civil Liberties and Civil Right,* 8(1), 91–116.

Lacasse, A., & Mendelson, M. (2006). The perceived intent of potentially offensive sexual behaviors among adolescents. *Journal of Research on Adolescence,* 16(2), 229–238.

Lackey, D. (1990). Sexual harassment in sports. *Physical Educator,* 47(2), 22. Retrieved from http://search.ebscohost.com/login.aspx?direct=true&db=a9h&AN=9609192477&site=eh ost-live.

Lamb, S. (2011). The place of mutuality and care in democratic sexuality education. In D. Carlson & D. Roseboro (Eds.), The sexuality curriculum and youth culture, New York: Peter Lang.

Larkin, J. (1994). Walking through walls: The sexual harassment of high school girls. *Gender & Education,* 6(3), 263. Retrieved from http://search.ebscohost.com/login.aspx? direct=true&db=a9h&AN=9512144251&site=ehost-live.

Lee, V. E., Croninger, R. G., Linn, E., & Chen, X. (1996). The culture of sexual harassment in secondary schools. *American Educational Research Journal,* 33, 383–417.

Lichty, L., Torres, J., Valenti, M., & Buchanan, N. (2008). Sexual harassment policies in K-12 schools: Examining accessibility to students and content. *Journal of School Health,* 78(11), 607–614.

Lindberg, S., Grabe, S., Hyde, J. (2007). Gender, pubertal development, and peer sexual harassment predict objectified body consciousness in early adolescence. *Journal of Research on Adolescence,* 17(4), 723–742.

Linn, E., & Fua, R. B. (1999). The role of school mental health professionals in resolving school-related sexual harassment compla. *Social Work in Education,* 21(4), 263–268. Retrieved from http://search.ebscohost.com/login.aspx?direct=true&db=a9h&AN=2397666 &site=ehost-live.

Livingston, J. A., Hequembourg, A., Testa, M., & VanZile-Tamsen, C. (2007). Unique aspects of adolescent sexual victimization experiences. *Psychology of Women Quarterly,* 31, 331–343.

Madson, L., & Shoda, J. R. (2002). Identifying sexual harassment: A classroom activity. *Teaching of Psychology*, 29, 304–307.

Marczely, B. (1993). A legal update on sexual harassment in the public schools. *Clearing House*, 66(6), 329. Retrieved from http://search.ebscohost.com/login.aspx?direct= true&db=a9h&AN=9402174994&site=ehost-live.

Meyer, E. (2008). *Gender, bullying, and harassment: Strategies to end sexism and homophobia in schools*. New York: Teachers College Press.

Michaelis, K. L. (2000). Title IX and same-gender sexual harassment: School district liability for damages. *Brigham Young University Education & Law Journal*, 1, 47. Retrieved from http://search.ebscohost.com/login.aspx?direct=true&db=a9h&AN=2919761&site=ehost-live

Miller, J. (2008). *Getting played: African American girls, urban inequality, and gendered violence*. New York: New York University Press.

Mitchell, K. J., Wolak, J., & Finkelhor, D. (2008). Are blogs putting youth at risk for online sexual solicitation or harassment? *Child Abuse & Neglect*, 32(2), 277–294.

Morrison, C. T. (2009). "What would you do, what if it's you?" Strategies to deal with a bully. *Journal of School Health*, 79, 201–204.

Ormerod, A. J., Collinsworth, L. L., & Perry, L. A. (2008). Critical climate: Relations among sexual harassment, climate, and outcomes for high school girls and boys. *Psychology of Women Quarterly*, 32(2), 113–125.

Pascoe, C. J. (2007). *Dude! You're a fag: Masculinity and sexuality in high school*. Berkley: University of California Press.

Pellegrini, A. D. (2001). The roles of dominance and bullying in the development of early heterosexual relationships. *Journal of Emotional Abuse*, 2(2), 63–73. Retrieved from http://search.ebscohost.com/login.aspx?direct=true&db=a9h&AN=9667951&site=ehost-live.

Pellegrini, A. D. (2002). Bullying, victimization, and sexual harassment during the transition to middle school. *Educational Psychologist*, 37(3), 151–163. Retrieved from http://search.ebscohost.com/login.aspx?direct=true&db=a9h&AN=7195823&site=ehost-live.

Pepler, D. (2006).Bullying interventions: A binocular perspective. *Journal of the Canadian Academy of Child and Adolescent Psychiatry*, 15(1), 16–20.

Petersen, J. L., & Hyde, J. S. (2009). A longitudinal investigation of peer sexual harassment victimization in adolescence. *Journal of Adolescence,* 32(5), 1173–1188.

Polce-Lynch, M., Myers, B. J., Kliewer, W., & Kilmartin, C. (2001). Adolescent self-esteem and gender: Exploring relations to sexual harassment, body image, media influence, and emotional expression. *Journal of Youth & Adolescence,* 30(2), 225. Retrieved from http://search.ebscohost.com/login.aspx?direct=true&db=a9h&AN=7657265&site=ehost-live.

Popkin, S. J., Leventhal, T., & Weismann, G. (2010). Girls in the 'hood: How safety affects the life chances of low-income girls. *Urban Affairs Review,* 45(6), 715–744.

Raspey, C., & Murachver, T. (2006). Adolescent sexuality. In R. McAnulty and M. Burnette, (Eds.) *Sex and sexuality,* Westport, CT: Praeger Publishers.

Rigby, K. (2004). Addressing bullying in schools: Theoretical perspectives and their implications. *School Psychology International,* 25, 287–300.

Rivers, Ian. (2011). *Homophobic bullying: Research and theoretical perspectives.* New York: Oxford University Press.

Robinson, K. (2000) Great tits miss!" The sexual harassment of female teachers in secondary schools. Issues of gendered authority. *Discourse*: *Studies in the Cultural Politics of Education,* 21(1), 75–90.

Robinson, K. (2005) Reinforcing hegemonic masculinities through sexual harassment: Issue of identity, power and popularity in secondary schools. *Gender and Education,* 17(1), 19–37.

Rowley, G. M. (1999). Liability for student-to-student sexual harassment under Title IX in light of *Davis v. Monroe County Board of Education. Brigham Young University Education & Law Journal,* 1, 137. Retrieved from http://search.ebscohost.com/login.aspx?direct= true&db=a9h&AN=1517707&site=ehost-live.

Ryan, C., Russell, S., Huebner, D., Diaz, R., & Sanchez, J. (2003). Family acceptance in adolescence and the health of LGBT young adults. *Journal of Child and Adolescent Psychiatric Nursing,* 23(4), 205–213.

Scott, H., Semmons, L., & Willoughby, L. (2001). Women and the internet: The natural history of a research project. In E. Green,& A. Adam (Eds.), *Virtual gender: Technology, consumption and identity.* pp. 3–27, London: Routledge.

Shakeshaft & Cohen, A. (1995). Sexual abuse of students by school personnel. *Phi Delta Kappan,* 76(7), 513–520.

Short, J. (2006). Creating peer sexual harassment: Mobilizing schools to throw the book at themselves. *Law & Policy,* 28(1), 31–59.

Shute, Owens, & Slee, (2008). Everyday victimization of adolescent girls by boys: Sexual harassment, bullying or aggression? *Sex Roles, 58,* 477–489.

Smith, P. K., Pepler, D., & Rigby, K. (2004) *Bullying in schools: How successful can interventions be?* Cambridge, UK: Cambridge University Press.

Stader, D. L. (2007). *Law and ethics in educational leadership.* Upper Saddle River, NJ: Pearson Education.

Stein, N. (1995). Sexual harassment in school: The public performance of gendered violence. *Harvard Educational Review, 65*(2), 145. Retrieved from http://search.ebscohost.com/login.aspx?direct=true&db=a9h&AN=9507051917&site=ehost-live.

Stein, N. (1999). *Classrooms and courtrooms: Facing sexual harassment in K-12 schools.* New York: Teachers College Press.

Stone, C. B. (2000). Advocacy for sexual harassment victims: Legal support and ethical aspects. *Professional School Counseling,* 4(1), 23. Retrieved from http://search.ebscohost.com/login.aspx?direct=true&db=a9h&AN=3665568&site=ehost-live.

Stone, M. (2004). Peer sexual harassment among high school students: Teachers' attitudes, perceptions, and responses. *The High School Journal,* Oct/Nov, 1–13.

Stratton, S. D., & Backes, J. S. (1997). Sexual harassment in North Dakota public schools: A study of eight high schools. *High School Journal,* 80(3), 163. Retrieved from http://search.ebscohost.com/login.aspx?direct=true&db=a9h&AN=9704241070&site=ehost-live.

Timmerman, G. (2002). A comparison between unwanted sexual behavior by teachers and by peers in secondary schools. *Journal of Youth & Adolescence,* 31(5), 397. Retrieved from http://search.ebscohost.com/login.aspx?direct=true&db=a9h&AN=6923155&site=ehost-live.

Timmerman, G. (2005). A comparison between girls' and boys' experiences of unwanted sexual behaviour in secondary schools. *Educational Research,* 47(3), 291–306.

Tinkler, J. (2008). People are too quick to take offense: The effects of legal information and beliefs on definitions of sexual harassment. *Law and Society*, 33(2), 417–445.

Tinkler, Li, Y.E. & Mollborn, S. 2007. Can legal interventions change beliefs? The effect of sexual harassment policy on men's gender beliefs. *Social Psychology Quarterly*, 70(4):480–494.

Tolman, D. (1991). Adolescent girls, women and sexuality: Discerning dilemmas of desire. *Women and Therapy,* 11(3-4), 55–69.

U.S. Department of Labor. (n.d.) http://www.dol.gov/oasam/regs/statutes/titleix.

Ussher, M. (1989). *The psychology of the female body*. New York: Routledge.

Vijayasiri, G. (2008). Reporting sexual harassment: The importance of organizational culture and trust. *Gender Issues,* 25, 43–61.

Walsh, M., Duffy, J., & Gallagher-Duffy, J. (2007). A more accurate approach to measuring the prevalence of sexual harassment among high school students. *Canadian Journal of Behavioral Science,* 39(2), 110–118.

Welsh, D., Rostosky, S., & Kawaguchi, M. (2000). A normative perspective of adolescent girls' developing sexuality. In C. Travis & J. White. *Sexuality, society, and feminism.* Washington, D.C: APA.

Wessler, S., & Preble, W. (2003). *Respectful school: How educators and students can conquer hate and harassment.* Alexandria, VA: Association for Supervision and Curriculum Development.

Winters, J., Clift, R., & Maloney, A. (2004). Adult-student sexual harassment in British Columbia high Schools. *Journal of Emotional Abuse,* 4(3/4), 177–196.

Yaffe, E. (1995). Expensive, illegal and wrong: Sexual harassment in our schools. *Phi Delta Kappan,* 77(3), K1. Retrieved from http://search.ebscohost.com/login.aspx?direct=true&db=a9h&AN=9512053716&site=ehost-live.

Yell, M. L., & Katsiyannis, A. (2000). Student-on-student sexual harassment: What are schools' responsibilities? *Preventing School Failure,* 44(3), 130. Retrieved from http://search.ebscohost.com/login.aspx?direct=true&db=a9h&AN=3505174&site=ehost-live.

Young, B., & Furman, W. (2008). Interpersonal factors in the risk for sexual victimization and its recurrence during adolescence. *Journal of Youth & Adolescence,* 37(3), 297–309.

Chapter 2: "Once a Slut, Always a Slut": The Impact of Sexual Harassment on Women's Lives

"Her sense of sexuality is informed by peers, culture, religion, violence, history, passion, authority, rebellion, body, past and future, and gender and racial relations of power" – Michelle Fine, 1998, p. 35

"Yeah, I think after that like when I got that reputation that was curtains, it was time to go. So I left school." – Pepsi

This chapter emerges from a research project conducted in 2001 in which we were concerned with the long term effects of the practice of labeling young women with adverse sexual labels. Data and interpretations from which this chapter emerged were initially developed and presented in Regina Moore-Rahimi's dissertation study (2002) and was subsequently also published in *Geographies of Girlhood* (Bettis & Adams, 2005). As we posit throughout this book, the practice of name calling/labeling young women is a form of sexual harassment that not only impacts the lives of the young women who are victimized, but it also serves to perpetuate the sexual double standard prevalent in our culture that positions men and women unequally. The study represents interview data from 12 women aged 25–35 as they reflected back on their experiences with being called names and receiving an adverse sexual label in school. For the purpose of this project, we relied on a definition of 'slut' provided by Tanenbaum (2000) who wrote, "There is no general consensus about what qualifies a girl as a 'slut.' Instead there are multiple, shifting distinctions between 'good' and 'slutty'" (p. 88). The shifting nature of this label illustrates the contradictory terrain through which girls have had to develop their sexuality. And, as we will articulate here and in other chapters, girls often receive this label for challenging the heterosexual proscriptions of remaining 'pure.'

As the women in this study revealed, they were given an adverse sexual label for a variety of reasons. Our contention is that the use of reputation is a form of marginalization and harassment that has continued to persist through the cultural practices of name calling and differential treatment of girls; and such labeling frequently occurs on school grounds (Epstein & Johnson, 1998; Ashbaugh & Cornell, 2008). The fact that this labeling seems to follow no set pattern contributes to the terroristic enforcement of gender discrimination.

While feminists, as well as other scholars, have made strides in helping to change the perceptions of gender and sexuality, little has actually changed to prevent girls from receiving such harmful stigmas and becoming victims of sexual harassment through negative sexual reputations such as the women in this study had to endure. As our more recent studies have found, as well as others reported in the research literature (Carpenter, 1998; Christian-Smith, 1998), adverse sexual labeling continues to serve as a detriment to the healthy development of adolescent girls.

This study examines how the experience of being labeled and harassed in school contributed to participants' constructions of their identities as women and affected their self-concept and their life choices. We will also examine the social context that continues to create a double standard of sexuality that applies to heterosexual relationships (the cultural acceptance of male's desire for sexual activity and cultural regulation of desire in females). The sexual double standard that permits and in many cases even encourages, harassment and labeling is considered, according to Capp, to be the "cultural thesis that female sexuality is regarded as a male possession so that sexual immorality by women has been regarded as a heinous fault while male lapses might be regarded as relatively trivial" (1999, p. 70). Butler goes even further in suggesting that the double standard of sexuality has been perpetuated by the assumption that the, "libido is masculine and is the source from which all possible sexuality is presumed to come" (1990, p. 53).

The prevalence of a male centered sexuality forms this double standard and has set up particular gender scripts for sexuality (VanRoosmalen, 2000). Those scripts have led to the view that women's worth comes not from a desire of their own, but as a result of their desirability to men (Kalof, 1995). Such a construction of sexuality leads not only to a muted development of female sexuality, but severely limits the choices for young women and presents them with a discourse of fear and shame regarding their own sexual experience (Tolman, 2000).

 Reputation is a powerful form of sexual harassment. For young adolescents who are in the process of developing their self-concept and identity these deeply embedded messages carry far reaching implications for their sexual and social selves (Lees, 1993). As a cultural institution, schools play a significant role in purveying 'acceptable' sexual behaviors, both explicitly through sexual education programs, but more importantly via the hidden curriculum experienced by students (Epstein & Johnson, 1998; Fine, 1988; Luker, 2006). When teachers and other school personnel ignore the name calling and ostracism, this is taken as condoning these behaviors (Stone, 2008; Meyer, 2008; Vijayasiri, 2008), and the burden on these young women is multiplied.

As we offer in numerous sections throughout this text, current messages regarding sexuality education are ineffective for addressing issues of harassment as they do not address issues of reputation and the sexual double standard. In fact, the formal sex education provided by schools is very different from that which the students learn through their daily experiences (Tanenbaum, 2000; Tolman, 2000). Further, the formal discussion of sexual education minus the inclusion of an examination of female sexual desire only further strengthens the inequitable effects of the sexual double standard and continues to perpetuate the masculinist orientation of sexuality discourse which encourages the sexual harassment of women (Hillier, Harrison, & Warr, 1998).

> A reputation acquired in adolescence can damage a young woman's self-perception for years. She may become a target for other forms of harassment and even rape, since her peers see her as 'easy' and therefore not entitled to say 'no.' She may become sexually active with a large number of partners (even if she had not been sexually active before her reputation). Or she may shut down her sexual side completely. (Tanenbaum, 2000, p. 229)

Indeed, as the women in this study revealed, many have in fact suffered from abusive relationships, have been involved with large numbers of sexual partners, or have admitted that they have no sense of their own desire at all, while there are a number of factors that have contributed to the formation of these women's lifestyles, they all experienced some degree of ostracism in school due to an adverse sexual label. Using reputation as a form of marginalization within schools is sexual harassment and serves as a cultural reminder to young and adult women that sexual power exists within a male dominated world (Kalof, 1995; Hunter, 2002; Wessler & Preble, 2003). How prevalent is this form of harassment today? The women in this study as well as the participants in our subsequent studies noted a ***daily occurrence*** of such misogynistic, harassing language and behaviors. Katz and Farrow (2000) note that while women may be experiencing greater freedom to participate in sex than in the past, they are "still constrained by a more covert but powerful double standard about morality" (p. 802). So, while some may argue that girls are 'enjoying' more sexual autonomy and expression, it appears that they are also more subjected to the discursive practices of regulation of their sexuality. Additionally, as we argue throughout this text, girls continue to be victimized in multiple places and in multiple ways. The messages that girls receive socially regarding their sexual behavior continue to be embedded in discourses of shame, while boys who are sexually active receive the message that their sexuality is healthy and their desire is 'natural' – as long as their sexual activities are heterosexual.

The women interviewed for this study re-visioned their experiences as girls who received adverse sexual labels and articulated how such labels subsequently affected their adult lives as women. The women here also recounted how the messages of sexuality presented to them through schooling practices shaped their experiences of marginalization. Examined through this study were the ways in which the system of patriarchy has set up parameters around female adolescent sexuality, how the construction and maintenance of the sexual double standard has been ardently performed by culture as experienced by young women, and the role of the school site in informing 'ideals' of sexuality.

Female sexuality has been historically viewed as threatening to the binary of femininity/masculinity. Janice Irvine has written that female sexuality is highly regulated because of its "dangerous potential to entrap men" (Irvine, 1994, p. 13). Women's behaviors, including the way they dress, are viewed as potential invitations to male sexual aggression, confirmed by participants' responses in this study as well as other studies presented in this book (see also Chapter 5). Since a woman's role is perceived to be the regulation of the sexual encounter, women who display sexual desire or encourage the sexual advances of men, are told they should not expect men to be responsible for their sexual aggression. This notion has served as a justification for violence inflicted upon women (Ramazanoglu & Holland, 1993; Miller, 2008). There has been plenty written on the subject of the feminine/masculine dichotomy that has been proscribed through hegemonic heterosexuality (Fausto-Sterling, 2000; Morozoff, 2000; Ore, 2000; Sterling, 2000, Thompson, 1995). This culturally mandated arrangement has rendered men's sexuality aggressive and women's sexuality passive and leaves women without a clear understanding of her their desire.

Female Sexuality as Deviance

Regan and Berscheid (1995) have written that the existence of male-centered sexuality "reflects common beliefs that sexual phenomena, including sexual desire, are inherently 'normal' aspects of the male, but not the female experience" (p. 355). Viewed from a historical perspective, young females have been subjected to a number of punitive measures aimed at regulating their sexual desires. Regina Kunzel (1993) in her examination of unmarried mothers through the social work movement of the early twentieth century, found an existence of prohibitive practices leveled against unmarried women and their sexual behaviors. She has written how practices have been systematically developed to keep young women from "gaining full control of their sexual and reproductive lives" (p. 22). Kunzel posits while little was done to reform male sexuality and behaviors, early reform movements aimed at regulating sexual practices were designed to "protect society from female delinquency" (p. 152).

Conforming to the traditional, heterosexual ideal of femininity has consequences not only on women's construction of their self-identities, but also on their physical bodies. Such practices present a 'disembodiment' for young women, as they become detached from their own physical pleasure and view their bodies as sites for the regulation of male sexuality. This disembodiment places the locus of control of their pleasure and body under male possession as deemed worthy by the male gaze (Holland et al., 1994). Female bodies have been and still remain viewed as public commodities (Durham, 2008). Women who do attempt to take back some of the power in sexual relationships and refuse to conform to the patriarchal hegemonic discourse of sexuality, do so through sacrifice of their social selves (Tanenbaum, 2000). These women are often ostracized and ridiculed, labeled and even abused. Thus, navigating the terrain of sexuality is treacherous for women, whether women conform to or rebel against traditional hegemonic gender roles. The stories presented here and elsewhere in this book highlight the conflicts of women's experience.

Ho, Slut and Jezebel: Stories of 12 Young Women

The women involved in this study were twenty-five to thirty-five years of age. They attended high school in the U.S. between the years 1985 and 1995. The women were identified through an advertisement placed in the local newspaper. The ad asked for women who had experienced "name calling in high school." We received over twenty calls; however, once we discussed that we were looking for women who had been called 'slut,' 'ho' or another similar adverse sexual label, we narrowed down the participant pool. The women's whose stories are revealed here experienced such name calling and were willing and able to speak candidly about those experiences. The decision to study women in this age group was made because of the overall goal of the project was to understand how sexual harassment, particularly in the form of sexual labeling, affects women's self-concept and life choices. The women in this study had the opportunity to reflect on their schooling. Our purpose in this study was to explore the long term effects of high school ostracism and sexual harassment.

We have chosen to begin this book with the study that began our research in this area, that is, with an exploration of the reflections of adult women upon their high school experiences. When looking at the experiences of adolescents, it is important to keep in mind that harassment has long range impact on students' lives. As the women in this study revealed, their lives were directly impacted by experiences with sexual harassment in school. In the chapters that follow, we examine contemporary experiences that echo experiences of women some fifteen years earlier. For this reason, we believe it is important to set the contemporary stage by sharing the stories of women who traversed this terrain more than a decade earlier. We must confront the fact that little has changed, and if we fail yet again to make change, we can expect the women we interviewed today to face similar challenges, and as the next chapter reveals, that is indeed the case.

While the experiences of the women in this study vary, they all shared the experience of being harassed in high school. The stories these women recounted provide a clearer understanding of the often painful road that adolescent women travel. Their words confirm the confusing messages that women must discern about our identities, our sexuality, and our relationships. The women whose stories are presented here had to contend with ridicule, harassment, verbal, mental and physical abuse, difficult decisions regarding pregnancy and childbirth, and other profound life choices.

What follows are the stories of the twelve women aged 25–35 at the time of these interviews. (Appendix A contains a quick reference for demographic/findings from each participant.) Eleven of these women identified as heterosexual, and one identified as bisexual. Five identified themselves as white and five identified as black. One self-identified as Hispanic and the remaining other identified as Jewish, but rejected racial classification. These women had to contend at some point during their middle and/or high school experience with being verbally harassed, and many dropped out of high school due to this harassment.

In this chapter and throughout this book, fictitious names have been used to protect the participants' identities. The accounts of the women we interviewed follow.

Tonya: Which Label Will I Take?

At the time of this interview, Tonya was a 27 year old white woman. Tonya appeared friendly and self-confident upon first meeting her. She seemed quite resolved, despite the very personal nature of the interview. She attended and graduated from a large, urban high school in the south. She described her family as "Christian and upper middle class."

Our interview first concentrated on discussing images in popular culture that Tonya could recall being exposed to during her years in school. She recalled reading magazines such as *Cosmopolitan* and remembers the predominant messages were about how to make one more attractive. A self-described "tomboy," Tonya said she remembered feeling awkward about her appearance and desiring to look more 'feminine." Tonya said she received more of her understanding regarding acceptable behavior from her older siblings. She recalled her older sister getting into a lot of trouble with drugs and dating a lot of guys and recalled her sister's promiscuity as "wrong." She said that she felt strongly that her understanding of appropriate sexual behaviors came from her education in the Christian faith. Tonya recalled no formal sexual education during her school years. We then turned our conversation to her high school years and her experience with being labeled.

> My junior year I had just started a different high school.... I transferred over to a different high school. I started dating a guy my junior year. We dated most of my junior year and a couple of weeks into the summer and we broke up. We were at a party of a whole bunch of mutual friends of ours and *he raped me*. That summer and I got pregnant. (p. 6)

She did not tell anyone she was raped, nor did she tell her parents she was pregnant. Rather she confided in her older sister who helped her arrange an abortion, an experience she described as 'traumatic.'

She recounted another experience with the same boy, who raped her a second time. She became pregnant again, and she recalled how, as her ROTC uniform began to fit tightly, her peers began to speculate on her pregnancy status. They started calling her 'slut.' After another abortion, the students began to call her "baby killer." Tonya said she made a painful decision to not address their comments. She said:

> I'm not going to tell them what I went through – I'm not going to give them the satisfaction – 'cause I'm stubborn. It was like I had a choice of telling them what really happened to me or letting them think that I'm just a slut and a baby killer. So I took that because it's not anybody's business what happened. It was very much a growing up period because to make a decision like that – which label do I really want? – because when you're that young, even me, I had heard somebody had been raped, yeah you felt sorry for them but at the same time, *what did they do to deserve it?* So, it's six to one, half dozen the other way. Which one do you really want to live with? An abortion will go away...rape doesn't. (p. 5)

So she endured the verbal harassment and instead lived in silent torment and shame. She said that she left campus as soon as her classes were over, withdrew from all people in her school and participated in no extracurricular activities. After leaving high school, Tonya became "very promiscuous." According to Tonya, "I have slept with over 200 men, which I am not proud of, but that is where I was at. I was going to get back at him [the rapist]". Despite her numerous sexual encounters, she never experienced desire, ac-

cording to her. She went into the military and married right out of high
school. She married right after high school and became pregnant. Her husband left her after her announcement she was pregnant; she placed the child
up for adoption and then married her second husband. Her second husband
was abusive, according to Tonya, and she remembered feeling like *she "deserved" the abuse*. Eventually, she left her husband. She has been called
'whore' by many of the men with whom she has been involved and she
called it painful. Her family has even participated in labeling Tonya, referring to her as "oversexed" and a "whore." Her painful high school experiences continued to plague Tonya, even as we conducted this interview. She
said that she has a great deal of resentment and pain. At the time of the interview, she was in counseling and taking anti-depressant medication.

Pepsi: Sexual Desire as Demonic Possession

I knew from my initial phone conversation with Pepsi arranging our interview that she had a lot to offer on the topic of women and their life experiences, particularly regarding relationships with men. As soon as she picked
up the phone, she nearly got in a physical altercation with her adult brother
who she said is "always f@!king with her." At the time of the interview,
Pepsi was a 35 year old black woman. She appeared self-confident and was
very friendly and warm upon our meeting. She did not graduate from high
school, but completed her GED when she was thirty. She described herself as
"self-employed" which during the course of our interview I found out to
mean that she was an escort and a prostitute. She described herself as heterosexual and had never been married. She grew up with foster parents in the
Christian faith. Intriguingly, she was one of the few women interviewed who
was able to articulate a sexual desire of her own. Pepsi recalled her early development of sexual feelings, although within her story is another example of
the dangerous lives adolescent girls live.

> Well I used to have an old guy that I called my sugar daddy…he paid for my abor-
> tion when I got pregnant at 17. I was messing with him from age 13, so you could
> really say that this was my first trick. So that's why I say I became very promiscu-
> ous. I might go with this man and that's just business, but I really want to be with
> you, so I don't charge you anything. (p. 3)

Pepsi's high school experiences appeared to be painful for her as she appeared very reluctant to discuss this aspect of her life, despite her openness
about all other areas. She did not stay in high school very long, she recalled
staying out until midnight having sex with men for money instead of attending school.

> I remember the first time I was called a whore. This guy said I was a "d*ck sucking whore" [she said laughing]. Pretty much once you get a reputation around schools, everybody looks at you in a different light.... Yeah, I think after that like when I got that reputation it was like curtains – time to go. So I left school. (p. 8)

When we asked her about how she felt when people called her names, she said that "It hurts because we are all sensitive and emotional. *We scar easy and we might play it off but deep down inside that we listen to it, it would take root and we are beginning to think, we start thinking that's all we are worth.* But this was my character, part of my character, I mean sex" (p. 11). Pepsi dropped out of school at fifteen and said she couldn't recall any pleasant experiences from school.

Pepsi said that her foster mother told her she was possessed with "masturbation and smoke demons" (p. 5). She believed that those demons were still possessing her. She believed that her strong sense of sexual desire, her enjoyment of her sexuality, and her choice to become a prostitute are demonic and stem of from an 'evil' that possessed her.

> Because the Bible tells you not to defy your temple, not to commit fornication, adultery. Yes, I definitely believe that. There is something that gets in your flesh that makes you want to go do this. I used to ride out just to meet guys just to go to bed with them. Give me some weed. I'd turn my stereo up blasting and I'm looking good here, I know I'm desirable. I know you want me, don't you. Come on let's go to bed. But then I've always had this thing about – I know I have a body and guys thirst after me, they want this, they want what I got- *it was a sense of power*. I got what you want, but you got to pay for it. I am your antidote. (pp. 4–5)

Pepsi's story stands out from the others because of the extremities of her life. While many of the participants' parents held relatively conservative Christian views, Pepsi's mother demonized her. Further, where many of the other participants experienced rape and domestic violence, Pepsi attempted to regain control over her body by becoming a prostitute. In this way, Pepsi's story represents an exacerbated response to the common contexts shared by all of the women in this study. It is as if Pepsi got the worst of the worst, with none of the ameliorating aspects coming in to play.

Tammy: Even Good Girls Are Sluts

At the time of this interview, Tammy was a 34 year old black woman who described herself as heterosexual. Tammy appeared extremely unhappy and withdrawn upon our meeting, and she did not smile throughout the entire interview. Tammy graduated from high school and said she had had "some college." She was in her second marriage. She described her high school experience as "generally negative" and herself as a student, she identified as "unpopular and shy." She grew up Baptist in an upper middle class home.

Our discussion first centered around the images in popular culture and the messages she received regarding acceptable behavior during the time she was in school. She recalled a general message and one that underscores the romantic narrative:

> Uh thinking back… pretty much if you love someone regardless of how they felt toward you, you show them. I guess you took whatever kind of punishment they gave out to you. As long as you love them, you thought you could change them. Turn them and make them love you. (p. 1)

Tammy's mother also contributed to her understanding of sexuality:

> My mother didn't talk to me about, you know, she wasn't open. The only thing she would say is that a woman can't do what a man can do. Because a *woman's name will become mud*, where a man can get up, he can walk away and he still holds his dignity. I also probably learned from church, maybe a few sermons may have touched base about what they would call *loose women*; they classified them as prostitutes. If you're not married, you're just the same. (pp. 1–2)

Additionally, she received a further conflicting message from school regarding sexuality.

> I think when I was in school that's when they really started talking about AIDS. That came into the picture and that's when they started talking about "if you are going to do it, wear a rubber to protect yourself." *But if a girl carried a condom, they would probably call her a whore.* (p. 3)

Many women in this study echoed the same dilemma, a dilemma that women continue to find themselves in today.

We then approached Tammy's experience with receiving an adverse sexual label. According to her,

> He [her boyfriend] wanted to have sex with me and I wouldn't. So what he did, he started spreading rumors that I did that and none of it was true. Because I didn't do it. A lot of people would just call me "trick" or names like that or "easy" or they wanted to go out with you because they think you're easy. In school I didn't have many friends because I felt defensive. (p. 3) For a long time I felt like nobody would accept me just for me because they couldn't get past the rumors. You get a feeling of worthlessness. It's like you're always trying to get people's approval or if you say something or do something, you wonder what are they going to say now? If I make a mistake are people going to talk about me again? Are they going to overlook all the good things that I do and just take that one little mistake and just cover everything over that I have done good? (p. 4)

Tammy said she married the first man 'who accepted her,' but she said he was physically and verbally abusive to her for several years before she left. She remarried and remains with her second husband today. She said she still struggles with some of the issues of her past and her painful experiences in school. Her school experiences of being withdrawn and never developing any friendships with anyone, according to Tammy, were largely a product of the shame she felt as a result of having this label, a shame that is reiterated by the many of the women in this book.

Shayanne: Pregnant Girls?

Shayanne was a 25 year old Hispanic woman. She seemed very unhappy, although she said she was interested in talking about her experiences. Several times during the interview, she became very emotional. Shayanne dropped out of high school in her 11th grade year; however, she received her GED and had "some college." She described herself as bisexual, but has maintained a purely heterosexual relationship for a number of years. She was raised Catholic and described her family as "poor." Our first topic involved her perception of the messages available to her regarding sexuality, and she recounted, "The whole Barbie doll image. You had to be very feminine and like the whole aura of smelling like flowers and just soft stuff." She said she never felt like she fit it because she enjoyed hanging around boys more. Her experience with receiving an adverse sexual label, according to Shayanne, happened as a result of a pregnancy.

> When I got pregnant, I heard it [slut] all of the time, and it was always little things like people would walk by talking about "only tramps get pregnant" and saying "only girls that were sluts and tramps are the ones that were pregnant." It didn't make any sense because they were all out there doing it, it just happened to be that I got unlucky that time. After my daughter was born, I would get tons and tons of "can I have your number, here's my number, give me a call." (p. 5)

After this experience, Shayanne said she had very few friends and didn't feel like she could get close to anyone or trust anyone. Boys would ask for her phone number, but it was clear they just wanted to meet up for sex, since she received the label, she began to feel like "open prey." She felt extremely isolated in school and didn't understand how she had become the subject of such ridicule. Her experience with sexual education or discussion of sexual issues in the school was very limited. She said she could recall no formal sexual education, but remembered the "safe sex campaign" from outside of school, not from within her high school curriculum. The message she received also was laden with contradictions for young women.

At the time I remember it was a big controversy about giving young girls protection. They thought that if you give them protection, you were encouraging sex and if you didn't then it would be you were asking for trouble. At the time it was just "don't do it" because you are going to end up with a baby. Not the guy.

She offered this for young women today,

They do need someone who can help them see what it is that they are. It gets so bad to where you hate the fact that there is a lunch time or there is a break – what are you going to do during that empty time? – I mean if there is things for those, even for young girls to hide from that little bit of time. (p. 10)

For Shayanne, social isolation and feeling like she had to adhere to white standards of beauty were the major obstacles for her in high school. These aspects of being labeled contributed to her feeling vulnerable in school and out of school.

Deanne: You Have to Give It Up

At the time of the interview, Deanne was 27 years old. She identified herself as white or Caucasian, and heterosexual. She was very friendly and did not appear reluctant at all to participate in the interview. She graduated from high school and has had "some college." She had been married once, but was divorced at the time of our interview. She was raised as a Jehovah's Witness in a middle class home.

Concerning prevalent messages she received, Deanne said she remembers reading popular magazines in high school, like *Vogue* and *Seventeen*, and she recited some of the confusing messages that the magazines espoused regarding female behaviors, "well, one you had to be beautiful, a certain size or whatever. You had to be seductive. Not so seductive that you were throwing yourself out there though." She explains how she became labeled:

It happened around my junior year, it started and it carried on into my senior year. I mean even though you don't do the act or whatever, you still fool around and you're known as a slut or whore or whatever. Basically, if you don't give it up they are going to call you that and that's what I experienced. They called me a whore because I didn't give them what they wanted.... It makes you wonder, okay why is there a double standard? Being called those names made me wonder why to even try for the opposite sex, I mean if that's all they want and if you're not going to give it to them, then they are going to call you those name or think that of you. So it is so hard to try to bond with males... The guy wants someone who is easy, but then if it gets around that the one he has been that way with a few times, then she is labeled a slut. It makes you think why even try. *It makes you wonder why there is a female species – for reproduction?* – who knows, but the males species can be brutal. They have no mercy on women and their feelings.... I'm in a relationship now that is over a year old and I try not to accuse him of wanting someone else, but it's always there and it's only because of my insecurity. Even though I give him what he wants, it's still there. I think that's where the high school experience – I mean that is what, I wouldn't say molds you, but it's your mind set as far as how men are going to treat you when you're older. (p. 7)

When asked about her experiences with formal sexual education, her memory was being separated from the young men in her class during Health class and getting information regarding certain diseases. Her recollection of the safe sex rhetoric seemed to be plagued with a high level of confusion and demonstrates how she, like many women, are taught and convinced that we are sexual gatekeepers and sexual responsibility is primarily our concern.

I feel the same way now that I did in high school. It's always up to the girl, the female. I mean basically what I got from 'just say no' was about using contraceptives. It's always up to the girl, because basically they are the ones that really have the say whether they are going to give it up or not. *Condoms were not acceptable for a girl to carry because you would be known as a slut or a whore. I didn't know of any girls that did carry them.* (p. 3)

The sexual double standard whereby males gain status by sexual conquest over girls, and females lose status and dignity by engaging (or even failing to engage) in sexual activities was a main focus for Deanne. Her story highlights the difficult bind girls are in as they navigate expectations to look sexy and "give in" to boyfriends, and yet to not be prepared to protect themselves from sexually transmitted diseases or pregnancy.

Camille: No One Was There to Help

Camille is a black woman who was 26 at the time of this interview. Camille was very concerned about privacy at the onset of the interview and commented before we began that this was going to be "hard." She described herself as heterosexual. She attended and graduated from an urban high school and was, at the time of this interview, an honor student in college. She had never been married and grew up an only child with a single mother in a Christian home. She described her high school experience as "very negative" and characterized herself in school as "disruptive, unpopular, and smart." She recalled messages she received regarding sexuality,

I remember the thing I got more than anything was that beauty was extremely important, *beauty would get you a man and you would be happy in some way, shape or form*. As an African American I got a lot of things from television and our own little teen magazines that maybe you have to be kind of aggressive with them, be willing to let men do the things they wanted to do and be willing to treat men with a lot of respect – make them feel manly by letting them do whatever they want to do to you. I think the ideal romantic situation for me in my era would be for a man to want to be with you. In retrospect, I don't really remember my own desires being addressed. I think, in any way my desires might have been addressed, might be to pick a man that has some money. I think that would be the extent of what I should want in a man-but never say I want him sexually. (p. 2)

Her perceptions of sexuality, the romantic narrative and belief that women should sacrifice for love, may have contributed to Camille's difficulty in her relationships. Camille had her first sexual experience at thirteen with a 20 year old man who was physically abusive towards her as well. When she was fifteen, Camille became pregnant and had an abortion. Her family members ridiculed her and said things like "you let him do this to you, you tramp." The much older male was not held responsible for statutory rape, and the young girl was made to feel shame and ridicule.

Camille recalled school being a very unpleasant place for her. She said that she didn't have any girlfriends because they didn't want to be associated with her since she was promiscuous. She remembered that she missed a lot of school, since school did not feel like a comforting place to be. Camille offered that her high school experiences impacted her life in a number of ways.

Let's start with men. I had bad relationships all my life, bad abusive, especially verbally abusive. The thing about it is you just begin to feel that nobody's every really going to love you. You really feel like why should they? Sex is like a chore to me because I've had so much and it's a chore to me. In my last two or three years of my life, it's massively degrading to me (p. 8)

Although Camille was a successful student at the time of this interview, currently serving a leadership role in the college, with plans to continue on to Graduate school, she feels as if she is a failure. She told me that she has been diagnosed as a manic-depressive, drinks heavily and has recently been prescribed an anti-depressant medication. She said she feels incredibly lonely and has no relationship with either men or women. Such isolation is another theme that permeates lives of women who are marginalized by sexual stigmas.

Jocelyn: He Was My First, Though

Jocelyn was a white, twenty five year old woman. She was very friendly and open before and during our interview. She attended and graduated from an urban northern, middle class high school. She earned a bachelor's degree

and was currently teaching elementary school. She described herself as heterosexual and was married at the time of this interview. She said she grew up
in a lower middle class family with her mother and stepfather and they were
involved in the Christian church. She described her high school experience
as "generally bad," although she described herself during high school as
"outgoing, popular and popular with teachers."

She recalls the primary narrative available to women involved women
"being very thin and working hard to please the man. Women were much
more polite, less sexual. The women that were sexual were considered sluts."
Her experience with sexual education echoed what other women in this study
recalled, that there was little and the message that was available regarded
safe sex or "just say no." However, she too cited the contradiction in that
message. "Boys were ok to carry condoms, but girls were sluts. It was okay
for a boy to go buy them. A girl wouldn't dare" (p. 4).

Jocelyn experienced harassment and name calling from her boyfriend's
friend who didn't like her. She said that she remembered how painful all of
those experiences were. She said that moving away from her peers was her
coping mechanism. She had been the victim of an abusive relationship before
meeting her current husband. She recalled how the reputation she developed
in high school adversely affected her life.

> It definitely made me, I mean I didn't like myself and I fell into the vicious cycle of
> dating complete jerks that were going to take advantage of me in some way. I just
> didn't have the confidence to take myself out of that. I felt like I had to have some-
> one, to be dating someone, to prove that I wasn't that way. I am very closed about
> sex. I think that it's probably thinking that it's wrong to be open. I don't talk about
> it. It's not something that is a big conversation piece for me. I guess it's kind of ta-
> boo. I think that the stigma that I got in high school, whether true or not, made me
> feel like I couldn't be a sexual person. So I think that that's part of it too... and I'm
> still just kind of scared to be open and honest because I don't want to get the door
> slammed in my face. (p. 9)

Through Jocelyn's story, we see the long term impact of social isolation.
Her way of coping with the name calling was to withdraw from social situations. Echoing the experiences of so many others in this study, Jocelyn became involved in an abusive relationship in her first marriage. Even in her
mid-twenties, she remained reluctant "to be open and honest."

Joanne: He Goes to College: I Have to Drop Out

Joanne was a 30 year old black woman. Joanne was extremely concerned
about confidentiality. She did not want to meet at the university in case anyone she knew was there. We met at her office, long after her colleagues left.

She asked several times for assurance that her name would not be revealed. (As with all of the names of the participants in our study, a fictitious name is used.) Joanne obtained her GED and she had "some college and vocational training." She described herself as heterosexual and was engaged to be married at the time of this interview. She grew up with her family as lower middle class. She described her high school experience as "horrible," and described herself during high school as "disruptive, popular, mean, and popular with teachers." Joanne said that she would have to cut the meeting short due to a prior engagement, however, her interview ended up being one of the longest and most engaging. It appeared her initial assertion about leaving probably had to due with her concern of being recognized. However, once she began talking, she became much more relaxed.

Her experience with receiving a sexual label came out of the way she dressed. She recalled one of her teachers saying to her "you're going to get pregnant before you leave school" (p. 1). She recalled her most painful experience in school:

> I got in a fight with a guy… he was a real big guy, he played football. One particular evening we were at the lockers and he came up and he felt me. At first I was like ah this is a big boy you know and my brothers ain't around and I didn't do anything. He did it again and we got into this real big fight and he was like "oh you're nothing but a whore anyway, why you trippin'?" There was a big old commotion and I got put out for 10 days. Ten days and I couldn't come back to school. I remember him specifically because he played football and when me and him got into it, it was like the whole football team and everybody hated me. Everybody hated me for that incident, and when you think about it, I didn't even do anything. After that when I got back to school it was like "oh there she go" – people would talk and stuff. They didn't care that he felt me up. I hit him with a locker, so that was assault. He didn't get put out, he didn't get reprimanded; *he didn't get anything.* He went to play with some school in Canada or something – I didn't go back to school. I ain't never gone back to school ever again in my life – *never, ever went back.*

> The school personnel didn't want to hear it. I seriously feel like he violated me because the first time he did it I didn't want to say nothing because this was a big man, you know he was going to beat me up. When he did it again, I just got tired of it because I felt like he only did it because he thought he could do it. He tried and because when I stood up the only thing I heard was me. He got a high school diploma. I had to get my GED. I had to do more than the average person had to do to go to college. I had to do more. It's not fair and I think back to it all the time. I never told nobody because *I just feel like I would get another label.* (pp. 2–3)

Joanne said she went on to become involved in abusive relationships when she left high school. In fact, the man she was with until she was twenty eight left scars on her back and arms from cutting her, she showed me some of these scars. She shared that she can't have children, because while she was involved with this man she contracted chlamydia and without adequate medical care, it had done irreparable damage to her reproductive organs. She left him and went to a shelter. She has recently remarried, but the memories of her high school experiences continue to haunt her today.

Kathryn: Confidence Is Dangerous for Young Women

Kathryn was a 25 year old, white woman. She appeared very friendly and was enthusiastic about the interview. She described herself as a homemaker and an actress. She grew up in a middle class home as a Mormon. Kathryn graduated from a southeastern high school and had "some college." She described herself as heterosexual and was married at the time of this interview. She, unlike most of the other women in this study, described her high school experience as "generally positive" and herself as a student, she described as "a perky cheerleader with long curly blond hair and blue eyes."

> I think the rules were different for different people. That's the weird thing about high school. It depends on the person. Well, I don't know; it's so weird. Obviously if you're in a relationship in high school it was okay to have sex with your boyfriend and that was just kind of accepted. It was basically not have you had sex, it was how long did you wait to have sex? That's how it was. But we all had friends, we knew girls that were at a party and got drunk and had sex, and it really wasn't frowned on. Well, I think it depended on how you acted in the school. Say like if you were a sweet girl and you had a one night stand, you were like 'oh yeah, I understand, you just got drunk or whatever.' They understood. But if you were viewed as someone who was maybe really confident and flirted or whatever, they would be like well that's just the way she is. (p. 2)

Kathryn felt like she developed a reputation because she was confident and boys tended to like her. Of all of the women involved in this study, Kathryn's experience with harassment seemed to be less harmful to her than they other participants. This may be in part because, as Kathryn described herself, she was a "perky blue-eyed, blond haired cheerleader." She resembled the ideal of femininity as expressed by other women in this study as well as the literature reviewed on popular culture (Hunter, 2002; Younger, 2009). However, her story serves to further illustrate the conundrum with which women are faced. While some of the women in this study felt as thought they weren't attractive enough and those feelings contributed to their sexually adverse label, Kathryn's experience illustrates that women who are viewed as confident are also in danger of receiving sexual adverse labels and are subject to harassment in schools.

Lee: Pick Your Friends Wisely

At the time of this interview, Lee was 27 years old. She was extremely articulate. She graduated from high school, held a bachelor's degree in anthropology and was at the time of this interview seeking to enter a graduate program. She did not identify herself as any particular "race" because she said she did not care to refer to herself in that manner. She was a single, heterosexual woman who grew up in a 'poor' Jewish family. Her high school experience was "negative" and she described herself in school as "unpopular and weird." Her understanding of the message provided through popular culture was in direct contradiction to her own notions.

> Well, my idea of their [celebrities] sexuality was not the same as my idea of sexuality for real non-famous women. My idea of their sexuality was that they were putting forth an image of women as being hypersexual and easily accessible to any man who wanted them. But my idea of real women's sexuality is there a gross double standard at play. Men can go out and party and pick up as many women as possible. If women do that, you would probably be living it down for the rest of your life. (p. 1)

Reflecting on her experience with receiving an adverse sexual label, Lee remembered much of the harassment she endured came strictly because of her choice of friends and dress and because she did not seem to 'fit in' with the mainstream student body.

> I hung out with a crowd of metal heads, everybody called them burnouts. While I was hanging out with those guys, just by association, I'd walk by and people would mutter under their breath a variety of unsavory comments. I would walk by wearing skin-tight acid washed jeans and somebody would go "slut" or "whore" or whatever. (p. 3)

Lee had sex for the first time when she was seventeen with a boy that attended her school; he came back and told the 'entire school' about the experience. After that her experience with being harassed and ridiculed only worsened. According to Lee,

> A guy named Tony had been picking on me a little bit for being Jewish, which is totally unrelated. After he heard the story of me sleeping with my boyfriend, he just really laid it [the harassment] on nice and constantly. At one point he stole my yearbook and wrote things all over it and returned it back to me with all sorts of derogatory words written in permanent black marker. Lots of comments about my ass. He even spit on me in the hallway. (p. 4)

Lee was asked to elaborate on how the experience of being labeled and called names affected her.

> They bothered me a lot, very deeply, but they didn't bother me in a sense of this person is calling me a slut therefore I am a slut. This person is calling me a freak, therefore I am a freak. It bothered me because I felt like an alien, like I was dropped onto a different planet. That I had no connection to these people and they had no connection to me. It was really depressing.

Just as Lee points out here, there is a great deal of isolation that girls who are marginalized and harassed experience. These feelings of isolation contribute to larger psychological and academic consequences.

Heather: The Whole School

Heather was a 32 year old white woman. She seemed very unhappy at the time of our meeting, and kept her responses during the interview very "matter of fact." She graduated high school and had "some college." She was single and described herself as heterosexual. She attended an urban high school that was mostly white. She said she grew up with "very liberal" parents in a middle class, non-religious home. She described her high school experience as "pretty bad" and described herself as a student as "outgoing and disruptive."

Heather, reiterated that while the "just say no" message permeated the discourse on sexuality; girls were told that they too were responsible for safe sex. Yet, according to Heather, the reality was that girls did not carry condoms because it was not acceptable. Her experience in school was painful for Heather. Heather said she received the label in high school as girls began spreading rumors around school that she was sleeping with everyone, and people began referring to her as "slut." It turned quickly into what she said was the "whole school" being involved in her harassment. They called her names whenever they saw her in the hallway, in class or in the lunchroom. She described school as "an uncomfortable place. I was extremely depressed all the way through high school. I was very depressed, with very low self-esteem." Her high school experiences contributed to her development as an adult woman, according to Heather, "I've been promiscuous off and on; mostly my self-esteem has never really recovered. I don't really know – the last time I can remember my self-esteem being really good was in the 6th grade. After that it's been pretty down the toilet" (p. 7). Heather said that she has not had a relationship with a male for a number of years, and that she moves very often. She has found little stability, and is still trying to reconcile some of her early experiences.

Kesha: He Was Supposed to Love Me Forever

Kesha, at the time of the interview was a 25 year black old woman. Kesha seemed very enthusiastic about the opportunity to discuss her experiences, and she was quite verbose in her responses. She graduated from high school and had "some vocational training." She described herself as heterosexual, married once and was divorced at the time of this interview. She grew up with her grandparents as the youngest child in a middle class, Baptist home. Her high school experience was "just bad, bad, bad," yet she described herself as "outgoing, athletic, and popular" in school.

Kesha first reflected on popular media that she recalled while she was in school and some of the images of women and the message regarding female sexuality. "Mainly I would say I read a lot of *Jet* and stuff. Women have to be perfect, have the perfect shape, be clean and everything. I always been thick, so I used to always not eat as much or whatever so I stayed thin" (p 1). Attempting to achieve the sexual allure of those pictured in *Jet*, left Kesha feeling worthless and imperfect by contrast.

Her experience with receiving the sexual label occurred for Kesha out of an "acceptable, monogamous relationship."

> When I first had sex, I was 17 and I never had sex with nobody else – just him – and he went back and told everybody that me and him had sex and stuff. Then it started – that's when everybody started labeling me – I hadn't been with nobody but one guy and everybody started labeling me and stuff and calling me a slut and talking about I'm a whore. He was one of the popular guys because he played basketball and football and he was very athletic. The girls just hated me for going with him. They wrote "whore" on my locker and wrote my number on the boys' bathroom. It had got so bad one time where when I went to class and everything – I would never say nothing in class. The teacher called on me and they would say "oh the whore got the wrong answer," I would be so upset and everything – I had ran out of the class – I was crying because I really had did nothing to her. (pp. 2–3)... I mean they harassed me the whole year. I mean continuously until the point – *you just don't want to go to school. I come home every day crying and everything and I end up... when I dropped out of school. I dropped out. The first time I dropped out was* like for a week or whatever and then the guy that started the whole thing well we ended up taking back to each other and he was coming around to see me and everything, and I ended up sleeping with him again.... I ended up pregnant.

She ended up leaving that school because she said she couldn't face any more ridicule.

> I jumped in a marriage right when I was eighteen. After I got married I had four more kids. I ended up with somebody abusive. I got scars and everything – I mean

scars on my arms and he put me in the hospital – my ribs had been broken – I had been unconscious – I mean all kind of abuse. Then on top of everything he kind of like push me everyday to have sex and even get pregnant, like "well you know we done been together all this long time and we had sex and all this and if you love me you will do this and everything" – and I'm like "oh yeah I do love you so I guess I'll go ahead and do this." (p. 6)

Like other women in this study, Kesha eventually was able to escape the abusive relationship. At the time of the interview, she was raising her five kids by herself. The high percentage of women in this study (50% of the participants in this study) who experienced domestic violence and/or rape clearly compounded the difficulties encountered by these young girls. The national averages for both domestic violence and rape are about 33%. Clearly, the women in this study have faced these traumas at much higher rates than the national average. The attacks on self-esteem and self-confidence open women and young girls up for continuing abuse.

I always had dreamed that when I got older I was probably gonna be in college or whatever and I would meet my husband in college. I always said I wanted to be a dancer. He was going to be a doctor and we was going to have a house with a white picket fence. I was gonna have two children, a boy and a girl. You know I'm going to have everything in my house that I want and my children are going to have everything they want and my husband is gonna be true to me. Be in love and live happily ever after. (p. 10)

Summary/Conclusions

The women in this study corroborate research literature findings that women receive messages that ideal femininity and womanhood rests in one's ability to be desirable and attractive to men (Irvine, 1994; Tolman, 2000; Durham, 2008). The narratives they encountered through popular culture confirm this. They also articulated some of the messages they received presenting acceptable behavior regarding heterosexual relationships and their sexuality. Many women expressed the ideal female sexuality as passive and discreet. Pepsi, for example, was the only woman in the study who openly expressed a sexual appetite, yet even her articulation of desire is plagued with a feeling as though that very desire is bad or evil and she will somehow be punished. Tammy also grew up remembering from her mother and her church that women who had sex outside of marriage were "loose." This view may have contributed to Tammy's inability (as well as many other women) to articulate desire and perhaps contributed to her staying in an abusive marriage to regain her good standing and to remain in a marriage where sex would be viewed as acceptable. For all of the women in this study, the label they received had something to do either directly or indirectly with their exhibiting autonomous sexuality. For example, some of the women were labeled for not having sex with their boyfriends, while others received the label *because* they had sex with their boyfriends. Other women in the study developed the reputation because of their dress, or level of confidence that may have suggested a carefree attitude regarding sexuality. Despite the reasons for first receiving 'the label,' all of the women in here cited feeling isolated and somewhat disenfranchised by their peers and the adults in the school.

Also quite clear in these women's stories are how often women are victimized by abuse, and this is often a result of the culturally proscribed "romantic narrative" (Carpenter, 1998; Christian-Smith, 1988). As Tanenbaum (2000) has written, the only acceptable place for girls to express sexuality is in a monogamous, heterosexual context. In many of the interviews, the women discussed how they would 'give up' sex to 'satisfy' their male partners, with very little of their own expression of sexual desire. As Tolman (2000) has written,

> The familiar story that organizes 'normal' female adolescent sexuality is a romance narrative in which a good girl, who is on a quest for love, does not feel sexual desire-strong, embodied, passionate feelings of sexual wanting. In this story, sexual desire is male; it is intractable, uncontrollable, and victimizing. (p. 70)

This seems to be Deanne's experience with desire and sexuality. Her experience with receiving the adverse label of 'slut' came when she refused to have sex with one of the boys; she came to view this as her fault for not "giving him what he wanted". This message of women as sexual gatekeepers responsible for taming men's strong sexual urges is a message that presides over women's lives. Because women are taught that being in a relationship is important and keeping men sexually satisfied is particularly important, women such as Deanne remain in unfulfilling relationships. Camille expressed a similar understanding during her interview when she discussed available images of African American women. According to Camille, African American women learn that being desirable and accessible to men is a most important quality. However, a woman who displays her accessibility in the sexual encounter would be perceived as a "slut" if the feelings are not reciprocated by the males involved. This dilemma presented for young women underscores the masculinist nature of the cultural standards for sexuality. A woman who displays her accessibility in the sexual encounter is at risk for the cultural punishment of developing the sexual label.

As the women in this study also illustrated, images presented to young women are often contradictory and do not represent the realities of our lives.

As we note in ***Geographies of Girlhood***, "Yet, there is some consistency found in the male-centered nature of the social construction of sexuality, in the denigration of female desire. As women we are to be sexually desirable to men, regulating with constant maintenance our physical bodies, yet we are to possess no desire ourselves" (Liston & Moore-Rahimi, 2005, p. 225). Young women learn very early on that "ideal femininity" should be pursued, however, that representation is unrealistic for most women (Holland et al., 1994; Irvine, 1994; Younger, 2009). Femininity is depicted as embodying sexual desirability to men, and meeting the requirements for standards of culturally specific ideals of beauty, in particular. As the young women in this study revealed, cultural representations of beauty caused them strife and struggle during their adolescent years. Tonya, for example, grew up feeling as though she was a 'tomboy" because she never felt as feminine as women depicted in the cultural media. She was athletic and "did not wear dresses" pointing to the construction of femininity which presents being a girl in her ability to display feminine characteristics. Shayanne recalled that messages she received regarding femininity were the "Barbie doll image" and "smelling good" and "being fresh." Lees (1993) has pointed out that women are constantly reminded to buy products and seek means of keeping ourselves clean and fresh in order to preserve the 'goodness' of our bodies. This policing of our own bodies is but one discursive means of regulating our sexuality, according to Holland et al. (1994),

> Young women are under pressure to construct their material bodies into a particular model of femininity which is both inscribed on the surface of their bodies, through such skills as dress, make-up, and dietary regimes, and disembodied in the sense of detachment from their sensuality and alienation from their material bodies. (p. 24).

Another way in which women monitor their bodies in an effort to display their sexual desirability to men is through the unrealistic representation of thinness. The women in this study provided examples of how this cultural ideal impacted their lives as adolescents and as adult women. Kesha, for example starved herself to try and fit the image she recalled being portrayed to African American young women, an image from which she felt completely 'disassociated'. She recounted how she nearly starved herself throughout her adolescence to remain thin, eating only one small meal a day. Even during her pregnancy, she was hospitalized as poor nutrition left her dehydrated and malnourished. Mary Pipher has written about the cost of femininity on the self esteem of young women. In her work, *Reviving Ophelia*, Pipher (1994) writes,

Girls have long been trained to be feminine at a considerable cost to their humanity. They have long been evaluated on the basis of appearance and caught in a myriad of double binds…. Girls are trained to be less than who they really are. They are trained to be what culture wants of its young women, not what they want themselves to become. (p. 44)

Not surprisingly, the women in this study remembered very little if any sexual education. This supports evidence that formal sexual education is not the source from where they learn about sexuality (Lees, 1993: Bay-Cheng, 2006). The courses described by the participants addressed none of their personal concerns and offered little meaning and connection to the young women to whom they were presented. As we argue elsewhere in the book, simply presenting information about possible diseases does little for young women as they leave that classroom door and are overwhelmed with messages about having sex, love, relationships, beauty, desirability, danger, harassment, abuse, and other realities of their lives which may pale the importance of protection from disease. Additionally, as many of the women in this study cited, carrying condoms still remains an unacceptable practice for women, and until some of these contradictions are addressed, women are continually placed at risk.

Despite the lack of formal education, the women in this study recalled messages they learned through the hidden curriculum in their schools. This supports the notion that school staff are contributive to those messages as well, in what they do and fail to do. Failing to recognize the name-calling of women as a form of harassment contributes to the message that this regulative behavior is acceptable (Stone, 2004; Meyer, 2008). The staff and teachers who allowed and continue to allow women to be degraded, picked on, and humiliated in classrooms, hallways, buses, cafeterias, and playgrounds of schools contribute directly to the harmful practice of labeling females; no formal lesson can rectify these real lessons that we as women receive. Six of the women interviewed recalled messages that girls are to be responsible in sexual encounters with regard to protection (Tonya, Tammy, Shayanne, Deanne, Jocelyn, and Heather), but all noted that it was completely unacceptable for girls to carry condoms, noting that girls who did were quickly labeled as "sluts." The reality for young adolescent women is that the risk of disease may seam less important than a tainted, damaged reputation (Kirkman, Rosenthal, & Smith, 1998). The reality of girls' lives, the potential for attaining stigmas and labels and being subjected to harassment for a variety of reasons, is never addressed or talked about by adults in authority at the school, yet is a prevalent part of young adolescent lives. Tonya's experience with being labeled after becoming pregnant as a result of a rape indicates some of the contradictions. She lived with the label of 'babykiller' after an abortion to save herself from worrying that people would think *she* caused him to rape her.

The 'real' education these women (and contemporary adolescents as we argue in subsequent chapters) receive regarding sexuality comes in through the hidden curriculum existing in schools. Deanne said she was certain that teachers and staff at her middle and high school heard students being ridiculed and called 'slut,' yet that behavior was dismissed and not formally addressed. Joanne's experience with the hidden curriculum and school climate regarding female sexuality directly led her to dropping out of school. After standing up to a popular athlete for sexually assaulting her, it was she who suffered the most severe consequences. She was suspended, shunned, and ridiculed. School staff did not listen to her as she told them of his touching her. Her 'reputation' in school seemed to 'warrant' such assault by the male student, leaving her with no recourse. She felt she had no safe place inside of the school and no one listened to her. The reality of girls' lives, not addressed by discourses of sexuality education, is that once a young woman has developed an adverse sexual label, she becomes "open game" for sexual suggestions, harassment and abuse, from males. Pepsi, Tammy, Shayanne, Joanne, Lee, and Kesha all recalled having boys approaching them about having sex after they heard they had sex with other males, noting that women find themselves treated as "open game" for the rapacious sexual attitudes of men.

These women's accounts prove that there is no road map through which girls must travel adolescence and that a sexually adverse label can become part of their lives for a variety of reasons (not always to do with their level of sexual activity). This label can serve to regulate behaviors of young women, how women dress, who they spend their time with, how long they wait to have sex, with whom they have sex, whether they protect themselves in sexual encounters, how to handle (or ignore) sexual assaults and advances, and much more. As Tonya articulated, women are often afraid to report sexual assaults, therefore, men can often get away with this abuse, since it is women who fear being labeled. This is also evident from Joanne's experience of being punished for fighting the man who assaulted her.

The real contribution this study has for this work on sexual harassment lies in the way in which women are impacted by the receiving a reputation and being harassed in school. The stories of the women we interviewed provide a glimpse into the potential futures of young girls in schools today. In the upcoming chapters we share studies of young women, young men, and teachers in contemporary school settings articulating their experiences or understandings of sexual harassment. However the stories of these women speak to the potential long term impact negative experiences in school can have on lives. Many of the women either married right out of high school or developed 'serious' relationships. Some of the women cited their feelings of not being accepted or fitting in as a reason to marry the first person that they felt accepted them. As women, we have been taught to seek a relationship with a man. Many of the young women in this study were subjected to abusive relationships. We do not wish to imply that the harassment of these women in school is the only factor that led to their abuse as women, however, as they recalled in their interviews, their school experiences contributed greatly to their developing relationships and life choices.

Dropping out of school is a reality for many young women that face harassment Peer acceptance is extremely important during adolescence, and for Pepsi as well as other women in this story, once that was lost, it was simply too uncomfortable to go to school. With little or no place to turn within the school for girls who face harassment, there is no alternative except to leave. Unfortunately, girls who do leave school, face limited life choices. The women in this study who dropped out have faced difficult decisions, decisions that led them to prostitution, abusive relationships, and struggles finding vocation.

Women are bombarded with regulatory messages that hinder the development of our sexuality. Women who are unsuccessful at the mediation of the constraints on sexuality are labeled and marginalized. The practice of labeling is an effective means of regulating women's behavior, as the women in this study articulated.

The stories of the experiences of these women illuminate the effects of labeling and harassment. During the final portion of the interview, the women were asked to reflect on what they would suggest to young girls struggling with some of the same issues they had. Their words contribute to the discussions of sexuality and adolescence we need to have:

(1) "I think that if there was more of an opportunity to talk to somebody to say this is what is going on. That would help." (Jocelyn)

(2) "I mean I've always gone back and looked at my life and thought of what I could have done differently. I guess that's why I have such a very low opinion of men right now. Because I know what men are capable of and it just always shocked me to think here I was 14, 15, 16, 17 with men that were old enough to be my dad at times. It makes me think why didn't they just – somebody should have probably helped me – somebody should have probably said" hey you need

this or this," but it didn't happen that way. When you're having sex with men that old and you're that young, the damage it can do to your mind, it just makes you have lots of problems." (Camille)

(3) "I would say don't give in to society and what they expect from women. As far as their looks – because your looks have a lot to do with what type of respect you get as you grow older. When I look in the mirror I look at something different. I look at something that was raised right, but then turned into something ugly and disgusting and I'm trying to get back to how I was raised. Just listen to your parents, because they know best." (Deanne)

The next few chapters present data collected more recently in which we sought to find young women, men and teachers who have more contemporary experience within schools. It should be noted here that little has changed. The types of harassment about which these women spoke are evident in the voices of the participants in the other studies as well.

References

Ashbaugh, C., & Cornell, D. (2008). Sexual Harassment and Bullying Behaviors in Sixth Graders. *Journal of School Violence*, 7, 21–38.

Bay-Cheng, L.Y. (2006). The Social Construction of Sexuality: Religion, Medicine, Media, Schools and Families. In McAnulty, R. & Burnette, M., (Eds.), *Sex and Sexuality: Sexuality Today, Trends, and Controversies* pp. 203–228.: Westport, Praeger Publishers CT.

Bettis, P., & Adams, N. (Eds.) (2005). *Geographies of Girlhood: Identities In-Between*. Lawrence Earlbaum: Mahwah, NJ.

Butler, J. (1990). *Gender Trouble: Feminism and Subversion of Identity*. Routledge, New York.

Capp, B. (1999). The Double Standard Revisited: Plebian Women and Male Sexual Reputation in Early Modern England. *Past & Present*, 62, 70–101.

Carpenter, L. (1998). From girls into Women: Scripts for Sexuality and Romance in *Seventeen Magazine*: 1974-1994. *The Journal of Sex Research*, 35(2), 158–168.

Christian-Smith, L. (1988). Romancing the Girl: Adolescent Romance Novels and the Construction of Femininity. In Roman, L.G., Christian-Smith, L., and Ellsworth, A. (Eds.), *Becoming Feminine* (pp. 75–98). Farmer Press: Philadelphia.

Durham, M.G. (2008). *The Lolita Effect: The Media Sexualization of Young Girls and What We Can Do about It*. Overlook Press: Woodstock, NY.

Epstein, D., & Johnson, R. (1998). *Schooling Sexualities*. Open University Press: Buckingham, UK.

Fausto-Sterling, A. (2000). *Sexing the Body: Gender Politics and the Construction of Sexuality*. Perseus Books: New York.

Fine, M. (1988). Sexuality, Schooling, and Adolescent Females: The Missing Discourse of Desire. *Harvard Educational Review,* 58(1), 29–53.

Hillier, L., Harrison, L., & Warr, D. (1998). "When You Carry Condoms All the Boys Think You Want It": Negotiating Competing Discourses about Safe Sex. *Journal of Adolescence,* 21(1), 15–29.

Holland, J. , Ramazanoglu, C. Sharpe, S., & Thomson, R. (1994). Power and Desire: The Embodiment of Female Sexuality. *Feminist Review*, 46(2), 21–38.

Hunter, J. (2002). *How Young Ladies Became Girls: The Victorian Origins of American Girlhood*. Yale University Press: New York.

Irvine, J. (1994). *Sexual Cultures and the Construction of Adolescent Identities*. Temple University Press: Philadelphia.

Kalof, J. (1995). Sex, Power, and Dependency: The Politics of Adolescent Sexuality. *Journal of Youth and Adolescence*, 24(2), 229–249.

Katz, J., & Farrow, S. (2000). Discrepant Self-Views and Young Women's Sexual and Emotional Adjustment. *Sex Roles*, 42(9–10), 781–805.

Kirkman, M., Rosenthal, D., & Smith, A. (1998). Adolescent Sex and the Romantic Narrative: Why Some Young Heterosexuals Use Condoms to Prevent Pregnancy but Not Disease. *Psychology and Health Medicine,* 3(4), 355–370.

Kitzinger, J. (1995). "I'm Sexually Attractive, but I'm Powerful": Young Women Negotiating Sexual Reputation. *Women's Studies International Forum*, 18(2), 187–196.

Kunzel, R. (1993). *Fallen Women, Problem Girls; Unmarried Mothers and the Professionalization of Social Work*, 1890–1945. Yale University Press: New Haven, CT.

Lees, S. (1993). *Sugar and Spice: Sexuality and Adolescent Girls*. Penguin Books: London.

Liston, D., & Rahimi, R.M. (2005). Disputation of a Bad Reputation: Adverse Sexual Labels and the Lives of Twelve Southern Women. In Bettis, P. & Adams, N. (Eds.) *Geographies of Girlhood: Identities in-Between*. Lawrence Earlbaum: New Jersey: Mahwah.

Luker, K. (2006). *When Sex Goes to School: Warring Views on Sex and Sex Education-since the Sixties*. W.W. Norton: New York.

Meyer, E. (2008). *Gender, Bullying and Harassment: Strategies to End Sexism and Homophobia in Schools*. Teachers College Press: New York.

Miller, J. (2008). *Getting Played: African American Girls, Urban Inequality, and Gendered Violence*. New York University Press: New York.

Morozoff, P. (2000). A Cultural Context for Sexual Assertiveness in Women. In Travis, C. & White, J. (Eds.) *Sexuality, Society, and Feminism* (pp. 299–320). American Psychological Association: Washington D.C.

Ore, T. (2000). *The Social Construction of Difference and Inequality: Race, Class, Gender and Sexuality*. Mayfield: Mountain View, CA.

Pipher, M. (1994). *Reviving Ophelia: Saving the Selves of Adolescent Girls*. Random House: New York.

Ramazanoglu, C., & Holland, J. (1993). Women's Sexuality and Men's Appropriation of Desire. In Ramazanoglu. (Ed.), Up against Foucalt (pp.239–264). Routledge: New York.

Regan, P., & Berscheid, E. (1995). Gender differences in Beliefs about the Causes of Male and Female Sexual Desire. *Personal Relationships*, 2(4), 345–358.

Stone, M. (2004). Peer Sexual Harassment among High School Students: Teachers' Attitudes, Perceptions, and Responses. *The High School Journal*, Oct/Nov, 1–13.

Tanenbaum, L. (2000). *Slut: Growing Up Female with a Bad Reputation*. HarperCollins Publishers: New York.

Thompson, S. (1995). *Going All the Way: Teenage girls' Tales of Sex, Romance, and Pregnancy*. Hill and Wang: New York.

Tolman, D. (2000). Object Lessons: Romance, Violation, and Female Adolescent Sexual Desire. *Journal of Sex Education and Therapy,* 25(1), 70–79.

VanRoosmalen, E. (2000). Forces of Patriarchy: Adolescent Experiences of Sexuality and Conceptions of Relationships. *Youth and Society*, 32(2), 202–227.

Vijayasiri, G. (2008). Reporting Sexual Harassment: The Importance of Organizational Culture and Trust. *Gender Issues,* 25, 43–61.

Wessler, S., & Preble, W. (2003). *Respectful School: How Educators and Students Can Conquer Hate and Harassment.* Association for Supervision and Curriculum Development: Arlington, VA.

Younger, B. (2009). *Learning Curves: Body Image and Female Sexuality in Young Adult Literature.* Scarecrow Press,: Landham, MD

Chapter 3: "The New Hello" and Girls' Views of Sexual Harassment in Schools

"My mother would tell me be careful because you are pretty." -Sheila

"The familiar story that organizes 'normal' female adolescent sexuality is a romantic narrative in which a good girl, who is on a quest for love, does not feel strong sexual desire. In this story, sexual desire is male; it is intractable, uncontrollable, and victimizing." (Tolman, 2000. p. 70)

Resurrecting the Conversation

As recent discourse surrounding school violence has increasingly focused on bullied boys, girls' experiences with sexual harassment and sexual violence have begun to be grossly overlooked. Although the experiences of boys is certainly worthy of attention, and boys are also victims of gendered harassment, we are contending that girls' experiences with sexual harassment are quite prevalent, impact their daily lives in multiple ways, and need more direct attention in the research literature and in daily life. While recognizing that males who challenge the norms of hegemonic masculinity (Robinson, 2005) also face ostracism and ridicule, emergent heterosexual male sexuality is virtually free of accountability (Pascoe, 2007). However, the development and cultural proscriptions assigned to female sexuality is full of double standards, social marginalization, harassment, violence, risk and blame discourses, and the constant reminder that their navigation of sexuality is a public commodity (Durham, 2008; Liston & Rahimi, 2005). Further, the various forms of harassment experienced by girls serve to ostracize and marginalize girls and can have detrimental effects on girls' psychological and sexual well-being (Fine & McClelland, 2006; Gruber & Fineran, 2008; Lindberg, Grabe, & Hyde, 2007). Additionally, while there is a myriad of ways in which girls are harassed, there are very few supportive environments in which girls can discuss their experiences with emerging sexuality and sexual harassment, violence, and abuse they encounter, including on school grounds. Therefore, understanding the experiences of girls who have encountered various forms of sexual harassment on and off school campuses is imperative, especially given findings that indicate other students and school personnel often overlook the impact of sexual harassment on school grounds (Rahimi & Liston, 2009). The study supporting this chapter, conducted in the fall and spring of 2009, examined how young women aged 18–20 define sexual harassment as they reflect on their recent high school experience. In particular, this study sought to examine what opportunities adolescent girls have/had within the context of contemporary high schools to discuss issues of sexuality, sexual harassment, and sexual violence. We seek to unveil the ways in which sexual harassment permeates the lives of young women, with a particular emphasis on their experiences within the culture of school. As the young women in this study shared their experiences, our suspicions were confirmed: On a daily basis girls experience harassment, little is done to counter sexual violence and harassment in school; and in fact, the culture of school often serves to perpetuate hegemonic notions of gender and sexuality which contribute to a climate of violence. Finally, it was clear through the participants' accounts, adolescent students have very little space within school to address these issues.

We interviewed twelve recent high school graduates attending a mid-sized public college in the southeastern United States. The girls were solicited through word of mouth, through flyers hung up on bulletin boards around campus and through an advertisement posted in the local school newspaper. Following IRB protocol, in-depth interviews were conducted with the girls who met the criteria of being between the ages of 18 and 20. As we did not interview students who were currently in high school, we wished to ensure the young women could recall their high school experiences, therefore participant criteria required that the young women had completed high school more recently than two years prior. During the interviews, participants were asked to reflect back on their high school experiences and discuss definitions of and experiences with sexual harassment and sexual education as it was provided both formally and informally within the school setting. Prior to the interviews, the participants were asked to provide some general demographic information. (Appendix A contains a quick reference for demographic/findings from each participant.) According to their self-identification, the demographic profile of the participants revealed: five African Americans, two biracial, four whites and one Hispanic. Eleven of the young women identified themselves as Christian and one as Atheist. Eight of the participants identified themselves as middle class and four identified themselves as lower middle class. All of the young women in this study identified themselves as heterosexual. Nine of the participants attended high school in the southern United States, while three attended school in the Northern parts of the U.S. Research questions focused on their definitions of harassment, and the influence of media, religion, family, and peers on those definitions. The research also focused on young women's experience with formal sexual education, perceptions of school personnel's response to harassment, culture of school regarding harassment, and personal experiences with harassment and/or violence. The interviews were recorded, transcribed, and analyzed for unique themes and compared to current literature.

While we recognize this research study is not without its limitations, we also assert the information gleaned from these participants is representative of young women's experiences. We acknowledge the rather small sampling size and the regional specificity of this study. However, these girls did not attend the same high schools. Participants attended schools all over the southeastern United States, with several attending schools in other regions. While this does provide a snapshot of the experiences with sexual harassment encountered by southern girls, we contend, as has been found in numerous preceding studies, that the sampling of participants' experiences further illuminates the existence of sexual harassment found nationally in U.S. schools.

Numerous thematic findings emerged from this study, many reiterating what the women in Chapter 2 recalled experiencing, demonstrating that not much has changed for women and girls since the turn of the century. The first finding relates to the ways in which females conceptualize sexual harassment within their own lives and the lives of others. While we have noted that the young women in this study provided a "classic definition of sexual harassment," (one closely resembling the definition provided by early feminists involved in revealing the concept, such as MacKinnon (1979)), laden within their notions of harassment is the idea that women are sexual gate-keepers and are ultimately responsible for male sexuality and aggression. Secondly, there emerged a distinct picture of how pervasive harassment is the lives of girls. The young women's articulations of their own experiences with sexual harassment underscore the assertion that indeed harassment occurs daily and permeates all aspects of girls' social lives. The young women in this study revealed that harassment occurs frequently (in some cases hourly) in their lives. Particularly troubling was hearing how numerous such experiences are within the context of their educational lives, we found harassment often comes both from peers as well as significant adult figures. Additionally, the young women cited instances of harassment outside of school involving same age peers as well as adults in their lives. Another emerging finding from this study is that young women experience a significant degree of shame and fear as a result of harassment, this was illustrated in the reflections of the women in Chapter 2 as well. Finally, the young women here also revealed their limited access to sexual education and/or discussion surrounding harassment. The participants confirmed a need for discourse on this topic and more direct response to sexual harassment within school settings. The women in this study confirm findings throughout the research literature; there is a hidden curriculum surrounding sexual education in which school faculty and staff fail to engage in discussions of harassment, and fail to address harassing behaviors they witness (Bradenburg, 1997; Meyer, 2008; Stein et al. 2002; Ormerod, et al, 2008). As represented by the young women in this study, young women's experience with sexual education is sparse at best.

Her Definition of Sexual Harassment

In articulating their conceptualization of sexual harassment, the participants in this study noted the unwanted nature of sexual advances and their definitions seemed clear. However, they demonstrated a disconnection between their definitions and their initial connections to their own lives and their circles of friends. That is, they could define sexual harassment, but many initially felt like it had not directly impacted them. Nonetheless, as the interview progressed, they revealed that sexual harassment (especially in the form of unwanted sexual advances) was a daily or even hourly occurrence in their lives.

As is common when asked to define a topic, the young women in our study had difficulty expressing a workable definition. They offered up statements that more or less set the stage for definition and exploration, and highlighted or overlooked various aspects of sexual harassment. For the most part, aside from using the term "sexual harassment" to start their definition, the women avoided saying the word "sex" or any derivatives thereof. Nonetheless, their definitions are insightful and help contextualize their understanding of the topic. Some definitions were vague and focused on sexual harassment making the one being harassed feel uncomfortable:

(1) "Sexual harassment is when anyone touches you and you feel uncomfortable about the situation." (Miranda)

(2) "Sexual harassment is where someone touch[es] you or talk[s] to you in a certain way that you don't feel comfortable." (Ariel)

Some highlighted or emphasized the fact that harassment can be physical or verbal:

(3) "Anything that makes you feel uncomfortable... from a touch to a comment." (Kia)

(4) "Someone coming on to you in any sexual way... verbally or physically." (Sheila)

(5) "It can be either physical or verbal, saying things like sexual comments to a woman or a man… touching them when they don't want to be." (Cassandra)

(6) "Sexual harassing… could be from any male or female to the opposite sex… it feels uncomfortable for the same sex … not even [just] physically but it can be verbal too." (Raven)

Others highlighted that sexual harassment is inappropriate, illegal or an invasion of personal rights or space:

(1) "When somebody touches you and you don't want to be … or they say something sexual towards you… [that is] not appropriate for the school setting." (Tricia)

(2) "Sexual harassment is unwanted sexual advan[ces] to the point… where the individual feels uncomfortable and sorta helpless …and feels… cross[es] the line of acceptable joking behavior… completely out of line comments or actions." (Kasey)

(3) "A male trying to touch you or saying things to you that is inappropriate with a sexual context to it, or just hinting things toward you." (Colleen)

(4) "It goes a little beyond physical harassment, I feel like it is any type of physical or verbal… just anything to do with your sexuality… or whatever." (Kelsie)

(5) "I define sexual harassment as violating the person's personal rights or abusing the privileges of an individual person's rights." (Dominique)

One person noted the persistence of sexual harassment, highlighting that generally the harassment is not a one-time event, but an ongoing situation:

"I define it when one person like touches another person where they feel uncomfortable, to the sense of it's constantly annoying." (Morgie)

Another person highlighted the perceived subjectivity and the importance of context in determining what constitutes sexual harassment.

"Calling it sexual harassment would depend on what the girl's reaction would be... if they don't like it or take it defensively, then... that is sexual harassment." (Ariel)

Finally, one person offered the following statement, showing a conflation of sexual harassment and rape:

"I had friends whose boyfriends would force them to have sex, like it's rape, but you know, just because they were in a relationship, they didn't see it that way." (Kia)

Clearly, the young women in our study presented sketchy and incomplete definitions of sexual harassment that ranged from comments and actions that are "uncomfortable" to more serious and persistent comments or behaviors directed at others, all the way to a conflation of sexual harassment and rape.

Undoubtedly, girls' experiences with sexual harassment are multiple, frequent, and occur in private and public spheres. The young women's articulations of their experiences indicate that many regard themselves as gatekeepers of male sexuality, revealing the troubling double standard that has plagued girls' lives deeply.

For many girls and young women, the message that permeates their lives regarding sexuality is one that places them in the position of gatekeeper. Noticeably missing from the comments provided by our participants was discourse reflecting young women's desire or sexuality autonomy. Rather, the conversations in their lives reflect young women as either mere participants in the narrative of ***male*** desire or as ***the*** person responsible for containing the dominant, rapacious sexuality of young men. One participant stated: "your virginity is sacred to your body; your whole body is sacred, especially being a female. I don't think it should be tampered with and just be given to anybody" (Sheila). Male virginity does not seem to be a precious commodity as they don't run the risk of being 'damaged property' with sexual experience. Another participant stated: "Because once we lose our virginity, we can't get it back. Like you can't tell if a man has lost his virginity or not, but you can tell if a woman has, so it's like, sacred and should only be given to, like in the Bible, should only be given to your husband" (Sheila).

In addition to pressure on girls (but not boys) to remain virgins, the girls in our study talked about the pressures of being the gatekeeper for the sexuality of others (especially males):

Going out with my friends, and I am the one like, "keep your hands off her", and they would be like, "look how she dress"... there will be those females who, even if it is a boyfriend, if they have too many boyfriends, and of course be sexually active with them, I guess like three or so, and if someone doesn't like it, you know you get labeled a "ho." Where with the guys, they can sleep with everyone, and it's ok for a guy, so yeah... Cause who's gonna wanna marry someone that everybody's been with? Who is going to actually wanna settle down with that person? (Kia)

The comments from the young women we interviewed give the impression that girls are to blame for the "bad things" that happen to them. One person stated: "I feel like there are some girls who are more likely to be victims because of the way they dress or their self confidence" (Kelsie). Another echoed this sentiment stating: "To me, what gives girls reputations, may be the way they dress is sending messages to the dude and maybe that is why they act the way they act, so maybe they should dress more appropriately for school" (Miranda). And another chimed in: "Sexual harassment probably wouldn't be as public as it is if girls respected themselves more" (Kia). Blaming the victim was a popular refrain, as yet another contributed: "Women are more sexually harassed because we are more passive by nature" (Kasey). This particular comment as well as this one presented by a participant, "if girls dressed more appropriately, they would get more respect" (Kia) imply that boys are free of responsibility regarding the harassment or mistreatment of young women. If only girls dressed better or if our 'nature' was such that it didn't allow us to be taken advantage of, we would be harassed less. The implication is that men's sexuality need not be put into check.

This progression of thoughts moved from girls as gatekeeper to girls are responsible for bad things that happen to them, into a definite double standard of behavioral expectations. Participants in our study reveal the sexual double standard that has silenced the discourse of desire (Fine & McClelland, 2006).

Some of the participants' comments reveal the heterosexual male centric rhetoric that has historically surrounded the discussion of sexuality as perpetuated largely by institutions such as church, but has served to permeate and silence the autonomous development of young women's sexuality. While there are some that assert that girls have 'come a long way' regarding taking charge of their own sexuality, interviews with our participants support the postulation that traditional and "old-time" messages still remain prevalent. The conversation regarding sexuality continues to be framed within a masculinist/pro-male discourse. Many of the women engaging in the supposed "new autonomous sexuality" have served only to further sexual subservience of women and continued the cultural role of fulfilling the male gaze.

The sexual harassment of girls, name calling, touching, marginalization for challenging the social constructs of feminine sexuality (which still exist) persist *daily* in the lives of young women. Young women are aware of the potential for harassment at every juncture of their existence. The participants in this study shed light on the ways in which harassment impedes and impacts their lives. Interestingly, one participant noted her encounter with receiving lewd comments from young men was "weekly, now that I am pregnant, it is daily" (Kia). Although it is beyond the scope of our study, this comment highlights the need for further study. Research on domestic violence indicates that incidents of violence often increase for pregnant women. According to this government report, homicide has become a leading and growing cause of "injury deaths" among pregnant women (http://www.ncbi.nlm.nih.gov/pmc/articles/PMC1449204/). Further research is needed to determine if sexual harassment is also more prevalent for young women when they become pregnant. Participants in our study indicated this could be the case.

Other participants corroborated one another's claims that harassment is daily or even hourly, in every class. They state:

(1) "Bitch,' 'slut,' 'ho' were words I heard everyday, in every class period. If the teachers heard them, they would say, sit down and be quiet... other than that, they probably didn't hear it, or they probably didn't care." (Cassandra)

(2) "Girls get called names a lot." (Tricia)

(3) "Hearing the words 'bitch,' 'ho,' 'slut' on daily basis, I want to say, this is true, I want to say that there hasn't been one day that I have been in school since 9th through 12th grade that I haven't heard one of those words." (Ariel)

And that prevalence seems to translate for many girls as the "way it is," so harassment has become an accepted, expected part of young women's experience. Even young women recognize this, as one of the young women stated:

(1) Most girls don't see it as sexual harassment, they just see it as, "oh, on TV they do it and this is what a guy wants so I am just going to allow it instead of seeing it as harassment. That is why I am saying, it is so reoccurring, it is not even harassment anymore in most public areas, it is just typical." (Kelsie)

(2) "When something is so common, apparently people disregard it, regardless if it is wrong or right, if it is common, it is disregarded,

there not anything wrong about it and there is not anything unusual then, I guess in a way, people, if it is usual people will assume that it is right, and that is not the way it is." (Dominique)

(3) "Oh it [sexual harassment] happens all the time." (Kelsie)

(4) "I don't think they realize how much sexual harassment goes on." (Dominique)

Who are girls supposed to be able to trust to deal with such issues of harassment? One would hope that the schools in which they spend so much of their time and certainly where they interact most with their age grade peers would be a place in which girls should feel safe from ridicule and abuse. However, as these young women attest, schools actually do very little to prevent such harassment and in many cases only serve to perpetuate its place as culturally normative. We do not wish to lay the blame for the hegemonic perpetuation of sexual harassment entirely on school faculty and staff (a point we stress numerous times throughout this book); we only wish to illuminate the impact failing to respond to harassment has on young women's and young men's perceptions of the acceptance of harassment. We will provide our discussion of what schools can do in the final chapter of this book. We also understand there are many reasons why school staff may fail to respond to issues of harassment; those will also be elaborated upon in Chapter 5. We do however, want to note the ways in which the young women in our study perceived the actions and inactions of school faculty; and how these inactions continue to silence the young women's understanding of their own sexuality.

Given the opportunity to discuss sexual harassment, young women have a great deal to say. One participant noted: "if a girl has a large chest, guys will say stuff about that. I had a friend who felt real uncomfortable in high school about her breasts. And I am like, 'Uh, you can't really control that'" (Cassandra). There is also sense of despair that the girls express; they feel as if there is no place on campus where they can go to have such harassment addressed. They feel they have no one they can turn to for help in stopping the harassment: "guys always comment about it. And it's like, you are in high school, who do you really tell?" (Kia). They clearly experience sexual harassment within the school walls during school hours quite frequently and often in view of peers as well as school personnel. Participants shared with us that they feel helpless and vulnerable.

Below the young women's experiences reiterate the multiple ways in which girls' lives are embedded in discourses of fear, shame and confliction.

Kia: Who Wants to Settle Down with a Girl Like That?

Kia is a, young black woman who graduated from high school in 2009. She described herself as growing up lower middle class in a Christian home. At the time of the interview, Kia was pregnant, and she said that she experiences sexual harassment 'daily' since she has become noticeably pregnant, but mentioned that prior to her pregnancy, she was 'harassed weekly.'

She received information concerning sexual behavior from her family, and much of that message appeared to be in the form of warnings about the risks of engaging in sexual activity in heterosexual relationships, a message of which most girls are very aware. "Oh, if you talk to a lot of boys, you are going to get that reputation." And, as girls learn, 'that reputation' serves as extremely problematic in their lives and precludes them from attaining participation in the 'romantic narrative' (Christian-Smith, 1990; Tolman, 2000) the dominant discourse surrounding female sexuality. Another comment made by Kia reveals how deeply embedded this narrative is in girls' notions of sexuality. "'Cause who's gonna wanna marry someone that everybody's been with? Who is actually going to wanna settle down with that person?" We would assert that "someone" here, while appearing generic, is clearly only meaning females. Males who have "been with everybody" are still considered worthy of "settling down with."

She also articulated some of the other conflicts facing girls as she mentioned the pressure she felt to dress "sexy" based on what she saw on television and movies. Girls who do not dress "sexy" are made fun of because they don't fit in. Yet, she admits that girls who "go out practically naked are the ones who get touched on and grabbed and felt up because they don't have respect for themselves." Kia said that boys "feel like they can do that because [the boys think] if she doesn't respect herself, why should I?" This reveals another 'common' message that permeates girls' lives and has served to police the behaviors of young women, and that is that girls have the responsibility for males' behavior and that male attitude toward women is governed by our management of our material bodies *and* theirs. "'Cause in high school, if I went to a party, I wanted to put on my short, shorts too and now when I look back on it, its like, you get more respect when you have on clothes."

Despite the earlier admission that she was 'harassed daily' by young men, many of the examples she provided regarding sexual harassment were experienced by her friends. This is but another example we have seen in our research where young women seem to distance themselves from their own experiences with being harassed. Kia described an instance of a 'friend' in high school who reported to her that she was being harassed by an older manager at work. In another example provided by Kia, she highlighted that young women are aware of sexual violence that permeates their lives. "I had friends, who, like I said, boyfriends, would force them to have sex with them, like it's rape, but you know, just because you are in a relationship, they didn't see it that way."

When I asked Kia to describe the way in which issues of harassment were handled in her school experience, not surprisingly, she illustrated the lack of involvement by school staff.

> Teachers didn't really get involved in that stuff, because it was more done outside in the classroom. Like it was in arguments and things like that. But they heard it, the teachers knew everything. It was small school, so the teachers knew everything that happened and small school, so the teacher looked at the students differently too.

We asked her to elaborate on the presence of school counselors to address some of the issues outside of the classroom; Kia informed us that they didn't have "that type of counselor" in their school. Kia divulged that there was very little sex education available, but she said she recognizes the value and potential it has for young women." She noted, "Where with the guys, they can sleep with everyone, and it's OK for a guy, so yeah, I think sex education would have helped those girls who felt they, you know, had to have sex."

Kia said that she did not receive any formal sexual education in her school. She attributed this to her attendance in a 'magnet school.' She said that the school viewed her student body as on a "higher level" so that sexual education was not needed. This view that only a "certain class" (read lower socioeconomic status) of student really needed sexual education, because only they were promiscuous is more obviously stated by the male participants in our study (presented in Chapter 4), but is also present, though more veiled in the interview data of the teachers (presented in Chapter 5). Kia did, however, note that sexual education would nonetheless be helpful for young women across the board.

> I think young women today need sex education and a counselor. Like in my school, we did not have a counselor, so if you had a problem, you just had a problem, because some girls need someone outside the home to talk to and say, "OK, this is not right, this is right" and a counselor has first had view cause they are in the schools.

Kia added that in her view school uniforms are a good idea.

> I think uniforms are a good idea because it takes one thing off your plate. So you don't have to worry about being in the latest stuff and it is kinda hard to be revealing

in a uniform. That is how girls feel, you gotta show your breast, your midriff, your butt, all this stuff, where if you are in a uniform, you can't really do that.

Girls feel pressure to display themselves as sexually desirable, and as Kia says, "taking one thing off a girl's plate" provides them less to worry about. The jump Kia takes here from sexual education to school uniforms is interesting in itself. She seems to think that policing girls' dress can be a substitute for sexual education.

Sheila: Be Careful because You Are Pretty

Sheila describes herself as "mixed"; her mother is white, her father is black. She described growing up in a lower class, Christian home. When I asked her to give a definition or example of sexual harassment, she was very quick to offer, "guys talk about your butt or they will say remarks like 'You gonna let me hit that tonight?' Guys would know I was online and say things like 'are you going to let me bleep you?' or 'Are you going to give me head?'" These examples also point to the existence of cyber sexual harassment (Barak, 2005). She characterized sexual harassment as existing to a high degree, but offered that most people don't consider it harassment because a lot of the language is in song lyrics, pointing to the existence of violence in daily language. She mentioned receiving 'sex education' in two courses in fifth and ninth grades. Sheila said that those courses contained primarily health related curriculum and the issue of sexual harassment was never discussed. She said that she learned about sex, sexuality and harassment primarily from older siblings and friends. Following the romantic narrative and 'good girl' ideal in which so many young women seem ideologically entrenched, Sheila said,

> Your virginity is sacred or your body, your whole body is sacred, especially being a female. I don't think it should be tampered with and just be given to anybody. Once we lose our virginity, we can't get it back, like in the Bible, it should only be given to your husband.

Yet, as Sheila expressed the common belief, virginity is more precious for women than men.

> Once we lose our virginity, we can't get it back, but men can't either, but it is different. Like you can't tell if a man has lost his virginity or not, but you can tell if a woman has, so its like, its sacred and should only be given to, according to the Bible, only your husband.

Adherence to the predominant sexual double standard is clearly taken for granted and never questioned. Sheila's comments also served to remind us about the message of risk associated with being a young female, "...*my mother would tell me be careful because you are pretty.* She would say that, and I think she was trying to warn me that it is possible for someone to harass you."

During the course of the interview, when I asked Sheila about experiencing harassment, she revealed that she was harassed by her step-grandfather.

> He would stare at me while I was doing my homework. I consider that sexual harassment. He would tell me I was pretty and he kissed me before, but it never went any further than that. He was a preacher and no one believed it [that he harassed her]. I remember when I was in the 8th grade and I remember going to school feeling dirty and nasty. 'Cause I felt like it was my fault.

In addition to shame and guilt which girls often experience as the result of sexual harassment or abuse, girls also fear retaliation if they stand up to or speak with their perpetrators. (We told Sheila about the resources available for dealing with issues of abuse; Sheila did not reveal any more detail regarding her interaction with her grandfather during the course of this interview. However, her disclosure of this event illustrates the numerous places and ways in which abuse permeates girls' lives.)

> It is hard when you are in that situation. 'Cause when I watch TV and I see girls experience those kinds of things, I always say that I would tell somebody, but when you are in that situation, you get scared, like someone is going to harm you, like either his family, or him and you just get scared.

Sheila said that she has access to very little sexual education. Like other people have mentioned in this book, in many cases, sexual education seems to be reserved for "tech track or general track" courses. Many of the students and teachers who participated in AP study or "college track" courses, revealed that sexual education was not part of their educational experience. They overwhelmingly presumed that more discussion of these issues was needed in the "general track," and that these discussions were actually taking place.

Sheila rarely remembered a teacher or staff intervening on comments directed toward her, and on the issue of guidance counselors, she offered. "We had guidance counselors, but that was more for the education part, and they were crap too, they didn't help at all."

Tricia: They Don't Think There Is Anything Wrong with It

Tricia was an eighteen year old black woman. Like Sheila, Tricia recalled only two sex education courses in high school, but she recalled receiving no information or discussion on the topic of sexual harassment. "One time this guy didn't like me because I didn't like him and he decided to call me a 'bitch' and there wasn't really much I could do, I could tell the teacher, but then they would say "oh you're a little tattle tale." This points out how few safe places girls perceive themselves having within school settings. Confirming what many of the other participants discussed, Tricia said the school staff, "would tell them to stop or whatever, but its not really like you are doing something wrong, it is just like, 'Stop, don't do that, don't call her this' it *just wasn't something serious."* Tricia mentioned incidents where young men grabbed her "butt," but she told them to stop, she never reported this to any of her teachers.

> I think guys think they have the right to do things like that, no one is enforcing it. I mean like me telling them 'no' didn't do much, they were just like OK, no to you, but the next girl is ok with it... and they don't really get in trouble for it, it is just like it's ok, that's it.

Tricia was asked how she felt about being touched by young men like this, she said, "actually you feel downgraded." She said a lot of the notion about the acceptability of this behavior comes from the music/video industry:

> Like it is fine, what they show in videos and things they say in songs, it is like, "You can do this, you can do that, we can call you hos, we can touch on your butt and touch on your body and its fine." Like if you meet somebody in the club or a bar or something, like it is supposed to be OK to dance up on them and like guys... you can go out to a club and guys just come behind you and put their genitals on you, like it is accepted, they don't think there is anything wrong with it...This is a known behavior, it happens all of the time, that is kind of their way of saying I wanna dance with you, so they come behind you. Sometimes they will tug on your belt loop or tug you, or pull you by the hips and it is just like, yeah you are touching me inappropriately, but there is nothing wrong with it.

When Tricia was asked about expectations she feels regarding her sexuality, the confliction of messages becomes clear,

> I think that, everything is accepted, I am supposed to have sex and at a young age and not necessarily get pregnant or whatever, but have sex at a young age, that guys are allowed to touch you, and allowed to kiss you anywhere, that guys can say anything they want to you, but as far as your elders, I think it is more like you are supposed to wait for all that, you are supposed to get married and then have sex. You

don't even have to have sex with the whole world, or two guys, it could just be one, you are considered a 'ho' by everyone once a lot of people find out. I think it is really hard through because it is like OK to do it, but then when you do, you are labeled for it, so what are you supposed to do? It is like a double standard in a way.

Tricia discussed the need for school programs to educate on and address issues of sexual harassment in schools, "Education is a good idea, I don't think any of my peers have a good, clear understanding of what sexual harassment is."

Kasey: Covering Up Won't Help

Kasey described herself as a white, lower middle class heterosexual woman. She expressed a great deal of enthusiasm regarding participation in this study, and it was apparent that she was very interested in talking about her experiences with harassment. We argue that this is due the lack of opportunity girls have to discuss these issues. Kasey revealed the way in which girls are often programmed to believe that harassment is our fault.

> I think females are definitely more harassed because we do, unfortunately, live in a male dominated society and females, by nature; we tend to be more passive, you know that the difficulty with sexual harassment is that if it does occur a big common trait with males is pride.

Recalling instances of harassment at work, Kasey offered, "I started working at this restaurant when I was 15 and there was this cook who brought filthy magazines to work and he would always make very inappropriate comments. He would slap girls' butts." Kasey at first asserted, "I can't recall any time when I felt sexually harassed." Yet, in the very next sentence she said:

> There were guys who would, you know, in middle school, especially once I developed, would make disgusting comments. I remember when I was in sixth grade this one guy was like, "Your boobs will grow if I watered them," and for a young girl, we see all these things in magazines, we want big boobs and we want a full body, and just you know, people commenting on it, to me, feels like harassment. I wasn't aware of the full effects and how hurtful it [the harassment] was, until as I got older, and you know, the looks I had received to me was sexual harassment, because I became so insecure about my body that to this day, still do it, sports bras and a shirt that is too big and occasionally jeans, most of the time sweat pants, the whole breast thing completely, uh, I just felt gross. I remember I used to go to the doctor because I would wear a sports bra and then a cami, I would wear a regular bra, a sports bra and cami over that and then a shirt and then a sweat shirt over that. And I would get red marks on my chest from boils because there was too much heat and then that is when I just started wearing regular bras.

These insecurities seemed to be confirmed by teachers that Kasey had, "I just remember the look in teachers' eyes when I would try to look pretty, like they thought I was just trying to show off what I had. That is when I just decided to transform myself into a boy. I was OK after that. I *would rather look like a slum that a slut.*"

Throughout our interview, Kasey mentioned numerous times, how difficult and painful adolescence was for her and is for other girls. She also articulated her understanding of romantic narrative and the desire for the male gaze.

> It is like females live to be accepted by boys and almost compete with each other for boys' acceptance. I go fake tanning cause I think I am hideous when I am pale and I dye my hair and put on makeup, none of that is for us. The pressure comes from us, a competition for men, because we hold men on a pedestal, we feel like we have to have a man. You will see 13 and 14 year old girls naming their children and talking about love when they haven't even menstruated yet.

For other girls, Kasey offered,

> I would pray for those girls who felt the same pain and I really, really hope that there is a way for it to be prevented cause because of this, I believe root so many different things, you know a girl will look in the mirror and find one imperfection but cannot see how beautiful they are and that's because we are always being knocked down and I think that if we were harassed and instead if we were told, 'you are beautiful' instead of 'your boobs are huge', that it would make all of the difference in the world.

Colleen: It Is More of a Baptist Thing

Colleen is a white female who described her background as middle class Baptist. She attended a parochial school for entire K-12 school career. Colleen said she received most of her information regarding sexuality and sexual behavior from her mother who gave her the message that "if someone is in your space or doing something that makes you uncomfortable, *be careful.*" The information she received in school was largely regarding how young women should behave. "I don't think I ever had a class or anything in high school that talked about sexual violence." When asked about the messages she received concerning appropriate sexual behavior, Colleen said that she learned that "the man was to be the enforcer." She explained, "With guys, if they want something then they have to go after and the girls pretty much just going to hang there." Much of the information she received from school was "more of a Baptist thing," according to Colleen, particularly surrounding the notion that men are responsible for making the 'first move.'

Colleen noted that sexual harassment was never discussed by any school personnel, according to her recollection. When asked if she ever witnessed sexual harassment, Colleen said she had neither witnessed harassment nor been a victim of it herself. Yet, she went on to recall how prevalent name calling was at her school. She said that the names "slut and ho" were used daily. She said there were a group of girls that were "sluts." Yet, she seemed to suggest that these girls deserved these labels. "The cheerleaders and their whole little group were the sluts. It was probably the way they acted or how they wanted the guys to see them, or how they dressed. But they had also done stuff to get the names." Colleen suggested that teachers probably would not have responded if they had heard the names being used. "I don't necessarily think they would jump on the matter right at the time. It is probably something that they keep underneath; they don't really talk about it or bring it up."

When Colleen was asked what could make it better for young girls in high school, she offered,

> I think girls probably have a hard time in high school with other girls and sexually trying to look a certain way to maybe get boys and I think there is more girls who are maybe more mature in that, where girls that aren't as mature get pressured into dressing a certain way to get a guy and feel like they have to do that. I felt that pressure, I wanted to do something so maybe the guys would talk to me. I was a freshman, but I did not want to get the name of being a slut, I just maybe wanted to get attention or something.

In Colleen's interview the challenge of being "sexy" and fitting in while not becoming labeled slut is evident. Even in her advice to the next generation, that struggle is highlighted – although with no resolution offered.

Cassandra: Just Keep Walking

Cassandra was a young black woman who describes her socioeconomic status as poor. Cassandra was asked the degree to which she thinks sexual harassment exists and she offered,

> I would say that it exists a lot. Because I know a lot of students complain about boys at my school, a lot of students complained about boys saying stuff to them, touching them, so it was kinda common in my school, but some teachers overlook and some didn't care about it, it was like, "You go sit down, it will be ok."

Her comments reiterate how many teachers overlook the harassment that takes place. Further, she illustrates that there are groups of male students, the athletes of the school, that seem to get 'free passes' regarding the harassment of young women,

> they were on the football team, most of the guys anyway, and boys would touch them [young women] on the bus, and since they were on the football team, and were winning, they would overlook it and wouldn't say anything about it, well the teachers would overlook and wouldn't say anything about it or wouldn't report them to the principal or nothing. Girls would sometimes go to the teacher and say 'he is touching me' and they [the teachers] would see it and would just turn the other cheek.

Cassandra's comments also reflect her perception of growing up in a poor neighborhood and her experience with harassment. "My parents didn't talk about sexual harassment, but I grew up around it, people that I stayed around were kinda lower class",

> so I learned it from society or the community. I think lower class is more accepting of it, but they know it is sexual harassment but it is kinda like they care, but they really didn't. Like when I went to school you would see females like, "I wish he would stop touching me" and stuff like that. Some would say that, but from where I stayed at, they would just brush it off and keep walking.

Jody Miller in her research found that sexual harassment exists to a much higher degree in lower socioeconomic areas and that girls have very limited recourses to such harassment and abuse (Miller, 2008). Miller found that women in this environment often had little recourse in terms of harassment and out of fear of retaliation learned to simply deal with the harassment, often by ignoring comments or touching, or as Cassandra articulated, by learning to 'brush it off and keep walking.'

Cassandra said she recalled one sex education class (titled health) in fifth grade. She recalled a chapter in her Family and Consumer Science course (a course offered to her in the tech track program). Other than that, she said she had no other experience with sexual education or discussion with any of the faculty or counselors at her school regarding sexual education or harassment.

Yet, she was able to recall instances of sexual harassment directly impacting her on her school campus, with little help from faculty and administration for truly addressing the issue.

> I remember my 9th grade year, probably, and I was in weight lifting class and this guy just came up and hit me on my butt and I went and told the coach and he was like, "ok, I am going to tell the office," and he actually did tell the office that it was a male and I think they gave him a day of ISS, and I didn't think that was good enough. I didn't invite him to hit me, but they just gave him a day of ISS.

Sexual harassment was a normal occurrence in her school, as Cassandra recalled, "The boys would say little things like 'let me touch you,' but they really didn't care cause they knew they weren't going to get in trouble."

Further, in discussing the use of names directed at girls, Cassandra said the use of such language was "very common. You would hear it everyday, every class period. I think people thought it was OK to say it, so they would say it just like any other word." Outside of school, Cassandra recounted instances where she has been harassed as well. "When you are going to the mall you get cat calls or call you names or come grab you or come touch you or come grope you and stuff like that." For Cassandra, harassment has become a part of her lived experience, to the point where she has come to expect some level of harassment.

> You know somebody is going to come touch you or someone is going to say some kind of thing to you, ***but most of the time you keep walking*** or like you don't hear it unless they come touch you and that is when you feel violated, and if you are in an area where you don't know anything you are just going to keep walking like, it just didn't happen to you, ***just keep walking like you really don't care about it.***

The 'just keep walking' refrain permeated Cassandra's interview. Having few places in which to turn for help, Cassandra and her peers had to learn ways to take care of situations for themselves. Laughing it off and walking away seem to have been the most popular ways to cope.

Kelsie: Protect Them from Themselves

Kelsie was a white, middle class, eighteen year old woman. When asked to comment on the frequency with which sexual harassment occurs, Kelsie offered, "oh [sexual harassment] happens a lot. I think a lot more than people realize, even if it is happening to them, I think a lot of people don't even realize what it is, or when it happens, but I think it happens pretty frequently."

Kelsie received most of her messages regarding sexuality and sexual behavior from her parents. Like many of the other young women in this study, Kelsie was reminded about being 'careful' from her family. Kelsie was brought up in a deeply religious environment and as can be gathered from her responses. When I asked her about messages she received regarding acceptable sexual behavior, she offered,

> It was to watch my body, watch my clothing, and watch my body language, be careful how I sat around boys, how I talked to them, how I dressed and that I had a role to play and they were not only men, but my brothers in Christ and I was to try to prevent them, to do what I could and do my ***part to keep them from stumbling and falling into that sexual sin***, so that was my role, it wasn't anything that was real

burdensome or that I feel like I had to take on, it was to just guard myself by doing certain thing, watching my clothing, my attitude, the way I talked, stuff like that. That is *boys' sin nature,* I guess you could call it. I have always been told that boys are visual and so therefore to keep them, we know that, like I know that is a foot hole for them. So in order to prevent that, or to help them in that, I am just supposed to do my part not giving them anything to look at basically.

Many of her responses indicated that the responsibility for violence against women largely falls on the women themselves. "I feel like there are some girls who are more likely to be victims because of the way they are as far as their dress or their self confidence." As with many others that we interviewed, Kelsie never once mentions holding males responsible for sexual violence or predation.

Kelsie was homeschooled for most of her educational experience; however, she said that once a week she attended a community school. I asked her to reflect on any experiences she encountered with sexual harassment from boys and she mentioned,

...typically the boys kinda tended to annoy us, because they were just so rambunctious, especially younger, so they would talk about how we weren't nice to them and we would never go out them and things like that, but it was always in a very joking, loving way.

Kelsie never had any experience with sexual education, but when I asked her about the potential of inclusion of it for young girls, her response echoed her earlier responses and underscores the fear/risk discourse available to so many young women.

I feel there needs to be education on the preparation, being careful and watching your surroundings and things like that. So, that is really the only experience I have ever had with it and really my personal feelings on it is just that girls need to be more aware of what to watch and as soon as they feel uncomfortable not to wait and to go ahead and bring a friend with you or just have somebody with you, have a buddy that you are with until either that person is gone or you have left or whatever.

Again, as Kelsie demonstrates, the focus remains on girls taking initiative to observe their surroundings in order to be safe from males' predatory nature. But, there is no suggestion that males need to be educated against acting out in these ways. The double standard remains firmly in place, as harmful male behaviors are dismissed with the phrase 'boys will be boys.'

Morgie: It is Not Even Harassment Anymore; It Is Just Typical

Morgie described herself as a biracial, middle class young woman. Morgie said she thought that sexual harassment was very prevalent in culture, and youth culture in particular. Morgie mentioned the practice of boys touching girls as 'common.' She said that boys put their hands on girls' buttocks "all of the time." We asked her to tell me why she thought boys do that and she said:

> I think it is a sexual gesture or like a gesture as, "Oh I like you, I am interested in you, wanna be my boyfriend or girlfriend?" This happened very often, like you would walk down the halls, switching classes and just wherever and it would happen, and especially like, when we were at events, basketball games and football games, it would go on there too, just like as a gesture of "you look good" and everything, most girls would think it's cute, most girls would be offended by it.

The instances of sexual harassment at her school were not limited to harassment by male students. Morgie mentioned that even school resource officers in her school were 'flirty' and would "be touching on the younger girls." I asked Morgie to discuss how school staff responded to the harassment at her school. Her responses confirmed inconsistency in the ways in which school staff address the issue.

> Some students would run around smacking girls on the butts and the girls would be OK with it and they defend themselves and everything, and some teachers, they wouldn't mind it, they will know everything is OK, they are just having fun, but some teachers would actually write up for it. It definitely happened in the hallway, just because some teachers, they knew around certain teachers it wouldn't matter and some guys, they are just so playful and whatnot, they would just do it and not understand how or what the purpose is behind the girls getting mad.

Even the administration at Morgie's schools seemed to do little to address the issue of harassment. "Some of the principals really wouldn't do anything about it, but like give them three days ISS and then they were out the door or like three days detention and then it is done, like it really doesn't seem like it was a big problem at the school, but it really is." Morgie did not note any pattern to explain adult intervention or lack of intervention. In Morgie's view, adult intervention seemed truly random and incoherent.

Within Morgie's interview, she revealed other sites of harassment for young women.

> It is common for boys to feel like they can touch you, especially once you reach 18 you will start going to the clubs and everything and that is where it gets major, cause they do stuff, they grab your butt and when you are dancing with them, like if you

see a guy you might like and might want to talk to you, you might dance and everything, but they get, most guys, with me, they will get to the point where if I wear a
skirt, even if I am wearing leggings or not, they will start trying to pull it up, while I
am trying to pull it down, then I will stop dancing with them and walk off.

She mentioned that she said she feels that may times ***girls' only recourse*** is to physically fight against the males that approach them, because
they can be so aggressive. Like the other young women in this study, Morgie
had very limited experience with sexuality education. She recalled a couple
of counselors coming into her health class to discuss issues of harassment.
She said there was some debate about what was harassment, but felt like her
classmates "couldn't care less because no one followed through." She reiterated what so many of the participants throughout this book have suggested
that teachers, for whatever reason, issue the ineffective threat to write students up for harassment, however, very little is ever done to truly address the
issue.

Miranda: Sit with Your Legs Closed

Miranda was a white, middle class heterosexual young woman. According to her, sexual harassment exists 'every day.' The messages she received
about harassment, according to Miranda, largely came from her family, her
mother in particular, and from her church. "When I was little, my momma
always told me, like, sit with your legs closed and always ***be aware of your
surroundings***, just not let anyone touch you inappropriately." She recalled
having very limited exposure to information concerning harassment or sexuality education in school. She recalled message from school staff such as,

I think it was mostly our P.E. coaches and stuff and they would talk to us about not
letting people touch you or you shouldn't...if you just feel uncomfortable about any
way someone is touching you, you shouldn't let them touch you, or if you feel like
you need to talk to someone else of authority, you should tell them.

However, as she and the other participants revealed, this message does
very little for young women who recognize that often those in authority fail
to respond to their claims. So, "telling someone" when there is really no one
to tell provides a false sense of security for young women and certainly does
very little to address the culture of a school in which girls would need to tell
someone.

Miranda recalled some of her high school experiences involving the harassment of young women, "boys would always refer to the girls as hos." She
related one story of a young girl who was probably gang raped, although
Miranda (and her peers) did not define it that way:

One time during prom this girl, they called her that [ho], because they said she was in a room with a whole bunch of dudes at prom in a hotel. When she got back to school they were laughing and picking on her at lunch. She didn't really want to come out and stuff and sit down with everybody else, I think she stayed in the bathroom most of the time.

Demonstrated here once more is the fact that males are not held responsible for their actions. Rather the girls are held accountable, even for crimes committed against them.

As we discussed in the previous chapter, resigning from school activities and dropping out altogether was a fairly common response from women who are harassed, abused, or ridiculed in school. Other instances Miranda recalled involving male harassment of female students involved the way in which the athletes in her school referred to girls, "Football players called everybody bitches." She noted how the practice of boys hitting girls was a common occurrence in school, "after the bell rang and stuff, I would see a dude walk by and hit a girl on the behind and something like that, but all she would be is just 'stop it' or 'don't do that', of course, we argue, this was probably the response because there was little else for girls to do in response."

Ariel: Cut that Out

Ariel identified herself as a heterosexual, black, middle class young woman. She said that that sexual harassment exists "a lot." She said, though, that she did not hear about sexual harassment very much at all in school. She recalled receiving the "code of conduct" book and school staff would "say sexual harassment is bad, don't do it, or you will be expelled or suspended from school, that was it," an all too familiar and grossly inadequate message it appears.

When I asked Ariel to discuss her experiences with sexual education in her school, she said,

The coach asked us one day in class do we want to talk about health today or do we want to talk about sex education today. And so, of course, the class raised their hand for sex education, so he was just saying you know not to do this stuff and that stuff, like not to touch a girl inappropriately and he was speaking to the guys mainly, and he wasn't really talking about the girls.

When I asked her if she ever witnessed boys hitting or touching girls, she said "oh, well, yeah, they were kinda like smack it or whatever, trying to be cool, and that is all I seen." When I asked Ariel if this constituted harassment, she said it depended on the girls' reaction, "if they don't like it, it's harassment." She said that no one ever touched her because she "wouldn't have allowed it." When we asked her about teachers' knowledge or reaction to this behavior, she offered,

> I think some teachers saw it and I believe some teachers would say something like they would just give them the little evil eye and that stare or they would be like, 'ok you guys need to cut *that out' and that was it."* Ariel said that girls were called 'b's and ho's all of the time, probably because of the way they dressed.

Again, she noted that teachers witnessed this name calling but did little to address it. Ariel has witnessed harassment on school grounds and to and from school campus, however, she claims that she has never been victimized herself. "Outside of school, I would see guys trying to feel up on the girl and if they were wearing a skirt or a dress, they would try to feel up their skirt or dress."

Dominique: I Know They Hear It

Dominique described herself as a lower middle class black woman. She said that she received information about sexual harassment from her school, and she referred to the good touch/bad touch message she received in elementary school. She did, however, mention that the issue of sexual harassment was never discussed in middle or high school. Yet, Dominique was able to articulate instances where sexual harassment occurred both on campus and off. "We actually had a teacher fired because of sexual harassment at our school, but the issue was never discussed. That was the only one time during my whole high school career that I even heard mention of it [sexual harassment]."

When Dominique was asked if she herself had ever been a victim of harassment, she noted an instance outside of school, "There was somebody I went to go see and my sister left me alone with him and he was just making unnecessary comments and touching me. I was kinda in shock. I really didn't expect that at all." This serves as another reminder that girls experience harassment throughout all social contexts in their lives.

When asked specifically about instances on her school campus, Dominique offered, "On **a daily basis I heard** words like ho, bitch, slut. Matter of fact, I want to say this and its going to sound a little unrealistic, but this is true. I want to say that there hasn't been one day since I have been in school since 9th through 12th grade that I haven't heard one of those words." When asked about how she recalled school staff handling that language, she said that she would recall teachers just saying things like "what did you say?" but never really doing anything about it. The existence and classification of misogynistic language as 'daily' in its use is extremely problematic.

Speaking directly about other instances of sexual harassment encountered in schools, Dominique said, "The majority of it I see goes on in school. Just you know, boys touching girls on their butts and all that stuff; it is *so common.*" Her reaction to this speaks about the difficulty girls have in trying to address this all by themselves. "Now I hate to say this, but because I was around my peers, I mean, I would look really bad if I was like stop. But if I were by myself, cause this has actually happened when I have been alone. I would say something then." Her fear of retaliation from her peers for standing up for herself, allowed her to just 'ignore' the harassing behavior. Meanwhile, as she asserted, school staff offer no assistance with the intervening. She stated, "When it happens in between classes or if they do, they (the school staff) just disregard it too, just like the names, *I know they hear the words they say.*"

Raven: Shanking and Hunching

Raven, described herself as a middle class, white woman. She recalled that she received most of her information regarding sexuality and harassment from her parents. She recalled not receiving any information from the school and said the only reason she heard about sexual harassment in high school was because she held a job and had to sign contracts stipulating the consequences of sexual harassment. As Raven points out, women are very aware of the sexual double standard. "Well, I guess they [young women] are expected to be sexually active, but not, it is looked as if you are promiscuous. If you are promiscuous, you know, you are a slut or a ho." This reveals the conflicting message young women receive regarding sexuality. When I asked her to elaborate on her statement that sexual harassment happened all of the time, she said,

> Not necessarily physical [harassment], but of course verbal, people would say things, even physical[ly] there would be times where girls would just be walking through the hallway and guys would just slap them on their ass, things like that, groping someone, or winking and kissing at them, making someone feel uncomfortable, stuff like that happens, if you walk through the hallway you see that all of the time.... Freshman year, the thing was, guys just pulled their pants down and showed you their penis, or shanked you; my best friend was shanked in high school."

She clarified this term for us: "shanked for me as when someone pulls down another's pants and panties." When we asked her if she thought teachers ever saw this behavior, she said,

> Of course, but it was thrown off like, "uh stop that or cut it out." It was always a slap on the wrist until somebody complained. Unless a girl complained about it

nothing was done and most of the time nobody complained because at that age you
want to be loved or you want to experience love. At age 15 when a guy gropes your
breast and grabs your butt, you are like, "oh that is so cute; he likes me."

This highlights the extreme entrenchment in the romantic narrative, how
important it is to be desirable to a male. She says that boys used to touch her
all of the time, and when she finally got sick of it she became 'evil and
bitchy' and stood up for herself.

Raven also recalled other instances in which she was victimized. She
discussed being involved in an abusive relationship as well as being molested
by an older male cousin. While she did not wish to go into detail about this
situation, she said that her cousin went to jail for her molestation. Raven's
experience further underscores pervasiveness of girls' vulnerabilities.

Summary/Conclusion

There have been numerous studies that document the prevalence of sexual
harassment and provide clear illustrations that girls experience such harassment at higher rates than do adolescent males (Gruber & Fineran, 2008), suf-
fer more profound consequences from harassment (Ormerod etal., 2008), and
often face repercussions for reporting or discussing instances of sexual harassment or violence (Miller, 2008). This study underscores those findings.
Girls face a barrage of messages that suggest their bodies, their sexuality are
public commodities to be touched, discussed, made fun of at the whim of
male pleasure, with little interception from the significant adults in the
school who have been given the task of taking care of these young women
and providing safety for them (Lindberg etal., 2007).

From the participants' responses, several findings can be gleaned. First, a
prominent discourse that follows girls' throughout their lives is the discourse
of fear and risk. As the participants revealed, their early messages about "being careful," "covering up" and "crossing their legs" serve to remind them of
the constant risk of violence they face. This risk serves to encourage girls to
police their material bodies constantly. This has been described in the research literature as objectified body consciousness (Lindberg et al., 2007).

Just as we revealed in Chapter 2, our participants' stories in this chapter
expose the way in which young women carry a great deal of self blame when
they are sexually harassed or witness sexual harassment. These young
women illustrate the fear under which women live in our daily lives. This
fear and risk narrative is so deeply embedded in women's lives, little attention seems to be given to it. One participant shares her perspective of the ur-
gency of reporting incidents as early as possible: "Girls need to be more

aware of what to watch for and as soon as they feel uncomfortable not to wait and to go ahead and bring a friend with you" (Kelsie).

Our participants reported feelings of guilt and shame. They described themselves as "feeling dirty and nasty." Feeling they had no one to turn to, many describe making attempts to hide by wearing baggy clothing. One went as far as to deliberately "trying to transform [her]self into a boy." She noted that she felt "more comfortable looking disgusting in these male clothes: I felt ten times more great about myself than when I would try to be pretty" (Kasey). These feelings of shame and guilt highlight the fact that girls are held responsible for the actions of males. Males are rarely held responsible, even when their actions are criminal. One participant even reported how a girl was blamed when she was gang raped by a group of males at a hotel during prom.

Our participants are not unique in their feelings of guilt, shame and isolation. Their coping strategies included laughing it off, ignoring it and just walking away. Although these strategies may help remove the girl from immediate escalation of harassment, the do not deter future harassment. Further, perpetrators and bystanders (peers, as well as teachers and school personnel) may misread these coping strategies as participation in or encouragement of the harassment. Similar effects and coping strategies can be found throughout the literature and in other studies (Larkin, 1994; Yaffe, 1995; Timmerman, 2005; Young & Furman, 2008).

Knowing that sexual harassment comes at them not only from peers, but also from adults, exacerbates their feelings of isolation and helplessness, magnifying the pervasive feelings that they cannot stop the harassment, all they can hope to do is avoid as much as possible and try to find ways to cope with seemingly inevitable incidents of sexual harassment. Participants in our study corroborate the findings of Ormerod et al. (2008) that experiences of sexual harassment impact young girls "negatively and directly."

Secondly, the romantic narrative available for girls continues to serve to position them in often compromising positions regarding their relationships (Tolman, 2000). Many young women in this study cited that they viewed the harassment almost as a form of flattery, a way of ensuring they were receiving coveted male attention. Yet, they also acknowledged that failure to negotiate perceptions of promiscuity would lead to their inability to successfully fulfill the romantic narrative of "settling down with the right man."

This study also reveals the multiple places in which harassment exists for young women, in school, in social events, in their homes, at work nearly everywhere they go. Additionally, our participants recounted experiences with being sexually harassed, ridiculed or even abused by adults both within and outside of school. While this book largely focuses on sexual harassment within school walls, it is important that the pervasive vulnerabilities that exist for young women are also recognized. Often, the persons engaging in the harassment were in positions of power and/or trust with the girls involved. The girls in this study seemed to have come to expect a certain level of harassment as it seems so much a part of their lives. Their first coping measure is to take it for granted that they will experience some harassment. As the girls' comments illustrate, girls are victimized by adults in numerous settings such as at work, in public settings, in others' homes and even in their own homes. Participants bravely shared with us stories from work where managers and bosses would touch them or other female co-workers inappropriately, at home where grandfathers would stare at them in sexually provocative ways and even kiss them inappropriately; even teachers, coaches and campus police officers were known to participate in the harassment of young girls. One of our participants shared that the campus police officer at her school was transferred because he liked to "get too friendly" with the girls. These stories reflect the research literature that demonstrates the tendencies of administrations (both in schools and businesses) to pass perpetrators along to other institutions or settings rather than take disciplinary action that might end a career (Shakeshaft &Cohan, 1995; Timmerman, 2002).

Correspondingly, the girls were left feeling shame, isolation and help-lessness. The pervasiveness of sexual harassment and abuse comes across clearly in our study. Young women have to navigate dangerous terrain at school, at home, at work, and nearly every place they go.

We have been particularly concerned with the perceived lack of attention to this issue given by school staff and lack of school faculty trained to address these issues. For a variety of reasons, as we will address in the concluding chapter, middle and high school faculty and staff often do little to intercept instances of harassment. Thus, as the young women here revealed, the issue does not seem to be important in the eyes of school personnel.

As we have argued elsewhere (Rahimi & Liston, 2009), teachers may not recognize certain behaviors as harassing, they may be too overwhelmed by the demands on them to "teach to the test" that the affective needs of students are disregarded, teachers may lack the training and preparation to effectively address instances of harassment, and without proper staffing such as an adequate number of well trained counselors, faculty and staff lack the resources to address the issue. Nonetheless, it is the perception of many young women that faculty did not deem their harassment as important and cited instances repeatedly where they felt teachers and staff overlooked such harassment.

Nearly *all* of our participants noted that teachers to some extent witnessed harassment and responded in the following ways that fell short for the young women: 1) The teachers did *nothing*, totally ignored it; 2) gave both perpetrators and victims a look that said "cut it out", 3) told the boys to "stop" but did not really act like anything was *wrong*; 4) occasionally the perpetrator was sent to principal and/or ISS. What is most glaringly missing from this list is *never* do they mention any full-scale investigation of reported incidents, or attempts to educate students to *stop* the harassment.

If teachers and administrators are making attempts to investigate sexual harassment claims more thoroughly, it seems from the participants in our study that this is done surreptitiously, which send the message that sexual harassment should remain secretive and hidden. So, we are troubled by the perceived lack of seriousness given to the subject of sexual harassment and the lack of education provided to both male and female students regarding sexuality education and the prevention of sexual harassment. These comments confirm for us the need to seriously examine the way in which education for both students and staff is made available.

The girls in our study reported limited access to sexuality education and few opportunities to discuss issues of harassment, violence, expectations, media/cultural literacy and sexuality. Sexuality education ranged from a one-time sex segregated distribution of pamphlets about menstrual cycles to slightly more coverage of sexual harassment in a "Health Occupations Class." None of our participants reported more than minimal exposure to sexuality education or school policies and procedures for reporting sexual harassment. Clearly, more formal sexual education classes could help address the isolation and helplessness that our participants in this study reported.

The girls' commentaries reveal the way in which our schools are severely ill-staffed to deal with the social and psychological needs of adolescents. As our schools have become increasingly focused on testing, school counselors find themselves exclusively riddled with duties surrounding the administration/assessment of standardized tests, attending to social issues impacting students' lives is overlooked. Without confidence that there are faculty and staff concerned with these issues, students are left to 'deal with' their harassment without guidance. This coupled with the fact that the adults they encounter tend to either look the other way, or are even the perpetrators of sexual harassment, exacerbates feelings of isolation and helplessness. When the young women in this study were asked about personnel to whom they could go with issues and problems specifically issues of harassment or abuse, they offered a dismal picture of their experience in school. The following comments represent this lack of important relationships needed for adolescents.

(1) "We didn't have that type of counselor." (Kia)

(2) "We had guidance counselors, but that was more for the education part, but, and they were crap too, they didn't help at all." (Sheila)

(3) "Some people don't get close to any faculty or staff. So some don't have the opportunity and they are always scared to tell someone, but if you had a particular person that dealt with that kind of thing, then it would be easier for you to express what happened." (Sheila)

(4) We had counselors, but to my knowledge, the majority of people just used the counselors for switching in and out of classes." (Kasey)

It is a sad fact that the people in the schools with the training to talk with adolescents about the problems they encounter in their lives, are "too busy" giving tests and helping them get into the right classes. Schools desperately need to examine the role of counselors in the school building and we need faculty/staff trained to deal with the realities of kids' lives and the pervasive vulnerabilities they encounter.

References

Barak, A. (2005). Sexual Harassment on the Internet. *Social Science Computer Review, 23*(1), 77–92.

Bradenburg, J. (1997*). Confronting Sexual Harassment: What Schools and Colleges Can Do.* New York: Teachers College Press.

Christian-Smith, L. (1990). *Becoming a Woman through Romance.* New York: Routledge.

Durham, M.G. (2008). *The Lolita Effect: Media Sexualization of Young Girls and What We Can Do about It.* New York: Overlook.

Fine, M., & McClelland, S. (2006). Sexuality Education and Desire: Still Missing after All These Years. *Harvard Educational Review*, 76(3), 297–338.

Gruber, J., & Fineran, S. (2008). Comparing the Impact of Bullying and Sexual Harassment Victimization on the Mental and Physical Health of Adolescents. *Sex Roles, 58,* 13–14.

Larkin, J. (1994). *Sexual Harassment: High School Girls Speak Out*. Second Story Press: Toronto, Canada.

Lindberg, S., Grabe, S., & Shibley, H. (2007). Gender, Pubertal Development and Peer Sexual Harassment Predict Objectified Body Consciousness in Early Adolescence. *Journal of Research on Adolescence*, 17(4), 723–742.

Liston, D., & Rahimi, R.M. (2005). Disputation of a Bad Reputation: Adverse Sexual Labels and the Lives of Twelve Southern Women. In Bettis, P., & Adams, N. (Eds.) Geographies of Girlhood: Identities In-Between. Pp. 211–230. New York: Routledge.

MacKinnon, C. (1979). *Sexual Harassment of Working Women: A Case of Sex Discrimination*. Yale University Press: New Haven.

Meyer, E. (2008). *Gender, Bullying and Harassment: Strategies to End Sexism and Homophobia in Schools*. Teachers College Press: New York.

Miller, J. (2008). *Getting Played: African American Girls, Urban Inequality, and Gendered Violence*. New York University Press: New York.

Ormerod, A. J., Collinsworth, L.L., & Perry, L.A. (2008). Critical Climate: Relations among Sexual Harassment, Climate, and Outcomes for High School Girls and Boys. *Psychology of Women Quarterly*, 32(2), 113–125.

Pascoe, C.J. (2007). Dude! You're a Fag: Masculinity and Sexuality in High School. University of California Press: Berkeley.

Rahimi, R., & Liston, D. (2009). What Does She Expect When She Dresses Like That? Teacher Interpretation of Emerging Adolescent Female Sexuality. *Educational Studies*, 45 6 512–533.

Robinson, H. 2005. Reinforcing Hegemonic Masculinities through Sexual Harassment: Issues of Identity, Power and Popularity in Secondary Schools *Gender and Education*, 17, 1.

Shakesshaft, C., & Cohan, A. (1995). Sexual Abuse of Students by School Personnel. *Phi Delta Kappan*, 76, 512–520.

Stein, N., Tolman, D., Porche, M., & Spencer, R. (2002). Gender Safety: A New Concept for Safer and More Equitable Schools. *Journal of School Violence*, 1(2), 35–50.

Timmerman, G. (2002). A Comparison between Unwanted Sexual Behavior by Teachers and Peers in Secondary Schools. *Journal of Youth and Adolescence*, 31, 397–404.

Timmerman, G. (2005). A Comparison between Girls' and Boys' Experiences of Unwanted Sexual Behaviour in Secondary Schools. *Educational Research,* 47(3), 291–306.

Tolman, D.(2000). Object Lessons: Romance, Violation, and Female Adolescent Sexual Desire. *Journal of Sex Education and Therapy*, 25(1), 70–79.

Yaffe, E. (1995). Expensive, Illegal, and Wrong: Sexual Harassment in Our Schools. *Phi Delta Kappan*, 77, 1–15.

Chapter 4: "It Don't Hurt Anyone, We're Only Fooling Around": Boys' Views of Sexual Harassment in School

"I think we do it to flirt or either, I think we did it more in front of the guys to just like, show off, like 'look I am slapping her butt,' like just to show off, just to say he did it." - Elijah

"Many of the names men were called also reinforced Mac an Ghaill's (1994) suggestion that schools were masculinizing agents, which required boys and young men to earn their masculinity through a process of conformity." (Rivers, 2011, p. 185)

His Definition of Sexual Harassment

As much conversation regarding sexual harassment and bullying both in academia and among the general public has focused on explosive incidences of school violence, more pervasive, but less dramatic occurrences of sexual harassment on school campuses go largely ignored. Further troubling is that often students and staff (teachers, counselors, and school administrators) fail to recognize its impact on students (Rahimi & Liston, 2009). As Owens, Shute, and Slee (2005) argue, many studies on bullying and aggression overlook the sexualized elements of boys' victimization of girls, a practice that continues to exist daily on school campuses. In our work, we have set out with a desire to have the conversation of harassment as a sexualized, gendered phenomenon, resurrected to draw awareness to the prevalence of this issue in the lives of young women.

Working to eradicate sexual harassment involves examining the perspectives that students have regarding their definitions of sexual harassment, experience with harassment, and means available for discussing such harassment on school campuses. While some of our past work presented in the preceding chapters has focused on women's and girls' perceptions of sexual harassment in school, we sought in this study to investigate the context in which boys understand, participate in, observe, or become victimized themselves by sexual harassment. Understanding boys' perceptions of sexual harassment is vital to addressing sexism as it exists in schools, since sexism undergirds and perpetuates both harassment and bullying. Hegemonic conceptualizations of sexuality and gender role expectations form the context within which girls and boys are harassed and bullied both as part of "fitting in" and "not fitting in" to these expectations (Meyer, 2008). Recognizing that boys themselves also are victimized by sexual harassment studies of their experiences as observers, perpetrators, and/or victims are necessary, this study examines boys' perceptions of sexual harassment on middle and high school campuses.

This chapter represents the study which examined how young men (aged 18–20) define and understand 'sexual harassment' in contemporary school settings. We were concerned with addressing the following questions: How do young men understand school culture relevant to gender and sexual expectations? How do they perceive gendered expectations from their racial and class perspectives? How do young men perceive their sexuality as well as the sexuality of young women? How do young men perceive societal, cultural, familial, and educational messages regarding sexual behavior of young women and men? What sexual education is available to them and how does that education frame the sexual experiences of young men and their interactions with women? What behaviors define sexual harassment and/or violence towards young women?

We interviewed 13 young men who were willing to participate voluntarily with this study. Also, because their experiences are potentially vastly different, the male subject group is further subdivided into heterosexual and homosexual or bisexual. (Appendix A contains a quick reference for demographic/findings from each participant.) As we will be discussing in the conclusion section of this chapter, there is a great deal of angst surrounding the punitive nature of the phrase "sexual harassment" that makes young heterosexual men less willing to discuss the topic. In our 'advertisements' for this study, we used the term sexual harassment, initially we received very little response from heterosexual males. We recognize that young men wish to distance themselves from association with 'sexual harassment.' This could be because sexual harassment is not an issue that they recognize as important, or they are not willing to view themselves as either victims or perpetrators.

Importantly, the participants involved in this study were quite diverse. A number of the participants attended rural schools, while others went to larger urban schools. Many of the participants were enrolled in Advanced Placement courses, while others participated in 'general tracks,' this distinction will be further discussed in this chapter. The participants represent African American, white non-Hispanic, Hispanic and Asian American. Additionally, the males in this study also represent heterosexual, homosexual and bisexual perspectives.

We asked the young men to reflect back on their high school years and discuss their perceptions of sexual behavior and attitude, following IRB protocol. Finding male participants willing to discuss this issue proved a little

challenging. At first flyers were put up on campus and a few male participants contacted the researchers. One of the researchers passed out flyers in
front of the school dorms. Still, we sensed some reluctance on behalf of male
students. We were able to conduct a couple of student organizations on campus to help elicit participation. It should be noted that perhaps the most enthusiastic of the male participants were part of the Gay Straight Alliance on
campus. Many of the young men who participated from this organization
expressed their desire to discuss harassment on campus and therefore were
very open to participating. We are very grateful for their candor and willing-
ness to participate. In-depth interviews based upon, but not constrained by,
open-ended questions were conducted with each of the participants. Each
interview took about an hour. While some of the males were more verbose
than others, each provided important insight into the climate of high school
and the perceptions of sexual harassment in middle and high schools.

Several findings emerged from this study highlighting the degree to
which sexual harassment and other forms of gendered harassment continue
to plague the lives of young people on school campuses. First, despite court
sanctions and the threat of lawsuits (Stein, 2007), sexual harassment continues to be overlooked and even tolerated on school grounds. As expressed by
all of the participants, there exists a great degree of laissez-faire attitude regarding harassment of young women. Second, many of the young men in this
study appeared to have a very narrow definition of sexual harassment. That
is, sexual harassment is something other guys do, not something they do.
Indeed, many believed young women do not mind having their buttocks
grabbed as a means of 'saying hello', or having overly sexually aggressive
comments directed toward them. Many of the young men in the study cited
the voluntary or even involuntary actions/inactions of young women as evidence that sexually aggressive behavior is somehow warranted or desired.
Additionally, we gleaned from these interviews, as well as our other studies,
perceptions of class and race contribute to views of sexuality. Further, this
research substantiates our other findings that there are few opportunities on
campus for students to learn about harassment and gendered violence, or discuss issues surrounding their emerging sexuality. What follows are each of
the thirteen males' perspectives. While each is very unique, there are some
themes which emerged.

Wayne: There Were Untouchables

Wayne identified himself as upper middle class. He said he was a Christian,
heterosexual male who attended school in a rural county in the southeastern
part of the U.S. We asked Wayne to define sexual harassment; his response

indicated that the issue had not been one that was discussed often with him. He said:

> I really have to think about that. I have never been asked. Approaching someone in a form that they did not feel comfortable with as far as touching or talking about certain topics, I guess, that pertain to sexual preferences or something of that nature. Sitting around the lunch table making... cracking sexual jokes that someone didn't feel comfortable with, that would be sexual harassment. Or walking the hall and grabbing someone's butt, or something like that, that would be sexual harassment.

Wayne was asked the degree to which he thought sexual harassment exists in the U.S. culture generally, and his response represents the way in which many young men fail to recognize the power differential in harassment,

> I think it depends on whose calling it sexual harassment, because *what you might see as sexual harassment and what I might see as sexual harassment is two different things.* Like, you might get offended by a guy coming and grabbing your butt, but me, it is like, football, you see that when you are on the football field, I mean, it is subjective in my opinion.

Wayne indicates that sexual harassment is context and person specific. As he notes, it is appropriate to pat another person's butt on the football field. But he presumes that these behaviors are merely subjective to each person and does not acknowledge that it is **not** appropriate to pat another person's butt as you walk down the hall at school. Rather, his position insinuates that one can't tell what will offend someone else.

Wayne goes on, "I would say sexual harassment is out there, but I think there is a lot of people that are not going to say anything because they are *scared that they shouldn't I guess...that they would get in trouble by somebody.*" For many males, "fear" surrounding sexual harassment doesn't come from being victimized, but rather for being caught and punished and 'getting in trouble.' However, in interviews with female students as discussed in chapter three, the discourse of *fear of victimization* surrounds all aspects of their social lives. From almost the time young women are born they are reminded of the possibility of harm; a perspective that many males seem to be unaware of. And yet, how can they be unaware of these messages that are so pervasive for girls? Brothers and fathers are as likely as sisters and mothers to give girls these warnings. Nonetheless, males seem oblivious to girls' perspectives on sexual harassment. For the males, they fear being accused of sexual harassment; meanwhile, they seem unaware of where such accusations may emerge from. To them, the accusations appear out of nowhere and cannot be anticipated.

Wayne was asked if he ever received information regarding sexual harassment in school,

> They had the people that would come by with the good touch/bad touch" and the "uh-oh feeling" and that is pretty much it. The last year in high school there was a big problem with sexual harassment going on and the principal would read the state defined code of conduct of sexual harassment every morning before school in the morning announcements, *so we have had it harped on us, but I never really paid attention.* No other discussions of sexual harassment, I have always been in A.P. (advanced placement) classes, so I guess they assumed that we knew about it. In our school, they kinda view A.P. students as the elite and you can kinda do anything you want.

Describing dating culture, Wayne said he "liked to keep it old fashioned." I asked Wayne what he thought gender roles should be in a relationship. Initially, he quipped in a tongue in cheek fashion, "Barefoot, pregnant, and in the kitchen!" Then, he added:

> I think in today's society they have just as much place, I think Biblically, it gives very specific roles and it is not so much the men are out working hard and the women are breaking their backs in the kitchen, it is the man's place to protect and to provide and the women's place is to nurture and protect the children. That is the specific Bible role, the Biblical roles that we are given and I still open the door for my girlfriend every time we get in the car and I don't let her open any door, that's my job, so I believe there is specific gender roles.

Wayne's views of sexuality have been largely framed by his religious upbringing.

Wayne recalled receiving no formal sexuality education outside of elementary school. When asked about the influence role media has had in the perceptions of sexuality, Wayne said, "The Caucasian culture, their main sex sells are through pornographic stuff then the African American culture, their main sex sells is through music videos, that is their pornographic stuff." Although, he offered, that he is influenced by neither, as he said, he does not interact with popular media often, his perception is interesting to note. As we have seen through other research presented in this work, constructions of race and media are important topics to be critically examined by students. While this study does not address that issue specifically, many of the participants' comments highlight the need for further exploration into notions into hegemonic notions of race and critical media literacy.

For some of the young men, including Wayne, there was a perception that some staff and faculty also engage in the harassment of students, indeed this supports research earlier provided by Timmermann (2002). As Wayne recalled:

> We had one male principal that when I got to my class, we always stood outside the hall and waited for the bell to ring, you could sit there and watch him and every time a girl would walk by he would...(Wayne made a gesture that the male principal would ogle the girls up and down). He was kind of a joke. When you walked by, guard your butt. *It was really funny.* We knew what he was doing and we knew it was wrong.

We asked Wayne if the girls ever expressed discomfort over this, and he said,

> Yes. They said that they would try to go to the other side of the hall, or if they knew he was on a particular hall, *they would dodge that hall.* It was a big high school, so to dodge a complete hall takes a bit of time. So, if someone is doing that just to dodge a principal obviously they are pretty uncomfortable. *It was always a joking matter, but you could tell they didn't like it.* But I don't think anyone ever went to anybody and said anything.

As his comments reveal, while girls' lives are disrupted by harassment such as dodging halls, changing routines, dealing with worry fear, boys can simply laugh off the event. Girls face this type of harassment, intrusion in our lives all of the time, a pervasiveness of vulnerability, a fear boys are not concerned with or even aware of. When Wayne was asked about whether or not sexual harassment existed in his school, he offered, "I am sure it was out there [sexual harassment], there is a bunch of immature guys; I just didn't pay much attention to it." I asked Wayne if he ever saw girls being touched in school. "Yeah, I did see that. They would just walk by and they [other boys] would grab their butts or whatever and be done with it. *The girls never expressed discomfort with it, so I don't know if you can call it sexual harassment. Some girls would flirt back.*" Wayne said that girls were called *a lot* of names in school such as "whore, slutbag, skank." in fact he said it was 'pretty common' to hear this language aimed at young women in the school. Wayne said these names were used in the "general population," but not in his A.P. classes. *"We were elite, we were above that.* We didn't date just to date and that was known among the general population that we didn't just date people just to date people, and to the general population, I would almost call it a game to see how many people you can date and so forth." This separation from the 'general track population' will be seen from several of the students in this study that identified themselves as 'advanced students.' It also should be noted that the A.P. students in this study, identified themselves as upper middle class, so we argue, as can be supported by national data (Killingsworth, 2011; Johnson & Kristonis, 2006; Ndura, Robinson, & Ochs, 2003) that advanced placement courses often represent students from white, upper middle class backgrounds. Additionally, Wayne and the other students identifying themselves as A.P., expressed there were very few African American or Hispanic students in their 'tracks.' Some of the attitudes regarding class and sexuality were revealed in this study at various junctures, and we point this out to suggest that it is important to highlight the continued disparity in representation of various 'tracks' within school. One negative outcome of the school within a school phenomenon is that students continue to maintain negative and inaccurate stereotypes of those in 'other' tracks. Wayne demonstrates this point in his beliefs about the racial typography related to pornography.

During our discussion of tracking, Wayne revealed that there was only one African American student that he could recall that participated in the Advanced Placement track. In trying to determine the perceptions of race within this context, Wayne was asked if students from various races were treated differently on his campus. He offered, "This is going to sound like really racially profiling, but it is really not, this is really how they separate, the white people tend to go to their class and hang out at the door and then the black people in the halls and congregate there. So, we separate."

Wayne was asked if there were different perceptions of girls from various classes. He said, "Back at my school, it was mostly perceived if they were not of the same class, *they were dirty*, so to speak, like the Indian caste system, *there are untouchables, you just didn't go there.* They didn't give them [girls from lower classes] the time of day. Just stay away that type of deal." He said that girls from lower classes were "more attention hungry and would do whatever it would take, if you get the drift." This implication that girls from lower socioeconomic classes are more promiscuous is a common hegemonic notion and is a means of marginalizing "others" (Malay, Laumann, & Michaels, 2005; Kent, 2007).

When Wayne was asked how teachers approached the name calling, he offered, "They didn't punish so to speak, say, it was always a chuckle and 'you know you can't say that' and 'even though it's true, you can't say that.'" Clearly, his comments suggest that it was perceived that teachers did not take name calling seriously at all. In fact, according to Wayne, teachers even contributed to the climate of harassment. "And then you got certain teachers that really don't care and they would contribute to the conversation. They [the teachers] would say, 'well I saw them walking down the hall with such and such the other day with her hand in his pants, and then I had to separate them" and so forth." He revealed that teachers would share information about other students and make comments such as "you know how they are," implying promiscuity, to other students. We argue throughout this book that teachers have to be more sensitive to labeling, name calling and their role in maintaining a healthy environment for all of their students. Clearly, Wayne was given the impression that teachers condoned name-calling and ostracizing behaviors.

Steven: They Hit Us Too

Steven described himself as a middle class, white, heterosexual male. He grew up in a Baptist home and attended a midsized urban high school in the Southeast. On defining sexual harassment Steven offered, "when someone is put into an uncomfortable situation that could be considered sexual, like, any means of inappropriate slander towards their direction and of course any physical touching of any kind that would make them feel inappropriate." Steven said that he received messages about sexual harassment "many times" growing up.

> My parents said to watch out for a lot of things. My sister said to watch out for a lot of things. Of course, we always had counselors who, because I have always had good counselors at every school, it was really been enforced into my head over and over and over again. The Golden Rule was enforced, to treat people as you want to be treated.

Steven is one of the only males who articulated a view that he as a male had the potential to also be a victim.

We asked him to discuss his notion of dating/gender relations. Steven offered:

> I think that the entire idea of it has kind of attempted to flip-flop, but it can't completely flip-flop because of so many little tedious ideas that we hold today from the old times and that we try and uphold in modern times. For example, women's rights was a very big deal coming up into our new age, and this is just based on kind of my personal opinion, the idea of chivalry kind of died with the birth of women's rights because now women have the rights equally as men do and with those equal rights, women should be able to do everything that men do, which would also mean that they should probably have more burdens to bear as well as men do. Now I understand the point of view that women also have to birth children, which is *why it kinda continually goes through my head, should women really have, like every single right that man has, or should they be held back on certain points of views and perspectives?* I do believe in equality to the greatest extent that is also a matter that provokes my head. Battery. Whenever a woman is hit by a man, that is a great crime, and whenever a woman hits a man, that isn't anything, like a man should be able to take that. I understand that not all women are quite as strong or as durable as men are, because of the way they were born and the way they were raised, so that is also the question in my head, like maybe they should have that right, maybe it is OK for

them to hit us, but that would take away from the idea of equality, that women are equal, and I still believe that women should have that equal right, *why then would we not be able to hit them the same way we hit men?*

This glimpse into Steven's thought processes as he spoke in a stream of consciousness manner, shows a conflict between a generalized belief that "women and men are equal today" and a value that "men should not hit women." But, he has not viewed these beliefs as being in conflict. Rather than acknowledging that women still have disadvantages, he believes that they have an advantage in that they could potentially harm him, and he would not be able to fight back. Therefore, he comes to express that men should be allowed to hit women, just as they would hit one another. His argument jumps right over the presumption that one does not hit those they perceive to be inferior, and therefore the injunction against hitting women belies an assumption that women are inferior. Thus, since he now believes women to be equal, one should be allowed to hit women.

In other of Steven's comments, he expressed concern about television programs that he sees has serving to promote 'pro-woman' agendas, according to Steven, these often are "anti-men" campaigns, although he did not offer any specific examples. Clearly, young men's views of sexism and gender related issues need to be further explored in and out of school settings.

Steven said he *never* heard or witnessed any sexual harassment, but there was other harassment in school. "It depends on where they are in the social status." He discussed the hierarchal relationships of various groups and the groups of kids at the "lowest levels" were the ones victimized by harassment, this supports other research on social class and victimization (Miller, 2008). He said that girls were referred to as "skanks or tricks" for various reasons, but he did not seem to classify this as harassment, despite the fact that he said these words were used '*daily.*' When I asked him if teachers or staff heard this he said. "I know school personnel have heard it. A lot of times they will come in and say 'you need to watch your mouth or you will get written up.' Occasionally they gave the blind eye because it was *simply just friendly banter.*" Steven said that he witnessed boys hitting girls on their buttocks, but "*it wasn't a big deal because girls hit boys too.*" So, by his own definition of sexual harassment, it did exist in his school, yet, he did not recognize it as such.

When I asked if boys ever experienced harassment, he said there was an openly gay boy at his school called "Tinker Bell" and he was called names 'frequently' at school. He said that teachers 'definitely' heard the name calling and did very little to intervene. As was articulated throughout these interviews, males who challenge the notions of dominant, heterosexual masculinity and sexuality, are also in danger of daily forms of harassment and ridicule, with very little consequence for the perpetrators.

Steven, like others in this study, said that he received some sexuality education in middle school, but that it was all male classes with "dude talk" mostly about sexually transmitted diseases. Outside of that experience, he received no formal sexual education in school and never recalled having a discussion with school personnel regarding issues pertaining to gender and or harassment.

James: Nothing Real Serious

James was a white, heterosexual college freshman who described himself as upper middle class. He grew up in a small southern town and attended a very rural high school. According to James, sexual harassment is,

> Like someone keeps going on and on, like won't leave someone alone and even when they tell you to stop, they just won't stop and they keep making comments about, like from a guy's point of view, keep making comments about girls that are just like, not appropriate, and they won't stop or even going farther than that.

James' only sexual education course that he could recall was in ninth grade and that course mostly talked about biology and consequences of un-protected sex. Outside of that experience, he was unable to recall any other conversation at school surrounding sexuality, harassment or gender related issues. When asked about gender roles in dating relationships, James said,

> I'm kinda like really conservative on stuff like that and I go at the girl's pace, like whatever she wants to do, if she says no, I don't bother about it at all and I think that is the way it should be is that the girl decides, because a majority of guys are going to want to go farther than girls actually want to do, so I think that the girl should kinda have the deciding factor on it. The *majority of girls want to find the right guy and just date before anything happens.*

This perception supports the notion of the romantic narrative that Fine and McClelland (2006) and Tolman (2002) suggest has permeated the lives of young women and served to stifle the articulation of their own desires. Although he does not put it in these words, girls are the gatekeepers of sexual behaviors. Girls determine how far sexual activities will go. The presumption is predicated on the sexual double standard that maintains the missing dis-course of female desire (Fine & McClelland, 2006).

James said that he had *never* witnessed any harassment at school. Yet, he said he heard, "people joking around, calling names, but I never *heard any-thing serious.*" When we asked if he ever witnessed girls being touched on the buttocks, he said, "It wasn't in a negative way, *just like joking around*. I would see that like *twice a day*." I asked James how the teachers responded to this, "They knew it was joking, like you can obviously tell the difference between when it is like a serious something and just like someone is messing around." James maintained throughout the interview that his was a "very tightly knit" school in which *all* of the kids got along; however, it became clear during this interview that this was the case for those kids who fit into the predominantly white, upper middle class student population; others did not fare so well. "Some of the people that were a little bit *different* [in sexual orientation and social class as he revealed later in the interview] got picked on, but it *wasn't anything ever real serious*." Our school is mainly upper middle class, the people that didn't have a car or could not get around or like dressed different or something and didn't dress appropriate, didn't have the right style, people would kinda mess with them, but it was nothing ever real serious."

James said that there were girls at his school that developed the reputation of being a slut for "sleeping with multiple guys at a party and if she dressed in that way, like wearing clothes that are revealing and stuff." He mentioned that there was a difference between girls who wore "Abercrombie," a symbol of middle class youth culture, and those who did not, implying that there was a huge class division in the perceptions of young women, yet he did not elaborate on this in the interview. There was an implication that the 'sluts' of the school seemed to belong to the latter group of less affluent students.

James did confirm that homophobia was present on his campus and said that there was a gay young man on the football team that ended up *leaving school* because of the harassment. He admitted this despite the earlier assertion that harassment at his school was never 'real serious.' He said that any male who acted 'effeminate' would get picked on in his school. According to James, teachers were not aware of these kids getting picked on because "it didn't happen in class." As we will discuss, the maintenance of hegemonic masculinity rests on the social isolation of those who challenge it.

Elijah: It Wasn't Like Any Big Thing

Elijah was an African American freshman who seemed a bit uncomfortable at first to answer the questions in this study. Elijah described himself as middle class with a strong religious background. Elijah said that he was very athletic and described himself as heterosexual. Elijah defined sexual harassment as, "going against someone's will to, I guess, sexually arouse yourself." This definition seems to be confused with sexual violence; however, within

Elijah's definition there was no mention of any other examples of harassment.

When Elijah was asked to elaborate on how he viewed gender roles in heterosexual dating relationships, he offered, "I think that the guy should make the first move, I guess because of *aggressiveness or dominance* or whatever." The maintenance of hegemonic masculinity rests on this principle that males are inherently sexually aggressive. James' views were the other side of this same coin, since he held that the girls should decide how far a relationship should go sexually, since males are presumed to want more than females.

In high school, Elijah remembers having sex education, but sexual harassment was never talked about. He said there were "little meetings" where the school staff would tell boys

> You can't sexually harass, and they gave examples of like the *little things that people don't really think are sexual harassment, like slapping a girl's butt* or something, but they were like, that is sexual harassment, *because people got in trouble and stuff before in high school for doing stuff like that.*

It seems even within this message that boys are not encouraged to look at it from girls' perspectives, but rather to think of harassment merely from the perspective of its potential for punitive consequences. Elijah said that boys grabbed girls buttocks all of the time in school, "but the only time I guess it was like really brought to the teacher's attention was if the girl didn't like him and he did it against her will or something like that. Girls got *their butts slapped a lot; it wasn't like any big thing."* According to Elijah, girls would respond to this by "flirting back", in the form of smiling or "laughing it off." Elijah differentiated when the act of touching a girl was harassment and when it's not,

> If you don't associate with her and you are not flirting with her and you know what basis ya'll are on, then yes, it is harassment, but *if you flirt with her a lot, I don't think it is harassment.* Or even if you are friends with her. I don't know, it is *not harassment unless you know you shouldn't do it.*

However, for guys butt slapping means something entirely different within the context of heterosexual masculinity.

> With guys it's like, don't touch my butt, but to me, that is how I am, but I mean guys smack each other's butt in the locker room, I played football and they smack your butt, the coaches smack your butt, being like "good play" or something, but it is just common knowledge really, you don't smack a girl's butt unless you know her and you like on that basis where it is not awkward.

On further elaboration, Elijah revealed that this behavior was largely a means of maintaining the approval of male peers and the establishment of masculinity. *"I think we do it to flirt or either, I think we did it more in front of the guys to just like, show off, like 'look I am slapping her butt,' like just to show off, just to say he did it."* Here Elijah demonstrates some understanding that girls are used by boys to show other boys that they are dominant, and to win approval for their dominance.

When Elijah was asked to recall how the faculty and staff in his school responded to harassment and or name calling, he responded,

> I guess if you said 'bitc*' [friendly tone of voice], which is more offensive than 'ho' and laugh it off, maybe they would just overlook it and not say anything, but if you said like 'bitc*' [hostile tone of voice], then it would be like, "watch your language in my class" or something, but I mean if you said it directly to a girl, like hey, I am sure they would pull you out of class and write you up or something.

Again, there seems to be some concern for punishment on behalf of a lot of young men. Rather than having discussions or working on developing empathy and understanding regarding gender issues, teachers simply threaten kids with 'writing them up.' Clearly, from the boys' perspective, the responses of teachers are ineffectual.

Ben: Not Like My Dad

Ben described himself as a Vietnamese, middle class, heterosexual student. For Ben, sexual harassment is defined as "unwanting of physical and/or emotional aspects of it. I don't know how I am saying that, but basically making the other person feel uncomfortable in any way. The simple brushing of your arms against someone else's leg can be sexual harassment in some areas, and some people might not think so, but say he makes you feel uncomfortable, but oh, he is not touching inappropriately, no one knows what their image of inappropriate is different from someone else's."

For males, the definition of sexual harassment seems arbitrary and subjective. Again and again, the males express bewilderment. They feel like the rules of engagement shift constantly. Therefore, they do not feel that there is legitimacy to the claims of sexual harassment. Rather, they believe that if a girl likes a boy, then it is not harassment. But if she decides she no longer likes you, then it is harassment. Either way, they do not feel responsible for their behaviors, because the same behavior might be acceptable in one moment and suddenly deemed unacceptable in the next.

Ben recalled receiving sex education in fifth and ninth grades which appears to be somewhat typical of all of the male and female students we interviewed. In both of these experiences, he said there was little discussion of anything related to harassment provided in those courses. The content, according to Ben, largely focused on medical terminology and information about sexually transmitted diseases.

When we asked Ben about dating relationships, he said,

> I think different races and different cultures have their different views on relationships and more of that goes on with time periods too. Say, in my culture, from what I know, I am from Vietnam, my parents are Vietnamese, my dad is definitely the dominant one, whatever he says goes, my mom can make suggestions, but it is whatever he says happens, so that is what is called a male centered society.

Ben was very careful to 'distance' himself from that vantage point. He expressed some disdain for the way in which his parents' relationship was structured.

On examples of sexual harassment Ben witnessed on school, he said that he recalled instances where a boyfriend and girlfriend are arguing and "he grabs her and pulls her back trying to get her attention, not as a trying to hurt her kind of way, but come back here I am not done talking to you kinda thing and she pulls away saying get off me and he tries to get her again." He said that he witnessed instances like that 'several' times during his school career. While, this study did not examine dating violence, his comments revealed that this form of harassment, dating violence and abuse is also prevalent in young adolescent experience.

He said that he witnessed boys touching girls on their buttocks between classes "all of the time." Ben, like several others in this study, (completely by coincidence it should be noted) was in the AP, advanced placement track in high school. He said that boys touching girls happened in the 'general track", but did not take place among his peers. We argued in this chapter and elsewhere, this stratification within the school perpetuates notions of class and race and the ways in which perceptions of class and race contribute to perceptions of sexuality, as can be seen in some of the attitudes reflected in this study and others.

Joseph: Stay Away; She's Friendly

Joseph was a middle class, white male who described himself as heterosexual. He described his community where he grew up and his school as very rural. His definition of sexual harassment was "anything as far as one person being uncomfortable with another in the way that they come off to them in a sexual manner, whether it be physically or emotionally, with words, and that person feels harmed or at risk." Joseph said that the only formal sexual education he received was in fifth grade when he learned about "good touch, bad touch," but that he received no sexual education in high school.

He said that his religious upbringing had contributed most to his understanding of sexuality. Joseph said that the messages that young women and young men receive regarding sexuality are different. He said that,

> It has always been more OK for guys to be sexual than girls, just cause of how people look at you. Girls are usually torn apart after losing their virginity or something, especially if they don't stay with that guy, but guys are more like ok with it. I don't feel like there was ever a pressure on guys to be that white flower all the way up to marriage.

When asked if sexual harassment was ever formally addressed by members of the faculty or staff of his school, he recalled having speakers who came and talked "mostly to the girls about being more active as far as if they feel uncomfortable, let people know, protect themselves in certain situation, carry mace." Joseph's comments here support the common perception that girls are the gatekeepers, and even in circumstances of violence and rape, the girls are responsible. Absent is any mention that males are responsible for their violent behaviors.

When asked if he ever witnessed harassment in school, Joseph said,

> I don't know if I would call it sexual harassment, but sometimes in the halls you would see guys being more aggressive to the girls, 'let me take you out, you need to go out with me' and the girls were kinda like trying to get away and they got kinda cornered almost, there was some of that, but nothing real serious.

When asked how girls reacted, he stated "almost intimidated. They would avoid certain situations like that or they would try to avoid the guy that was bothering them." Joseph said there was a "lot of touching on the butt." We asked him how faculty and staff treated the issue, and he said, "either with a detention or they would write them up, they were classified as P.D.A. [public displays of *affection*]. "Clearly, these harassing behaviors are not considered out of the norm. The males doing the harassing, the females being harassed, the males and females looking on, the teachers and administrators passing by – all take these behaviors for granted as "nothing serious."

Joseph was a student athlete in school and he recalls that he was warned, even by his teachers, to stay away from 'certain girls.' His male teachers, according to Joseph, would warn him to not talk to particular female students because "they heard she was 'friendly.'" According to Joseph, these teachers were 'good guys' that tried to protect him from promiscuous young women. Joseph said that as an athlete he enjoyed a great deal of privilege in school and that he and his friends rarely got reprimanded. According to Joseph, there were a "couple" of gay people in his school. He said that homophobic language was 'sometimes' used. His recollection was that teachers, upon hearing the use of that language, would reprimand the person saying it by writing them up. However, according to Joseph, coaches treated the issue differently, "they are the tough guy, macho coaches of high school and they are not going to cut down on you for calling something gay and things like that, as much as a math teacher would." Hegemonic masculinity is particularly protected in the culture of sports in school (Majors, 2001; Burn, 2000; Foley, 1990) as players' and even coaches' aggressive behaviors are often overlooked or even rewarded.

Shawn: Harassment? Never Saw It

Shawn described himself as lower middle class and white. He described himself as heterosexual and said that his high school was very rural. According to Shawn, sexual harassment is, "any sort of unwanted advances of that nature, I guess, coupled with, I don't know, physical contact unwanted." Like some of the other male participants, sexual harassment and sexual violence seem to be synonymous which could indicate that behavior that falls short of sexually violent is not viewed as offensive to young males.

Shawn said that he received a "very basic explanation" of sex education in the fifth grade, and that the boys were taken out of class for that experience and it was very awkward according to Shawn. He said that he remembered the conversation in fifth grade was largely about how the body develops. His only other experience with formal sexual education occurred in health class in his freshman year of high school, although he said that he did not recall the information he received through that course. Shawn said that he remembers the issue of sexual harassment being brought up in "a couple of assemblies." Like another students in this study recalled, the discussion during that assembly largely focused on the issue of the student code of conduct and the consequences for sexually harassing someone on campus. Shawn said that he did not think many of his classmates paid attention or took the presentation seriously. We asked Shawn if he ever witnessed sexual harassment and he said that he *did not*, yet when I asked him if he ever saw girls being touched in school, he said, "oh yeah, I saw that." He did not elaborate much during his interview. But he did say that one of his friends, who was transgendered, was the victim of a great deal of harassment in school. He said that teachers did very little to address his harassment.

Mike: Don't Get Accused

Mike was an "upper" middle class, white male who preferred not to respond to the status of his sexuality. He defined sexual harassment as,

> an umbrella term used when you make unwanted sexual advances on somebody else and they say, "Stop" and if you are accused of it, your name goes on the sex predator list and if you are in an employment opportunity, then the person filing the complaint can sue the crap out of you. If it is falsely accused, you have to raise a sh*t storm if you want to get out of it.

This indicates, again, that many young men's understandings of harassment and sexual violence is predicated on the possibility of punishment. Mike said that he "googled" sexual harassment when he was younger to make sure he wasn't "violating any laws," although we are not certain the context for his concern. He said he found that "it is a very big civil problem and if you are accused of it, you are basically screwed if you are a male and you are in a position of power. Apparently, it is harder to prove if the woman sexually harasses you and you may get laughed out of civil court."

Through the course of the interview Mike offered ways in which hegemonic masculinity is attempted to be maintained with his peers. "I do think if you are a dude and you want to go ask out somebody and you are under the age of 40, you probably have to make the first move, otherwise you are a raging pu**y and your buddies will continue to berate you and they are allowed to berate you." Of course the use of pu**y as highly negative is also a misogynistic manipulation of language.

I asked Mike what form of sexual education he received, he said the

> Nancy Reagan, "No means No" crap and if you have sex, you will get AIDS and die. There is a double standard which has existed forever, but if you are a man, you are supposed to have sex with as many women as humanly possible, assuming every party is consenting, and if you are a woman, then you are not, and there are various reasons for that. Probably because *most people who have sex addiction are women* and if you are a dude, the worst you can get is AIDS, but if you are a woman, you can get a kid.

No other participant mentioned "sex addiction." Mike fails to see the conflicts in his presumptions. It is bewildering that men are constantly seeking sex and yet women are "sex addicts." Nonetheless, Mike's views may shed light on Joseph's more delicately stated position that some women should be avoided because they are "friendly." Again, the predominance of the male sex drive is never questioned, although embedded in Mike's diatribe may be an indication that males feel a lot of pressure to appear even more sexual than they may actually feel.

Regarding the harassment of young men on school campus, Mike was concerned that faculty in his school were homophobic, and gave an example of when the principal took out Cross Dressing Day because it "encouraged gay people." He also mentioned how open affection in a heterosexual context was sanctioned in his school, but any possible homosexual display was immediately squelched. He mentioned that there was a great deal of "P.D.A." in the hallways of his high school with little being done to address this by the school faculty.

We asked Mike if he heard the use of derogatory terms toward women and he said,

> *Yeah, I heard whore, slut, any form of ethnic slur, those can be kinda funny actually,* you know stuff like that. But these people are generally, you know the people who just sorta scream 'I am a horrible train wreck, never go near me' and I know they won't shut up about drug use and stuff like that, so I think it may have just been the social stigma of them just not being good people. It wasn't just their sexual activity; there was a bunch of other contributing factors.

According to Mike, those being sexually harassed are clearly to blame, and it is ethically acceptable to have social pariahs. In Mike's view, there is not just one factor that leads to harassment (sexual and other), but the combination of factors. In this, his view is supported by the research literature, as we have also found that race and social class (as well as other factors, often beyond the control of the victim) contribute to conditions in which one person is labeled while another is not.

When Mike was asked if school personnel did anything to address the name calling he offered,

> Our school personnel is overworked, or either underworked; I don't think they actually do anything. Our counselors, for the most part, sucked. They lived in their little enclaves and you needed to do a bunch of passing and have a perfect dress code and do all sorts of crap if you wanted to get in to talk with them, so I figured the best way of dealing with the counselors was never, never speak to them. I was in the *advanced kids program, we had our own special counselor,* but she just mostly came in to go through and talk to us about college crap. In the advanced classes, *we didn't have broken people,* the people who do lots of drugs, have lots of promiscuous sex and generally have a lot of social stigma, we didn't have any of them, and for the most part, everybody in there, they saved their public displays of affection for outside of school. I don't know if it was the program did it, or they *were not just raging animals.*

So, this leads one to wonder how the general track students were viewed. Again, while Mike is more crass in his expression, his views reflect the same general assumptions presented earlier by James. According to these "upper class" males, "If *they* don't wear 'Abercrombie' *they* aren't worth one's time."

We asked Mike if he ever witnessed girls being touched in any way on school grounds. He responded, "There was a grope fest, yeah, randomly, when you walk down the hall, it doesn't matter who you are, apparently this happens to a lot of people, somebody will randomly grab your ass and you won't know who it is." He too responded that while this was a common oc-currence, little was done to address this behavior. He recalled teachers and other staff overlooking this behavior and the issue of harassment never being formally or informally addressed by school personnel.

The following participants identified themselves as homosexual or bi-sexual. Their stories further illuminate the heterosexist, misogynistic views that seem to be reinforced in school. While this project did not aim to address homophobic harassment, the stories of these young men clearly underscore the need for further research. Additionally, as we have contended throughout this book, recognize the relationship of heterosexual masculinity to issues of the harassment of those that challenge it. An important part of the establish-ment of that performance of masculinity in schools is the degradation of young women and gay youth, gay young men in particular (Pascoe, 2007).

Ian: Only If Things Got Serious

Ian was a white, middle class freshman who described himself as homosex-ual. Ian attended a midsize urban high school in the southeastern U.S. Ian seemed very enthusiastic and willing to participate in this study. Sexual har-assment, according to Ian, is "attention, unwanted attention like touching, groping or comments or even looks." Ian offered that in fact both males and females can be victimized and he articulated a very interesting perspective by suggesting that the peer pressure that heterosexual males feel to have sex with a girl on the first few dates was a form of sexual harassment and that young men who didn't perform that way were ridiculed or criticized. We would agree with Ian; indeed, the maintenance of hegemonic masculinity and the pressure to conform to the notion of male, heterosexual aggression is a form of harassment (Quinn, 2002; Pascoe, 2007). This is also in line with Mike's views that males are expected to have sex with as many women as humanly possible. Ian said that pressure to conform is presented to males as a way to prove their masculinity. Ian said that guys "play it up when they are with their friends and have to behave a certain way, like a group mentality. But separately, you see the real deal."

According to Ian, he was offered a formal class on sexual education during his ninth grade year. He said part of his health class, *two days*, according to him, was spent talking about STDs, and during that time there was one discussion about sexual harassment. He recalled that message, which he viewed as largely directed at girls, was "just say no." When asked about the existence of sexual harassment on his campus, he said that it was hard to determine if touching was harassment because "sometimes the girls acted like they liked it, they would laugh and play along with it, so how can you tell if it's harassment?" This further confirms for us that open discussion between students needs to be allowed to examine contradictions regarding harassment. Again, as Ian confirms, males' view of sexual harassment is that it is arbitrary and unpredictable.

Ian's recollection was that teachers rarely intervened when girls were groped. According to Ian, teachers didn't address it unless "it got heated. Like if a guy grabbed a girl's butt, no teacher intervened. But if it got like serious where she was like yelling or they were yelling, then the teacher intervened. *Only if things got serious.*" According to Ian, guys would even touch girls in class, "Guys would make sexual comments towards them and everyone would laugh. So I guess the guy thought it was ok to be that way since everybody was laughing and encouraging him along and the teacher isn't punishing him."

Ian told us that he personally experienced harassment while in school. Ian said that he "came out" as a homosexual in 12th grade, and prior to that he recalled a great deal of harassment of gay and lesbian students in middle and high school. He recalled *daily* use of derogatory terms, and perceiving teachers as "*not caring at all.*" He said that the harassment "was not that bad because no one ever got beaten up." However, there was daily use of verbal harassment directed toward him and other gay males in particular. He said he experienced harassment mostly by heterosexual males in the school, as Pascoe (2007) and Rivers (2011) have found, derogatory language aimed at women, as well as gay men, is part of the process of maintaining hegemonic masculinity in schools.

Ian took classes in the A.P. track, but he also took courses in the general track. He was asked if there was a difference in the perceptions of the two groups. He said there was 'definitely' a difference, "the teachers didn't care in the general track, they were lax; they just wanted class to be over." He said that apathy carried on into how they addressed issues of bullying and harassment as well. Ian said that teachers teaching A.P. track students were more apt to address issues of harassment and monitor student behavior more closely. Males in our study have repeatedly made claims that there are differences between A.P. and general tracks in the treatment of sexual harassment. We believe this constitutes an important area for future research, neither the girls nor the teachers made these observations as directly during their interviews.

Ian concluded our interview by suggesting that homophobia needs to be addressed more in classes since it is "never really talked about." We argue teachers' perceptions regarding homosexuality need to be explored with greater care in teacher preparation programs. Just as the sexual harassment of young women is a daily occurrence that is often failed to be recognized or addressed, the daily harassment of gay and lesbian youth is ignored and sometimes even promoted by school faculty and staff (Rivers, 2011). We must work to eradicate the culture of intolerance that seems to exist for so many young students.

Sam: Not Harassment, Just Disrespectful

Sam was an African American freshman who identified himself as bisexual. His definition of sexual harassment was, "physically touching someone or abusing them when they didn't want to be touched." This definition leaves out anything non-physical. We argue that many young men fail to see harassment as such unless it involves physical harm. Sam's experience with sexual education, like the other participants in this study, was limited to a brief discussion in middle school in which he encountered the 'no means no' message. Harassment, according to Sam, is primarily directed at women, because if a man gets harassed, he is considered a "punk." Sam said he attended a small Christian school during high school, and he clearly got the message that abstinence was encouraged in a primarily heterosexual context. He said that homosexuality was highly discouraged "from a religious aspect and also because this is the South." He remembers being told how wrong homosexuality was his entire life and having no place to discuss his sexual feelings and thoughts. While Sam is bisexual, according to him, he has chosen to remain a virgin because of his religious beliefs.

Sam said that he *never* witnessed any sexual harassment of any kind. Yet, he said that *every day* boys would say something to girls about what they wanted to do to them. "They would say it in class, in text messages, on cell phones, on Facebook, everywhere." Of course, this corresponds with what (Barak, 2005) has found regarding the newest forms of cyber sexual harassment. When Sam was asked if he identified this as harassment, he said "only if the girl tells them to stop and they don't stop. I don't think it is harassment, it is just very disrespectful." He recalled the use of 'bitch and ho' daily. He said that heterosexual males would direct this term to girls who turned down their sexual advances. According to Sam, teachers would only sometimes address this name calling, and often the consequences did very little to address the issue. According to Sam, teachers would often threaten kids with writing them up to stop the name calling. However, as Sam offered,

> Nowadays writing somebody up, doesn't really scare them, it doesn't do anything. It is like sitting somebody in a corner; it doesn't do anything, so they would just continue to do it over and over again until they got switched out of class or something. I think teachers get lazy. I think because they hear it so much and they aren't going to be like 'hey don't say that.'

Sam said that he has witnessed a lot of male aggression directed towards young women. According to him, "African American males are very aggressive. Most of my friends are female, and their butts have been grabbed, slapped; we have been at parties before and they have been like grinded on and like, *I mean it is just common.* Everyone is dry humping each other at parties." This behavior at parties and clubs is confirmed by our female participants as shared in Chapter 3. Sam said that he thought African American males were aggressive sexually because they were so angry. Miller (2008) in her research has argued that the maintenance of hegemonic masculinity is particularly encouraged in the African American community. However, the touching of girls and harassing language seems to be part of contemporary youth culture, and not specifically relegated to one segment. Sam said he avoided being harassed due to his sexuality because he kept it hidden, but he said he recognized 'coming out' in high school would have caused him to face harassment by his peers.

Ryan: Has It Become the Standard?

Ryan was a white, middle class, homosexual male. Ryan attended high school in a very rural part of the southeastern U.S in a public school setting. His definition of sexual harassment was, "any form of unwanted touch that was not consented to." According to Ryan, sexual harassment can happen in a homosexual context with older men intimidating younger men. However, according to Ryan, it largely impacts women.

> I have seen it happen numerous times on the street, guys will objectify girls and say things, *grab them inappropriately; it has become the standard.* If a girl looks at a guy and smiles, they might think a girl is cute, so they will try to walk up to them and grab their butt, or try to grab her side or hold her. That also happens a lot with homosexuals in bars and stuff like that.

Ryan had a "little bit" of sexual education in middle school, but he remembered that it was largely a heterosexual discussion and mostly geared toward abstinence. He recalls feeling very isolated and disenfranchised by those discussions. Ryan directly recalled witnessing sexual harassment in high school. "Guys trying to grab girls' butts or making lewd comments towards them in the hallways, it happened. And girls would shrug it off, laugh or objectify the guys. It *was all in a joking manner and never serious.* I didn't really witness any aggressive behaviors."

Like other students, Ryan recalled male teachers participating in the harassment of students. He recalled some of the male teachers looking at girls inappropriately and even recalled one of them asking a female student when she "would be legal." He cited other examples of 'perverts' in the school who would ogle young women in the building.

His own experience with harassment began in middle school when all of the students would call him gay 'all the time.' He said his harassment was not severe, and he physically confronted many of his harassers who eventually left him alone. Ryan said that he approached his principal in his junior year about establishing a Gay Straight Alliance on campus. Ryan met resistance as the principal responded with how tolerant the school was and that they didn't need one. He said he realized at that juncture just how intolerant the school really was.

Christopher: They Looked at Them Like Prey

Christopher was a Hispanic, middle class freshman who identified himself as homosexual. Christopher attended a mid sized urban high school in the Southeast. Christopher defined sexual harassment as, "someone physically doing something to you, verbally saying something about the way you physically looked, if you didn't like it and it made you uncomfortable, then it is harassment." He said that he received little information about the concept of harassment in school. Like most of the others interviewed, he recalled receiving the "good touch, bad touch" message in elementary school, very little sexual education in middle school, and almost none in high school. Christopher said that he recognized that in a lot of music women were spoken about very negatively, and he said that he viewed this as a source of sexual harassment. Christopher said that he thought there was a difference in the way that Hispanics view their own image regarding sexuality. "Hispanic women, they have to have makeup on and look pretty, do their hair when they leave the house. My dad would always have to dress nice. Also, with other cultures they don't show any skin, but for us, it is ok to show a little skin, *without looking slutty.*" When asked to articulate what constituted 'slutty,' Christopher, like so many other participants, was unable to provide a clear definition.

Christopher's experience with sexual education was provided in 7th grade in the last two weeks of health class, according to Christopher, during which he said, "Abstinence was hammered into our heads." Outside of that, he received no other formal sexual education. Christopher said that there was a great deal of harassment that took place in his middle school. When asked to elaborate, he offered,

> I mean there was just a lot of slang going on, guys would talk about how a girl looked; they would say "oh she is fine, look at her ass" and stuff like that. Stuff like that. *I mean, which in their sense, would be a compliment*, but in the female sense, it would be more like don't talk to me that way. It was also the way they looked at them. *They looked at them like they are prey almost.*

He also suggested that the language of 'ho' and 'bitch' was part of 'everyday' language. Christopher said that he didn't think many of the teachers addressed the use of this language because, "they don't want to deal with the confrontation with the students, cause where I went to high school, the students would definitely talk back to the teachers, I guess they didn't want to deal with it."

Christopher said that he experienced a great deal of harassment during middle school. He said that during his middle school years, he was still confused about his sexuality, but the kids would 'constantly' call him gay. He said that he heard that daily in high school, but it lessened during high school when he joined the ROTC, where, according to Christopher there were many other homosexual students so he did not feel isolated with this group. He said that he escaped a lot of harassment by hanging out with his group of friends and avoiding contact with possible harassers.

David: Even the Teachers Scared Me

David was a lower middle class white student. David described himself as homosexual. His definition of sexual harassment was, "possibly negative remarks on a person's appearance or possibly rumors of someone, maybe there was sexual activity, or making movements that feel personal, violate, or any words with sexual content." When David was asked the degree to which he thought sexual harassment existed in culture, he said,

> A lot… I don't know if I would blame the culture for a rapist, but we are so desensitized to what we can say to each other, people just don't think when they speak.

Honestly, *male posturing is something that is really expected of them, so they are expected to treat women as if they are objects or something to be degraded.*

The fact that males are so clear on this aspect of gender relations, in a general social context where there is presumed equality between the sexes is quite telling. According to the males we interviewed, it seems that underneath the veneer of sexual equality is an assumption that females "are something to be degraded." According to David, this exists in primarily a heterosexual context, because according to him, sexual harassment is not that big of a deal in terms of heterosexuality.

When I asked David to discuss any sexual education he had in school he said,

> My high school was in such a rural area that homosexuality was not talked about at all and if it was it was in a negative context. In my school, we never talked about anything related to sex. Teachers never addressed sexual harassment, because honestly, they were more focused on shirt tails being tucked in and ridiculous things like cell phones.

David said that he recalled girls being touched on the butts all of the time, with little interference from faculty or staff.

David said that he was frequently the victim of harassment by homophobic males in the school.

> I was bullied all through grade school, called "faggot" and "gay boy." By fifth grade I was sick of it and it had gotten to a point where I didn't want to tell my parents about it, but because I was being bullied so often and nothing was being done about it I had to. It happened in classrooms, hallways or at lunchtime or if we went outside or something. *I was always really afraid of my teachers; I never felt like I was very liked by them.* I would get shoved into lockers and called "queer." I started smoking, drinking and then my parents started to realize there was something wrong with me. I told them I was fine, but I tried to attempt suicide. I got caught trying to hang myself and then I got sent to therapy.

David says he is doing fine now and has overcome much of the pain associated with his harassment in school. Yet, he maintains that high school was a very hostile place for him and that harassment exists daily in school buildings.

Conclusions

There are several very important conclusions which can be gleaned from this study. First, male definitions of sexual harassment seem to be entangled with sexual violence and concerned with the punitive consequences for harassment. Several of the male participants when asked to provide a definition of sexual harassment provided example of what we would call sexual violence. Their understandings of harassment seemed to suggest that unless someone was physically assaulted, it was not harassment. Clearly, through the course of the interviews, we determined that behaviors such as name calling, the use of adverse sexual labeling and even touching a girl's buttocks were not immediately considered to be forms of harassment. For the most part, males consider these activities merely joking around.

Second, laden within many of their constructions of harassment was the concern for punishment. When discussing harassment, the male perspective does not seem to be sympathetic to female's positionality. Rather, there seems to be a fear, not due to their own victimization, but rather a fear of being wrongly accused and punished for sexual harassment. This fear is in contrast to the fear that girls live with involving the *constant* potential for being victimized. In the interviews with the young men, there was no discussion of the victimization of young women or the way in which sexual violence or harassment is a harmful practice. This is in large part, we will argue, because male students are given very little opportunity to learn about female experience and in particular, girls' sexuality (Fields, 2007). Opportunities for young men to understand and view the world from the position of young women would create more sensitivity to the issues of harassment and violence.

Arbitrary, subjective and unpredictable

Another finding that emerged from this study is that instances of harassment that were discussed by the participants were seen as joke, as not serious enough for concern of alarm, or even as a form of flirting. Many of the males construed the girls' failure to become noticeably upset as an indication that girls also viewed their behaviors as acceptable or even part of a joke. As the participants recounted, as certain experiences with harassment cause girls to alter their appearance or behavior (i.e., avoid certain places or people), males perceive these same experiences as sources of comedy, but not cause for alarm or concern. This confirms what Jodi Miller (2008) found in her research that boys view harassment in terms of just "playin." Boys perceive the touching of girls or even name calling as a form of 'flirting,' and they view the girl's response as form of flirtatious banter, causing this behavior to continue. Yet, as Miller (2008) discusses in her work, girl's failure to respond in a more aggressive manner is often more a result of her fear of retaliation rather than approval of the behavior. So, again, providing young men the opportunity to view these experiences more critically would allow them to examine the ways in which many 'common practices' often serve to violate young women.

Another finding which emerged from our study related to the definition of sexual harassment. Over and over again, the males in our study highlighted the arbitrary and unpredictable parameters of what constitutes sexual harassment. For the males, behaviors that are perfectly acceptable one moment could be labeled sexual harassment in the next moment without warning. This spurious context leads to males dismissing sexual harassment as beyond their control and responsibility. This view allows them to push responsibility for the harassing behaviors back onto the victims of sexual harassment.

The young men's discussions also highlight the degree to which hegemonic masculinity is discovered, promoted, and maintained through the culture of school. As the young men offered, male participation in the name calling of young women is very much alive and well on school campuses. Wessler and Preble (2003) found that when boys use highly sexualized words directed at girls and that goes unchallenged, then the behavior becomes accepted. This behavior, according to Wessler and Preble, has the potential to escalate as boys view this behavior as acceptable, then groping becomes acceptable, then potentially dating violence and rape may become acceptable, so a culture of denigration and violence against women in created and maintained. As we have seen through these interviews and other research we have conducted with other groups, clearly behaviors that serve to denigrate women are present in school and even thriving, maintained by the lack of a comprehensive approach to dealing with the issues of harassment.

Likewise, the harassment of gay youth, in particularly gay males, who challenge the hegemonic perceptions of masculinity are ridiculed and harassed in school as well. Throughout the interviews with heterosexual and homosexual males, it is clear that there is a daily existence of homophobic harassment and that is also maintained and even promoted through the inattention paid to these students. This harassment involves common behaviors in the establishment and maintenance of masculinity and male dominance (Duncan, 1999). As Pascoe (2007) found, masculinity is often achieved in schools and in social contexts for youth by the use of homophobic remarks and explicit remarks about girls' bodies. These practices are still very prevalent and, as the males in this study corroborate, go largely unchecked by school personnel, as school personnel do little to address these behaviors (Pascoe, 2007). Therefore, the perpetuation of such behaviors continues, creating a climate of harassment in school.

Another finding from this study which emerged is the degree to which class and race stereotypes regarding sexuality influence perception. We have discussed this issue in previous work, but it is reiterated through this research as well. As many of our participants noted their positions in middle class contexts, they suggested that sexual aggression and harassment happened to/by 'others,' and in particular to students in the 'general track' or 'vocational track' in their high schools. Intersections between social class, race and educational tracking have been documented throughout research literature (Oakes, 1990; Johnson & Kristonis, 2006; Ndura, Robinson, Ochs, 2003). This coincides with the literature (Malay et al., 2005; Kent, 2007) as well as findings from our other work in which middle class 'othering' of persons from lower socioeconomic status as displaying "deviant" sexuality is still present in current day psyche. As Radkin and Berger (2008) found, male bullies and harassers tend to come from higher social classes than their victims. As our participants here cited, in some of the Advanced Placement programs, students feel as though they have the run of the school and that they are 'above' the behaviors of those students not involved in that program. This may contribute to the power differential in the school that can lead to the harassment of students. It is certainly an issue that needs to continue to be explored further, particularly if the Advanced Placement courses serve to code or alienate students from lower socioeconomic status.

These beliefs also contribute to a 'blaming the victim' stance as demonstrated in the interviews presented here. Many of the males we interviewed made clear that those who are harassed are in many ways 'asking for it.' The teachers also demonstrated similar views in their interviews as presented in the next chapter.

Lastly, this study underscores our assertion that sex education is sparse and grossly inadequate. Female and male students have very limited access to a sexuality curriculum that addresses the contemporary issues present in their lives. There are very few opportunities for male students (as well as female students) to examine interpersonal relationships from a variety of perspectives. As the males in this study articulated, most could remember only one or two opportunities within their entire school experience where they were privy to formal sexual education. Much of the education they recalled centered on sexually transmitted disease and the consequences of engaging in intercourse. Yet, there were little to no discussion of sexual harassment and understanding sexuality from a female perspective. The school culture which seems to pay lip service to dealing with harassment by threatening to write kids up (turn in a disciplinary action to the principal) is largely ineffectual in dealing with the larger gender issues which continue to highlight power struggles within the school. The daily experiences of harassment that young women and gay youth experience on campus can not be addressed simply by tossing out threats of punishment. We argue that it involves creating a culture of sensitivity and tolerance beginning with providing more opportunity in school to explore social issues from a critical perspective. Issues surrounding sexuality, gender, dating, violence, name calling, etc. must be examined more thoroughly and discussed more openly in school buildings. We also understand that this begins with opening this discussion up in teacher education programs, so that teachers are better prepared to recognize the forms harassment takes and the affective toll such harassment can take on its victims. We assert that eradicating harassment and establishing a truly safe climate for all students involves a holistic, systematic approach. Schools must do a better job of providing well trained counselors in the schools. We owe it to our students to provide spaces where pervasive vulnerabilities do not exist.

References

Barak, A. (2005). Sexual Harassment on the Internet. *Social Science Computer Review,* 23(1), 77–92.

Burn, S. (2000). Heterosexuals' Use of 'Fag' and 'Queer' to Deride One Another: A Contributor to Heterosexism and Stigma. *Journal of Homosexuality,* 40(2), 1–11.

Duncan, N. (1999). *Sexually Bullying: Gender Conflict and Pupil Culture in Secondary Schools.* Routledge: New York.

Fields, J. (2007). Knowing Girls: Gender and Learning in School Based Sexuality Education. In Teunis, N., & Herdt, G. (Eds.), *Sexual Inequalities and Social Justice* (66–85). University of California Press: Berkeley.

Fine, M., & McClelland, S. (2006). Sexuality Education and Desire: Still Missing after All These Years. *Harvard Educational Review,* 76(3), 297–338.

Foley, D. (1990). The Great American Football Ritual: Reproducing Race, Class, and Gender. *Sociology of Sport Journal,* 7, 111–135.

Johnson, C., & Krstonis, A. (2006). A National Dilemma: African American Students Underrepresentation in Advanced Mathematics Courses. *National Journal for Publication of Doctoral Student Research,* 3(1), 1–8.

Kent, T. (2007). The Confluence of Race and Gender in Women's Sexual Harassment Experiences. In *Gender Violence: Interdisciplinary Perspectives,* 2nd ed., L. O'Toole, J. Schiffman, and M. Kiter Edwards (Eds.), 72–180. New York University Press: New York.

Killingsworth, M. (2011). Equity in Education: Minority Students' Participation in Honors/AP Programs. A Dissertation Presented to Graduate Faculty at Auburn University for Doctorate of Philosophy.

Majors, R. (2001). Cool Pose: Black Masculinities and Sports. In *Masculinities Reader*, S. Whitehead, and F. Burnt (Eds.). pp. 208–217. Polity Press: Cambridge.

Malay, J., Laumann, E., & Micheals, S. (2005). Race, Gender, Class in Sexual Scripts. In *Speaking of Sexuality: Interdisciplinary Readings*, J.K. Davidson and Nelwyn Moore, (Eds.) pp. 144–158. Roxbury: Los Angeles.

Meyer, E.J. (2008). Gendered Harassment in Secondary Schools: Understanding Teachers' (non)Interventions. *Gender and Education*, 20(6), 555–570.

Miller, J. (2008). *Getting Played: African American Girls, Urban Inequality, and Gendered Violence*. New York University Press: New York.

Ndura, E., Robinson, M., & Ochs, G. (2003). Minority Students in High School Advanced Placement Courses: Opportunity and Equity Denied. *American Secondary Education*, 31(1), 21–38.

Oakes, J. (1990). Multiplying Inequalities: The Effects of Race, Social Class, and Tracking on Opportunities to Learn Mathematics and Science. Rand Corp: Santa Monica, CA.

Owens, L. Shute, R., & Slee, P.T. (2005). In the Eye of the Beholder…Girls' Boys and Teachers' Perceptions of Boys' Aggression to Girls. *International Education Journal*, 5(5), 142–151.

Pascoe, C.J. (2007). Dude You're a Fag: Masculinity and Sexuality in High School. University of California Press: Berkeley.

Quinn, B. (2002). Sexual Harassment and Masculinity: The Power and Meaning of 'Girl Watching'. *Gender and Society*, 16(3), 386–402.

Radkin, P., & Berger, C. (2008). Who Bullies Whom? Social Status Asymmetries by Gender Victim. *International Journal of Behavior Development*, 32(6), 473–485.

Rahimi, R., & Liston, D. (2009). What Does She Expect When She Dresses Like That? Teacher Interpretation of Adolescent Female Sexuality. *Educational Studies*, 45(6), 512–533.

Rivers, Ian (2011). *Homophobic bullying: Research and Theoretical Perspectives*. Oxford University Press: New York.

Stein, N. (2007). Locating a Secret Problem: Sexual Violence in Elementary and Secondary Schools. In *Gender Violence: Interdisciplinary Perspectives*, 2nd ed. L. O'Toole, J. Schiffman, and M. Kiter Edwards, (Eds.) pp. 323–332. New York University Press: New York.

Timmerman, G. (2002). A Comparison between Unwanted Sexual Behavior by Teachers and by Peers in Secondary Schools. *Journal of Youth and Adolescence,* 31(5), 397–404.

Tolman, D. (2002). *Dilemmas of Desire: Teenage Girls Talk about Sexuality.* First Harvard Press: Cambridge, MA.

Wessler, S., & Preble, W. (2003). *Respectful School: How Educators and Students Can Conquer Hate and Harassment.* Association for Supervision and Curriculum Development: Arlington, VA.

Chapter 5: BET Encourages Immorality: Teachers' Views of the Current Generation of Students

"The biggest "diss" that you can give to a woman is she is a slut or a whore, but the biggest "diss" that you could give to a man is that he is feminine." - Catherine

"We can teach our daughters that shame belongs to the act of abusing or de-valuaing female sexuality, not to that sexuality itself"- Wolf, 1997, p. 229

This chapter is largely reprinted from *The Sexuality Curriculum and Youth Culture* (Carlson & Roseboro, 2011), Chapter X: Title X... by Rahimi and Liston. In order to present a fuller context for *Pervasive Vulnerabilities*, the data presentation has been expanded to include sections elaborating the perspectives of the participants and including more quotations from the interviews. The portions of this chapter that are original to this book are indicated in the text.

Sexual Harassment as Hidden Curriculum

Over the past decade, we have collaborated on a number of studies exploring how adolescent sexuality is experienced in schools. Our studies have documented that the sexual double standard persists; sexual harassment is prevalent, and yet in many ways invisible in schools; and that hegemonic representations of race and class play a role in establishing the context in which adolescent sexuality is interpreted (Liston & Rahimi, 2005; Rahimi & Liston, 2009).

In this chapter, we seek to explore the hidden curriculum of sexuality through examination of the way in which middle and high school teachers perceive the sexuality of their female students and relate that sexuality to past and contemporary cultural and social contexts. We have conducted open-ended interviews with eleven middle/high school teachers currently working in both urban and rural contexts in southern Georgia, deep within a very conservative, often religious, landscape of sexuality. (Appendix A contains a quick reference for demographic/findings from each participant.) Our research explored the teachers' perceptions of adolescent sexuality both in a general context and related directly to their particular student population. We found these teachers' perceptions were formed largely through religious institutions (church) and "mainstream" popular culture. While relaying their definitional understandings of sexuality and the role of images in popular media, these teachers showed distress over a cultural, racial, and generation gap between themselves and their students. This demonstrated a hegemonic socialization (in)formed by and within those understandings. Many of these teachers seemed to yearn for Mayberry, or a nostalgic time of presumed innocence with little regard for the spaces in which youth cultures reside. As we will discuss in this paper, this social and cultural disconnection has direct impact on the implications of/for democratic sexuality education for developing adolescents.

Teacher-participants in our study repeatedly derided students for their participation in and reflection of Hip-Hop culture and BET, in particular. The prevailing presumption among our participants was that the "black media" (code for black culture, we argue) is invading the mainstream (code for white culture) and spreading morally repugnant behaviors. Thus revealing how the hidden curriculum of sexuality in education entails a cultural clash between perceived "mainstream" views and "black" views. This entails, from the mainstream view, a perpetuation of the sexual double standard in which females are held accountable for the behaviors of males, and abstinence is presented as the only morally acceptable stance regarding sexual activity. Meanwhile, "black" views are one-sidedly associated with BET and hip-hop, leading teachers to assume that the values entail "if you got it-flaunt it", "if it feels good-do it," and in general anything goes sexual mores. It is important to note that both "mainstream" and "black" views represented in our study reflect teachers' perceptions and not an independently established "real" reflection of these positions. Nonetheless, we find it disturbing the degree to which racial and class biases by these teachers form the context in which the adolescent sexuality of their students is developing. As white, middle class women interviewing these teachers, the participants assumed comfort in revealing their racist views. It is imperative these views be disclosed and analyzed as these are the very views which impede social justice minded education and prevent the development of democratic sexuality education.

As their perceptions were revealed, our findings highlight a number of potentially harmful consequences resulting from adults' perceptions of adolescent sexuality. In addition to the very dangerous misunderstandings these teachers (and we argue many, many others) have regarding the sexuality of "others," our findings indicate a significant paradox for young adolescents in general, females in particular, to negotiate: on the one hand church and some "mainstream" sources tell girls to remain abstinent, denying their very real sexual desires; while on the other hand contemporary entertainment and fashion industries tell girls to flaunt their sexuality and express their desires.

So, female youth must sort through this contradictory terrain and face ostracism by peers, or negative perceptions from teachers, perceptions which as we will discuss have direct implications on student expectations and serve to dangerously silence issues of sexual harassment and sexual violence in schools. Also quite troubling, as our study indicates, is the lack of opportunity for youth cultures facing such contradictions on a daily basis to have spaces for discourse on school grounds. What can du

Additionally, contradictions of expectations which, young women especially encounter on numerous fronts, heightens the tensions of trying to strike a reasonable balance. As many scholars have pointed out (Fine, 1988; Tolman, 1991; Ornstein, 2000; Phillips, 2000), there are numerous conflicting discourses provided to young women, particularly in the hetero-normative context in which sexuality education is presented. Girls are forced to face discourses of love, power, violence, purity, attractiveness, fear, choice, romance, pain, immorality, harassment, voyeurism with very little guidance from school personnel, parents, or counselors, even given that schools are an important site through which many of these discourses are enacted and reified as forces in girls' lives (AAUW, 2001; Epstein & Johnson, 1998).

In this chapter, we will present ways that teachers view their role in helping students navigate these contradictions. To do this, we will first address the context in which the teachers in this study identify themselves morally regarding sexuality. As the teachers' identities seem to collide with their perceptions of their students, many of the teachers we interviewed seem to purposefully highlight the 'difference' between themselves and their students. We will discuss their views of sexuality as framed by their religious experiences as well as the messages provided to them through popular culture in their own adolescence. We have chosen to term this "Mayberry" morality, a reference to the white, middle class context in which many of the white middle-class female teachers in our study have framed their own sexual development. While not all of the teachers we interviewed grew up watching *The Andy Griffith Show*, they demonstrate a uniformity of cultural assumptions that seems to look back to the mores the show advocated. Set in the North Carolina mountains, this show epitomizes traditional white southern cultural mores. Although set in the south, the town is composed entirely of white people. Poor whites are sometimes characters in the show, and these are often the people who cause trouble. But, "somehow" in the end, all the characters are redeemed (or they leave town). Even the "town drunk" displays enough moral rectitude to lock himself in his cell if he drinks too much. The lead character, Sherriff Andy Taylor, is a widower living with his aunt and young son. Although he has a girlfriend, the series is careful to show them only holding hands, and does not even imply that they are intimate. Similarly, the teachers we interviewed seemed to expect students in their classes to demonstrate comparable asexual mores.

Secondly, we will examine through interview transcripts the way in which the teachers' experiences influence their perception of the sexuality of their students. Understanding the way in which teachers' identities intersect or sometimes collide with students' identities, we examine in particular how the white, middle class teachers we interviewed seem to perceive the "invasion" of black culture into the "mainstream," a theme that presented itself in this study, and one we did not originally seek to examine. Finally, we will conclude with the implications for democratic sexuality education. We argue that teachers need to become aware of the limitations of their perceptions and generate a reconstructed sexuality education curriculum that takes into account changing social contexts and adolescent desires, provides space for discourse on/for/by adolescents surrounding the contradictions in their lives, and serves to eradicate gendered harassment and sexual violence. We concur with others (Duncan, 1999; Meyer, 2008; Tolman, 1991; Wolf, 1997; Tanenbaum, 2000) who have argued that, as researchers and educators, we must advocate contemporary discourses of sexuality education on school grounds that account for the issues existing in the lives of students from the standpoint of their lived experiences and must offer youth a place in developing that sexuality education on school grounds. Rather than excluding adolescent culture, pretending it does not exist, we as educators must find a way to help adolescents frame their own sexuality. We must refrain from analyzing the experiences of our students from the contexts of our own adolescence. As we reveal in this study, attempting to impose our own sense of moral superiority, while castigating "kids today" as deviant and degenerate highlights and strengthens the generation gap, further isolates and subjugates youth culture, and stands in the way of adolescents' development of healthy sexual lives. While understanding that teachers' sexual identities have themselves been historically questioned, persecuted, and remained a source of tension and debate (Cavanagh, 2006), teachers in this study seem to remain determined to distance themselves from the public discourse on sexuality in which many of their students wish to engage.

One of the most striking themes that arose from the transcripts of teachers we interviewed concerning the sexuality of their adolescent students was the reverence in which the teachers discussed the context of their own adolescence and the apparent *pity* they have for girls growing up today. This dichotomous characterization of the teachers/students presents more than just the teachers' harkened desire for nostalgia, it represents a direct form of 'othering' that serves to stifle the opportunities young women have to discuss issues of sexual education.

It appears, as the participants' comments below will reflect, that there is a sense that sexuality 'formed out of guilt' is superior to the perceived sexuality of 'rap culture' and that these two ways of expressing sexuality are diametrically opposed. The first places women in the role of gatekeeper on both female and male sexuality, while the second presumes there are no gatekeepers at all. Further, the presumption that there is "no place for women in that culture" betrays an assumption that the 'true women' are not the ones depicted in rap and hip-hop, essentializing a white middle-class version of womanhood as the only 'true' image of women.

In the juxtaposition created by the teachers in discussing the influence of popular culture on sexuality, it becomes quite clear that the religious experience of the teachers tends to encourage the framing of their discussion of adolescent sexuality as a 'deviance discourse' in which the sexuality of others does not equal the 'moral majority.' Clearly, these perspectives reveal coded language (Weiler, 2000) disparaging views that deviate from the rose-colored nostalgic ideal of Mayberry. This is an ideal mythic past that is reflected in these interviews, showing the belief that culture has declined from a romanticized 'Old South' where white culture was safely segregated from black culture.

During the interviews, the participants were asked to reflect on their own adolescence and messages they received concerning their sexuality and sexual development. As the participants discussed their own experiences, it became clear that their own affiliation with the church frames their beliefs of the perceived *im*morality of their students.

The 'othering' of contemporary youth culture is evident. But, going to church is seen as having a redemptive value. In addition to regular church attendance, our participants believed that two parent, heterosexual, households can be a good predictor of high moral behavior, and abstinence from sexual activity. This assumption is in contrast with research literature which show that teens in two parent households who attend church regularly and even make chastity vows are no less likely to be sexually active than those who do not (Regnerus, 2007; Morin, 2009).

Even here, the assumption is that the 'old time religion' serves as an inoculation against premarital sex and other harbingers of bad moral character. But at least there is some recognition that even kids who attend church might not be entirely immune from sexual promiscuity.

Taken as a whole, the teachers we interviewed showed dramatic consensus that kids today are headed in the opposite direction from the paths the teachers and their peers took. They seem to agree that regular church attendance and two-parent (heterosexual) households are key elements in their own moral development, and would ensure better moral development among the youth of today. These participants further agreed that while not attending church is one factor contributing to immorality today, the gap left by not attending church has been filled by mass media. Here also, there is a clear sense that media today is more detrimental to developing adolescent morality than it was when teachers were growing up. Further, there is no compulsion on behalf of the teachers to work to address these tensions in girls' lives.

In addition to their experience with religious institutions, teachers also shared how popular media they were exposed to in their own adolescence was vastly different from the popular culture of their students, yet such acknowledgment did not seem to effect their perceptions of students' emerging sexuality or provide opportunities for discourse of such matters. Many of the teachers seem to yearn for a perceived lost innocence. Additionally, the largely inaccurate imposition of twin beds as seen on TV sitcoms that many teachers grew up watching, played out a middle-class mystification and denial of sexual desire.

There is this acknowledgment on behalf of the teachers that the cultural and social context in which adolescents are growing up is different, and yet there is a suggestion of moral superiority in the way in which the teachers developed. Additionally, the teachers openly acknowledged that there is no space within the school to discuss issues involving sexuality with students. Indeed the white middle-class norms as cited above highlight that sexuality is something which ought not be discussed or acknowledged.

Perhaps one of the most remarkable outcomes of this study, and one that has a great deal of implication for democratic sexuality education, and democratic education in general, is the degree to which perceptions of race and class (Weiler, 2000; Meyer, 2008; Kent, 2007) impact the teachers' views. Framing the above section within the context their own white, middle class, and often religious upbringing, demonstrates the antithetical view the teachers have of their students' sexuality, and allows us to examine the ways in which the teachers view the students' cultural/social contexts as 'deviant', perhaps even 'immoral.' As researchers, we felt a bit of angst at first regarding reporting the teachers' comments. As white middle class researchers, and as many of the participants were white, middle class teachers, the participants revealed rather comfortably, explicit racist, classist, and sexist views.

As the teachers in this study elaborated on their perceptions of the popular media that students interact with/exist in, there seems to be a great deal of angst resonating from the teachers. With regard to the sexuality of their students, in particular, the teachers seem to hold black representations in popular culture responsible for 'deviant' messages. Of grave concern to us is the prevalence of hegemonic depictions of students made clear through the teachers' responses. As the teachers revealed their perceptions of the sexuality of their students, it became clear that the hyper-sexualized portrayals of black men and women (Collins, 2007; West, 2008; hooks, 1981) clearly remain existent to some. Hegemonic representations of family clearly influence the teachers' perceptions. Additionally, many of the teachers present a level of discomfort with the increased prevalence of black representation in popular media, and further hegemonic notions of race by essentializing the representations of Black media. As the teachers' comments reveal, their understanding of BET and black media in general refers only to sexually explicit music videos and does not account for any other programming available for/by black youth.

As noted, many of the teachers made reference to "that culture" as being "blatantly sexual" and a dangerous image of hypersexualized, welfare dependent black men and women. There is also present a notion that race and class are inextricably linked, the black students must be coming from poverty and thus are "blatantly sexual". This very narrow misunderstanding of BET and its programming only furthers racist assumptions made by the teachers. This highlights the need for teacher preparation programs to fully immerse in cultural studies and media analysis as part of their programming as a means of eradicating bias and providing discourse on issues of sexuality.

Many of the articulated perceptions of the teachers have deep historical ties can be linked back to the notion of purity and the Victorian ideal which marginalized women of color (Pratt, 1992; McClintock, 1995). Phillips (2000) has termed this "the pleasing woman discourse." The conceptualization of this view can be traced all the way back to Imperialist discourse around the 'cult of true womanhood' and the importance of purity, a notion that purposely and fervently perpetuated a dichotomous virgin/whore representation of women (hooks, 1981; Collins, 2007). Such representation characterized white, upper middle class femininity as moral, and contemporaneously represented women of color and poor women as possessing immoral sexuality, as West (2008) has written, this depiction served as justification for much sexual abuse of women of color and precluded them from being viewed as victims of sexual assault. We argue that the perceptions expressed by teachers in this study represent a view that contributes to the lack of attention given to issues involving sexuality education, sexual bullying, and sexual harassment in schools. As the teachers expressed their discomfort and lack of understanding regarding their students' sexuality, it is clear that the opportunities for discourse for/by youth remain limited.

Teachers' Views: Their Own Words

The teachers' comments below help to illuminate the way in which teachers' perceptions counter or contribute young girls' pervasive vulnerabilities. *The following sections which are subtitled with pseudonyms from participants in our study have been added to this chapter as an enhancement from the in-depth interviews of the teachers.*

Catherine: My Babies Are Having Babies

At the time of this interview, Catherine was a young, middle class white teacher. She had only been teaching for one year, and was teaching in an urban middle school. Catherine suggested the demographical makeup of her school was 80% free/reduced lunch and 90% African American. When asked how love, romance, sex and desire were represented in culture, Catherine, offered:

> I think that romance is often seen, or described, or used, or treated like a fantasy and that romance doesn't have to be a fantasy, it can be real, but it is so idealized, especially for girls and women. We as females tend to think that we can never have it and shortchange our own levels of romance by pretending or wishing that it was something that it wasn't.

Catherine was the only participant in this study who articulated that women could have an autonomous desire.

> The thing that drives me craziest is that women often are not taught from their families and from television that they can be actors of love, they can be initiators of love, and that they can be sexual without being sexed upon, you know, without being taken advantage of, that they can have desire without being desired upon.

This brief affirmation of female sexual desire was the only instance we encountered in our interviews of the teachers wherein it was acknowledged that women also experience sexual desire. Here, rather than women only being viewed as gatekeeper against male sexual desire, Catherine notes that women too may be "sexual without being sexed upon." Still, even for Catherine, this agency is reserved for mature women and does not apply to the adolescents in her classroom.

Catherine elaborated on the role school should have in sexual education:

> I have pretty strong feelings because I work in an urban environment, because I have little babies that think they are pregnant, that are sexually active, I think that it is imperative that schools address sexuality with children before they enter puberty, before they become sexually active.

Catherine said she is very confident her students are having sex, and as a sixth grade teacher provided a couple of scenarios she has encountered.

> I have one child who wrote a letter to me about how she believes she is pregnant, for the second time, and she had sex with her boyfriend without a condom a few months ago, and she has an upset stomach and she thinks that she might be pregnant. She doesn't want to tell her mother because she doesn't' want to be forced to have an abortion. I have another student who spread some rumors about being pregnant.

When Catherine was asked whether there was sexual harassment that happened in class and in hallways, she said:

> I think that there is an intense amount of harassment going on. I think that it is primarily not sexual in nature, because of the age of kids, they think that playing and...they see harassment as playing. Particularly the little boys see harassment as playing, but the girls too. The girls participate less often, but the same percentage of them participate as the boys. Sometimes ... the most sexual harassment that I have seen or that I feel is inappropriate is usually done in notes that are written about who wants to see who or who wants to date who, or who is the hottest and I don't know...I'm not sure whether it would be sexual harassment or not, it depends, I think, to a certain degree, on the intent of the notes that are written, because they can be seen as harmless in some ways, as bullying in some ways, and I don't know that it has come to the level of sexual harassment.... The biggest "diss" that you can give to a woman is she is a slut or a whore, but the biggest "diss" that you could give to a man is that he is feminine.

On observing other staff/faculty reaction to name calling on campus, Catherine said:

> The word "gay" has come up a lot, particularly in association with boys, and it is even more of a hot button than slut or hoe or whore. I think I personally, have friends that are gay, I react very strongly when kids use that word, I look at them as thought they just said, "f*#k"; I take it seriously. I don't react as strongly towards slut or whore or whatever else, but I do treat it as thought it is a cuss word in my classroom, and I look at the kids and let them know that it is not OK and that they should not say that in front of me, and I don't want to hear those words and I don't appreciate their attitude in saying them.

On her students' development of sexuality and cultural proscriptions, Catherine offered,

> Now with most kids that grow up, particularly kids that I serve, their understanding of sexuality comes from the hip-hop and rap culture that incredibly sexualizes women, there is no place for women in that culture, apart from being seen as a sexual object, in most of the representations of that culture. I think there is a pressure

within the African American community for black men to represent their entire race all the time, and I think there is not that pressure for women, so I think there is an emphasis when there is a black male that doesn't live up to whatever it is. Many of my children come from parents who were in middle or high school when they were born and those tend to be the kids who have the most issues, those are the kids who think they are pregnant, those are the kids who get involved with catty arguments with sexual slurs. Those kids are so influenced by the idea that being sexy is being accepted, that is what love is, that it is all about sex, where I kinda grew up in the opposite environment, that sex is bad, wrong and evil.

Clearly Catherine's views, though somewhat liberal, harbor allegiance to what we have been calling Mayberry morality. Although she deviates from this somewhat in acknowledging that women experience sexual desire and should be able to express these desire apart from merely being acted upon, overall, her views remain somewhat nostalgic for "the old days." Two parent families who don't let their children watch BET or listen to Hip-Hop music would still be Catherine's ideal.

Jane: That's What Children from Poverty Do

Jane is a middle class, middle aged white teacher who serves as an academic coach in an urban middle school. Jane described the demographics of her school as:

Typically 100% African-American, 95% free/reduced lunch. When we get the statistics from the surrounding housing projects, we pull from 5 standardized housing projects. When you look at the statistics that we get from them, like sometimes out of 800 families in the project, there will be three that a father lives in the house.

Throughout her interview, Jane attributes poverty and "living on welfare" in single parent families as major contributors to declining morality among her students. The first questions she was asked pertained to her perceptions of love, romance, sex and desire. She said,

Sex to me is a celebration between a husband and a wife, just a glorious thing, a gift from God.... Their own special thing to be shared with them and no one else, which of course is nothing like what our culture teaches, and I hate it for the girls that are growing up nowadays because I feel they are missing, they are settling for plastic beads when they could have had diamonds, but they don't know any better unless somebody teaches them because our culture teaches women to be used. I think desire means physical desire. I think desire is something that you can control. I think it is something you are responsible for. Our culture doesn't teach this; our culture is very much in conflict with my personal view.

Jane references "our culture" but in talking with her, one gets the feeling that she is distancing herself from the culture of the children. Several years older than Catherine, Jane feels she is teaching students who she feels are not like her. She notes:

> I think boys are given the message that it is okay to disrespect girls, and I see that in school all the time. They [girls] are disposable. You do not have to stick with them; there are no monetary consequences for what you do. I think the role a school should have in sex education is teaching people to respect each other because this is just an everyday thing. Because all the time, every day, it is very common for me to hear a boy make some negative slam about a female that is particular to females. I walked by two kids the other day and he was saying something about the crabs between her legs and she's just laughing. I think if teachers don't say something, which I did, you know, that is rude, that's disrespectful; you don't do that to a girl…. Even the slapping around kind of stuff that they do…. I think formal sexual education is fine, but it is not going to help the attitudes they have towards each other unless it's an ongoing, everyday thing. In my situation it is more common to see a boy slap on a girl, girls slap guys too, but I'll correct a boy for doing it…. I see this kind of behavior all the time. Friday as I was leaving school, and the kids were going out, *some boy slapped the fire out of a girl*, and one of the other black female teachers said to her, "Are you going to let him hit you like that?, then you are going to grow up and have some man hitting on you, which is *probably more common in the neighborhood where I teach than it would be in the neighborhood where I live.*

Jane continues distancing herself from her students. Remaining separate, on the other side of town, Jane's values reflect Mayberry morality. The last part of this story, where she relates the reaction of a black female teacher, helps Jane justify her position. Ultimately, both Jane and the black teacher in the story reinforce the belief that girls are responsible for the ways they are treated by males.

Laying the immorality she perceives in her black students at the feet of BET, Jane explains:

> We are very careful about girls being picked up from the nurse, because it might be that older boyfriend picking them up, not the dad or the uncle like they say. The boys…I watch BET on occasion, just because I know that is what my kids watch all of the time, and they very much copy what they see. They are all about the chains and the gold teeth and the thug look. They are really unhappy they have to wear uniforms. The girls, they are stuck with uniforms too, but they are able to, even with uniforms, show more of their bodies because they can wear a uniform skirt and still wear really short skirts, which some of them do. More often, they will wear a low top. That is the kind of thing I see the most, because a lot of girls wear pants, so the thing that is more blatantly sexual is their tops.

In Jane's point of view, the students in her school mimic BET in dress and attitude. Girls foster a "blatantly sexual" look while boys go for "the thug" look. But, the attempts to mimic BET go further than mere appearance. As Jane expresses it, these mores pervade the environment.

> Guys are really bad about saying mean things to the girls. We have had a student put out for harassing teachers. Putting their hands on girls... and what I mean is like around the shoulder and such, and they will try to do that to you as a teacher too... and I think that is just a way to show dominance, and I don't allow it, neither do other teachers. But those boys do that a lot, and they do it to girls and the girls usually let them.

Seemingly unaware of the relative lack of power of the girls, Jane holds them accountable for how the boys treat them. The girls' "blatantly sexual" attire, and laughing off of the boys' advances provide enough evidence of promiscuity, that Jane (and the other teachers) feel comfortable in blaming the girls for the boys' behaviors. Dismissing the fact that even teachers are sometimes touched inappropriately by the boys, girls become the target of needed correction.

During this interview, Jane described a situation involving one of her students which highlighted the existence of homophobia in the school. Also, it appears worth mentioning that girls can easily become the target of correction even when they aren't really central to the events.

> I don't know how this happened, but apparently some girls got hold of a boy's journal and in there he wrote about his sexual desire for another boy. The place just blew up. We have had parents in and out of the building ever since. I wonder how their writing is going to be affected after this. It would never have had happened if the teacher had been there, but it has blown up. And the boy he wrote about is so angry, so angry. I am still thinking there will be more fall out from this. You know they have written about it now and all this has gotten out, they may not be as free to write anymore.

Jane described how the kids tore this boy's bookbag apart and threw it in the hallway. "I think the best thing to do is to take that child out of the room when there is a sub in there." Rather than address the homophobia, Jane suggests that the gay male be removed. This mirrors the reaction of teachers against the girls as well. The actions and reactions of the dominant group (males in the case of sexual harassment, and homophobic students, teachers and parents in the base of the journal) remain unchecked and unquestioned, while the subordinate group (females, LGBTQ students) are held responsible.

Jane's interview continually returned to the twin ills of poverty and BET. After relating the story of the boy and his journal, she returned to her refrain. "They watch BET all the time. Children from poverty that is what they do. When they want to disrespect the teacher, one kids will sing a line and the rest will chime in with them, because they know the same music and lyrics." When we asked Jane to comment about other cultural influences on her students' development of sexuality, she said,

> The culture they live in. If a woman doesn't have an education and she is trying to raise children by herself, then she has got to have a way to support those kids, so of course they will talk about "Father's Day," when the welfare checks come, you know, some of this is just a poverty thing. Those if you see that that is the way your mother lives, and most of our guys I would characterize them as angry, very angry, and that anger comes from not having a father in their lives, I think spousal abuse is more common in their neighborhood and more accepted in their neighborhood. It is accepted and they get that from their own culture. The whole idea about getting married, you know, they have very different ideas about that. They get benefits. Some of them have a lot of family pressure to get pregnant because it increases the family benefits. You are doing something to help the family if you get pregnant. The whole pregnancy issue is just totally different in their culture. Marriage is a different thing in their culture; the financial thing is different in their culture. Even when you do go to church where they hear that it isn't right to participate in sex outside of marriage, they still do. It isn't like something...*it just isn't as taboo as in my culture.*

Perhaps Jane is attempting to relate to generational poverty, but her views on the culture of the students in her school show little sympathy and understanding of the material conditions of the students' lives. Her belief in the value of traditional two parent families carries through in her interview, even to assuming that there is less domestic violence in traditional families. But in her view, the "culture of poverty" perpetuates loose mores, welfare fraud, teen pregnancy, domestic violence and other forms of moral degeneration. She states,

> I have only worked with children from poverty, so I have just that particular view and I feel so badly for the girls. I feel so bad for them, because I feel like they got so much that could be so much better, and it's really disheartening to watch them get pregnant in middle school and just repeat the same cycle that they have been in themselves. Yet, on the other hand, girls are doing better academically than males are, which says to me, that this whole message to males, that it is ok to treat girls this way also teaches them that they are dispensable, because girls can get along without you, they make it without you, they can raise their children without you, so what is their purpose in life? So, why should they break their necks to achieve in school and try to make something out of themselves to start a family? It takes their

purpose away. So, it is affecting both genders very negatively and I feel really bad for them.

No doubt Jane "feels bad" about the whole situation. She sees one vicious circle in which generation after generation of impoverished black girls succumb to negative influences of a popular culture that rejects "traditional" (read white and middle class) values. But her bad feelings seem to be focused on disgust rather than any recognition of the difficulties faced by her students. Jane seems to believe that if only the Hip-Hop loose morals could be substituted with the Mayberry morality – if only her students would adhere to more traditional mores with which she was raised (in which "good girls don't"), boys will act with respect and the negative influences of poverty will fade away.

Ali: Undermining of the Family

Ali is a middle aged, white woman also teaching in an urban middle school. Ali commented that she believes young women and men receive different messages from culture and that boys are allowed to do "anything and it is ok."

> It is ok for you to go out and get three girls pregnant and not support your kids and I think that comes from the media, I think that comes from the culture, especially the culture at the school I teach at right now where its all the children are coming from a single mom/parent household where they have six kids and each kids is from a different father and those fathers, none of them are really keeping up with what those kids are doing, and she has to take care of all of them, and I think that men are definitely given a different message.

The demographic makeup of Ali's school, according to her, is 99% African American, and a "low socioeconomic status with a lot of single parent households." Ali said that she thought the message young women and men should be receiving is one of abstinence with an understanding that they should not "value themselves based on how many boys/girls they have sex with."

When asked if she ever observed sexual harassment in her class or school building, Ali said,

> Yes, actually I only observed it one time, last year; I haven't seen that this year. Where a kid was constantly at this girl, constantly at her, they were a little bit older, making suggestive comments, but again it seemed more *of a cultural thing,* because when teachers approached the child and said, 'this is sexual harassment', the kid was kinda taken aback, like, "Well that is how we talk to each other all the time."

So, other than that, no I haven't seen that in the school, or witnessed it being said verbally or seen that action.

When asked if she heard students using the words, ho, slut, whore to describe other students, Ali replied that she had not heard those words, only "your momma." This is quite contradictory to students' accounts in which they say that language is used frequently and daily. Obviously, there exists a disconnection between students and teachers.

In addressing similarities or differences in the messages regarding sexuality that Ali received compared with her students, Ali offered,

> I grew up in the 70s, so I probably heard more than they did! Actually, what is different about it is that my generation, we grew up with two parents in the household, so we knew if we did something bad, dad was going to beat us when he got home from work. I grew up on Leave it to Beaver and Andy in Mayberry and these kids are growing up on offensive stuff. So, I think they are exposed to a lot of things, and by being exposed to it, they are told it is ok. It is really being undermined, the whole family is being undermined.

Ali said that one of her biggest concerns had been the number of female students exposed to abuse. "I can think off the top of my head of five instances that I know of, where girls have been sexually abused and sexually molested by a step-father, stepbrother and uncle. You know that is five that I know of.... If it is something that is just being exposed more, but it concerns me." Ali also commented that she knew of very little opportunity within the school that girls had to discuss issues involving sexual education or other current social issues of concern.

Melissa: Teaching to the Test

Melissa is a middle aged white woman who at the time of this interview was serving a dual role of teacher and academic coach in an urban middle school. Her school, according to Melissa, is a Title I school with 95% free or reduced lunch and predominantly African American. Melissa was first asked to discuss the various messages that female and male students receive regarding love, desire, romance, sex. She said,

> I know that little girls learn to think they are nothing if they don't have a man and if they are not sleeping with someone, or if they don't see "my baby daddy." I know that men, young men and boys, are applauded when they are promiscuous and they are intimate with more than one person, so whether the message is explicit or implicit, then end result is the same. I think the sexuality and the physicality of it are just so much more blatant today than they were a decade ago, or decades ago, and I think for guys, I think culture says, "Be brusque, look down upon women, subjugate

women, insult them, show them how tough you are, cause they are going to love it, that is what they want," and I think the videos that our kids are watching shows them exactly what society believes. You know you can look at the halls, *just look at the way they are treating each other in the halls.*

When asked to elaborate on this treatment, Melissa said,

You know, boys will insult the girls, or the boys will ignore the girls and you know, maybe give them time, maybe not, but look away at them, or if they are going to look at them, they are going to look at them up and down. I can't tell you how many girls I have, you know they wear their shirts under their uniform shirts, and all I have to do now is go like this (a gesture tugging at shirt), and the girls know to pull it up because they just want to show cleavage and I think that is what the boys want to see.

Melissa said that she felt like many of her sixth grade students if they were not already sexually active, at least wanted people to think they were. This is in direct conflict with the way Melissa perceives that things were when she was in middle school. She opines, "I took a little note from a kid talking about 'I wanna do you', and the girl was so proud to receive that note."

Melissa was asked the role she thought sex education should have in middle school curriculum, and she said,

I don't think we should be like Maine, passing out birth control, and I don't know if you are familiar with how to justify it to 11 year olds, because parents have given them permission to treat their children. I don't think we should take the place of the parents. Medically, I certainly don't think we should issue birth control of any kind. On sex education, let folks know how it works, when it works, why it works, what you don't have to have happen to you. We have moved into so many areas of parenting, that we simply can't afford to do anymore, you know, at the cost of instruction, so I am very conservative, very, very, conservative.

Clearly, Melissa would be content to live in Mayberry. Her self-proclaimed conservative views put her at odds with the students in her classroom. Her understanding of sexual harassment is steeped within this context. When Melissa was asked if she had observed any sexual harassment of students in her building, she said,

Not so much this year, again, because I am not in the classroom as much. Every once in a while I see guys poke at girls and push and play and girls do the same thing back, and a couple of bigger guys, you know, I will stop them and say, "You can't touch each other!" Knowing that we have sixth graders who, for whom this is the first year without recess. I take the big guys and I say, "You know what? I know she just touched you, I also know that society is going to think that because you are a big guy, that it is more wrong when you do it... now I don't think it is more wrong, but you need to protect yourself, and you need to stop playing now, you need to start thinking that folks might think of it, someday, as sexual harassment." I will tell you that I have a couple of eighth grade boys who won't pull their pants up, I said, this is sexual harassment, why do I have to look at your butt!' So I have used the term sexual harassment, and I have told the kids I am writing it up as sexual harassment next time, because I am sick of seeing your private parts. So I am the one that has used the term. Some of the eighth grade guys have gotten indignant, so they evidentially have the knowledge of what sexual harassment is.

Her examples of sexual harassment move from "play" to how students dress without stopping to address the context of these events. Rather than helping students develop a more genuine understanding of the threat of sexual harassment, she highlights for the "big guys" how they may be wrongly accused. Then, this is underlined when she conflates contemporary fashion trends of wearing pants well below the waist with sexual harassment. Granted, no teacher should have to be exposed to their students' 'private parts' when trying to teach. But to make the claim that exposed body parts is "sexual harassment" is inaccurate. If this were the case, then every female whose blouse shows cleavage is sexually harassing those around her. Indecent exposure is not the same as sexual harassment. Blurring these lines does not help students understand the broader context.

Melissa was asked to elaborate on how the staff respond or react to the perceived sexuality of their adolescent girls, and Melissa offered, "I think that some teachers are so tired right now and our morale is in the basement, so teachers have just decided that is not a battle they are going to deal with."

Melissa was asked what teachers can/should do to address sexual education in the middle school.

Well the little things, if you are going to have a dress code, take it seriously. We need to build it in contractually, no form fitting clothing, ok? These little girls are so developed, you know you can't help but notice their bodies and their breasts when they are wearing things two and three sizes too small, and they are allowed to, because males aren't going to tell them not to, it needs to be in the code of conduct from the district level down.

Melissa, like so many teachers, feels the pressure put upon teachers in 'teaching for the test.' "I think that if we weren't always testing our children than we could have more of these conversations." Although we sympathize with Melissa in thinking that standardized testing has gone too far, eliminating testing will not bring these conversations to the forefront. Indeed, before high stakes tests were the norm, sexual harassment existed as a problem, and a problem that was not addressed.

Louise: Your Name Is All You Have

Louise is a forty year old African American teacher who at the time of this interview was teaching in an urban middle school. She described the demographics of her school as "low income to the poverty level, inner city students, predominantly black. 75% of my students are female."

Responding to her view of desire, love, romance, sex, Louise said, "Desire, that's overly done because you see the young boys panting after the girls, running up to the girls, trying I guess, trying to express their feelings or their desires to be with that woman, the little girls running behind the little boys expressing their desires, letting everything be known. Desire is too openly done." She said that the way in which boys and girls express desire is different.

> As far as the little boys, they start hitting on the little girls, so therefore you know that little boy, *doing like the caveman scene*, I hit you, you run or whatever. But the girls verbally express their desires or write their desires for the young man, so one is an open way and one will be discreet, they pass notes through girlfriends who stop the chain for reading. The girls try and express it that way because they don't want to mess up their name because I tried to extend to all my girls, *your reputation, your name is all that you have, and you should keep that to yourself until you are married, cause once a young lady loses her name, or herself, it is hard to regain it* back. In other words, if they start being too open or other folks say too loose, their reputation is torn and very hard to get it back and they could be one of your most prominent citizens in the city or the state, but they are still known for being that whore, that slut, by males later on in life.

Louise begins by noting how boys and girls express desire differently, but she quickly moves to assert the existence of the double standard whereby girls' reputations are hurt by expression of desire, and this may follow them beyond high school. Although she does not specifically mention BET, Louise stands with her white teacher peers in viewing the negative influence of popular culture, and music videos in particular, on youth. On how the media influences the perceptions of sexuality, Louise offered,

> The kids I deal with most on a day to day basis, I would say they watch mostly music videos, because in the inner city that is what a lot of kids refer to on TV, on those it is OK to wear shorts showing half your behind, it's OK to show your chest, but we need to find some way to redirect our girls, it's not OK. It's OK if you are in your comfort zone in your home behind your closed doors, but not publicly and out like that, even the dancing some of them do is too vulgar and what it is giving is like it's OK, not stating that these women's names may never be the same, *they may never be looked at as a housewife,* even though they try to portray the housewife role.

Clearly, Louise advocates are more "chaste" moral code than the one that her students appear to be living by. The type of sexual education that she feels should be available to students would encourage abstinence, but provide a more realistic view than she feels she got:

> They need to hear the truth, instead of everything being sugar coated to them. Like back in the day, they would tell a young lady, if a man kisses you, you get pregnant. We need to tell them this is how a child is conceived, let them see a video of a woman in labor of a man dying of disease. They need to feel it, and talk openly about it.

There is a 'scared straight' quality to the tenor of sexual education that Louise would offer to students. Missing still is the dynamic of power, friendship, desire and love between men and women. Missing still is a solid conceptualization of how sexual harassment and sexual pressure may be brought into the picture. Louise was asked if she have ever observed any instances of sexual harassment and she said, "No I haven't personally observed any." In the next question she was asked, have you ever heard the terms: slut, whore or hoe used to describe girls in your school, "I have heard it, seen it daily. Mostly girls use it to each other, "what's up ho? But I have heard boys use it among themselves, 'that's a ho' because they know the girl has been with several other boys or they think or presume they have been with other boys." When asked how the staff in her building responds to such names, Louise said, "those are almost like immediate write ups." Louise was asked how she responds when she hears girls using those words toward each other,

> I say, "come here and let me talk to you, do you know what the definition of that word is? Why would you want someone to refer to you in that way? It is very degrading to a young woman." A lot of times you sit and you explain to them because a lot of them only have street terminology, which sometimes street terminology is correct, and those terms are correct, but you need to let them know it is not acceptable, they shouldn't degrade themselves in this manner. See, a lot of times, especially dealing with your black inner city girls, they see things like women walking the streets at night, prostitutes, they see mothers getting beat up at night, during the day, whenever, it seems to be the norm. Momma grew up on welfare, Grandmama was on welfare, Great-Grandma was on welfare, it is like a generational curse. You just have to take them and love them and let them know it is not acceptable.

Louise makes an attempt to take the girls under her wing and explain a different way of being. However, she simultaneously holds the girls responsible for the names they get called. Still missing is a challenge to the sexual double standard and regulatory status quo that holds the girls accountable and sends boys off with a 'boys will be boys' kind of attitude.

Sonja: And the Boys- Bless Their Hearts

Sonja was a white, young, middle class woman teaching in her third year in a rural, southeastern high school. She described her school as having about 500 students. The population of the school, according to Sonja, was predominantly black with

> Anything from low, low, low socioeconomic status to very high. Whether they are white or black, there is a good variety of kids. I think education-wise, with the kids, a lot of parents have not gone to college, especially the blacks, they have not gone to college to get a degree, they grew up locally and they stay here.

On sex, desire, and romance, Sonja said,

> I don't think there is any romance with this group whatsoever. I think it is probably just sex. I hear stuff that goes on with the middle school kids that was unheard of when I was growing up. We have seventh graders having babies or sixth graders getting pregnant. In the high school I hear what the girls have been doing, what the boys have been doing. When I was in school, you didn't tell anybody because then you were considered bad. Here, it is almost like you are an outcast or you don't really fit in if you're not part of that group as having sex. We have had some girls where the big thing to do in high school here when you get up in the 11th and 12th grade is have parties where they go out and make a bonfire or whatever they may have – they call it 'camping', they tell their parents they are going camping. I hear more stories of people hooking up behind the car in any way shape or form.

When Sonja was asked about her perception of girls' sexual aggressiveness, she offered,

> I believe it is almost swapped from when I was growing up. Now it is more the girls chasing the boys. The girls are more aggressive. I think they use their bodies to get attention. I tell them, "they didn't grow them that way when I was growing up." They just look different now. They are more mature, their bodies are more mature and they use that. They wear tighter clothes. *And the boys, bless their hearts, they can't concentrate as it is,* you know having two or three cute girls around them, that's all they're focused on and I think the girls take it to their advantage. So they (the girls) are very aggressive, almost to the point where I kinda wish it was the other way around.

Sonja's statements are remarkable in that she is one of the younger participants, and yet feels less connection to this younger generation than her older peers. Further, her hostility is more squarely centered on the girls rather than the boys. She offers the most direct "boys will be boys" attitudes exhibited in our study as she throws in the typically southern expression, "bless their hearts." Sonja's views excuse the boys from accountability. On the kind of sexual education that is need in high school curriculum, Sonja said,

> Seeing the trend of girls being more aggressive, I think that we shouldn't be so prim and proper. They need a slap across the face kind of message. *There is more to it than just getting pregnant. You might catch something now, but the chances of that are slim, we are a small town, so you don't have to worry about that, but still there are diseases.* I think that *if the girls are going to be more aggressive, we need to be more aggressive.* As far as the boys, I don't think the message has really changed much, I don't know how to handle boys.

Sonja's hostility toward the girls is very thinly veiled. Clearly, Sonja feels that it is the girls who have changed, while the males have stayed the same. And although she claims that she does not know how to handle the boys, she also expresses little concern for their behaviors. It is the "aggressive" behaviors of the girls that distress Sonja.

Sonja was asked if she ever witnessed sexual harassment, and she said, "I don't think so, other than I have had a girl come to me about someone grabbing on her butt. I tell them when they come into my room these are my babies, and no one better touch them."

At the conclusion of this interview, Sonja was asked if there was anything else she wished to add regarding educating today's young women, and she offered quite a bit that added some insight into the role teachers' perceptions of race as well as gender and homophobia:

> I got a least three girls that I teach that I know have been in relationships with each other as well as boys. *I got one, she has even had relationships with black males and she is white, but I look at* her and she just wants to be loved, she doesn't care who it comes from.... I've got one student who says, "I'm not bi-sexual, I'm bi-curious" and that scares me, 'cause if she is bi-curious, there is no telling what she might try. I think the bi-sexual thing is definitely more common in the white group, where the black thing is male/female – even the girls that are – I don't know, I think they are very sexual too, the way they dress, the way they act; they are probably more aggressive than the white girls are. They have a tendency more to get pregnant and I think that is more of who they are having sex with, but for some reason they don't always pick the brightest boy. My thing is a bubble, I tell everybody to get out of each other's bubble, cause they cannot quit touching each other and I see that more with the black group, with the kids in my classroom or whatever, they are just touchy feely all of the time. I have a student that is probably six months pregnant now, and I would have put money on it that would have happened sooner.

Sonja's outpouring of issues and concerns at the conclusion of her interview, essentially unprompted by the researchers, is very revealing. Although, young enough to nearly be of the same generation as her students, Sonja harbors a lot of hostility. This rant raises so many flags that it is difficult to address them all. Clearly, her first and foremost fear is related to the sexual aggressiveness of women. But, the racist view of the white girl who has "had relationships with black males" jumps off the page. She also hits the homophobic area hard with her presumption that "bi-curious" means the girl will "do anything with anyone." Then, this rant jumps back to race, indicating that black girls are even more "sexually aggressive" than the white girls. This hyper-sexualized view of blacks is discussed earlier. Here Sonja bares it out clearly for all to recognize.

Dana: Girls Want Love

Dana was a middle class, young white teacher teaching in a rural high school in southeastern U.S. The school, according to Dana, was about fifty percent white, nearly fifty percent African American, and a very small percentage of Hispanic and Asian students. According the Dana, this school has a great deal of impoverished families. At the start of her interview, Dana was asked about the messages that young men and women receive regarding sexuality. She said,

> Seeing some of the things on television… they watch these dating shows where it is just flip about it and there is one on now that the woman is a bisexual and she's got men and she's got women, and I have never watched it, but just flipping through it, I think this is crazy, it just encourages kids to do whatever. I think boys and girls get the same message because I feel it is just out there, anybody can do whatever they want and I think not long ago it was different that boys were encouraged to go out there and be more sexual and girls were, you know, you need to kind of refrain, but I don't think it is that way anymore.

When Dana was asked if she ever witnessed sexual harassment, she was one of the few who started off her response in this area by saying "yes." She went on to explain:

> Well, this school year we had a student that would put his hands on girls and I would see him touch like their shoulders and things and wanting to give them messages and things and I would tell him to 'stop.' To me, touching like that is harassment, and he is in the alternative school because I think he did something to somebody else here at school.

Presumably the "something" he did to "somebody" involved more than just "touching their shoulders." The fact that Dana at least acknowledged that she had personally witnessed sexual harassment, sets her off from the majority of the other teachers.

On discussing how girls/boys portray their sexual desire, Dana offered, "I think it is the same for the girls and the boys. It seems to me that boys have always been boys like that, 'I am this big studly man that does all these girls' and most boys are like that I think. Girls think that everything is about love."

Again, the pervasive assumption is that 'boys will be boys,' so they are pretty much left alone to do what they will. But, the view expressed again here is that the girls have recently changed. Dana assumes that the pervasiveness of sexual availability on television makes everyone think they should be sexually available. Like Sonja, Dana conflates bisexuality with "anything goes," and blames the televised portrayal of a bisexual woman for loose morals among her students.

Caroline: Does Your Tape Still Stick?

Caroline was a middle aged, middle class woman teaching in a rural middle school in southeastern U.S. In fact, this is the same school setting in which Dana works. Caroline's views regarding love, romance, desire as well as her views of what messages students should receive versus what messages they do receive were in line with the views of her peer teachers:

> I think the message is the same; I think the perception is different. I think the girls think that what they see is true love and it is not. We used to comment in my classroom a lot that, how do they say…that boys use love to get sex and girls use sex to get love, I think that pretty much sums it up. Sex is a relationship between a husband and a wife – a committed couple. I use a demonstration in my classroom all the time, I given them a piece of tape and tell them to put it on their arm and to pull it off and they say "ow it pulls the hair" and I say, now stick it again and we keep doing it until it won't stick anymore and I say, 'when you give yourself away so many times, eventually nothing is going to stick, you are never going to have that bond between a special person, because you have given so much of yourself until there is nothing else to give away."

Caroline teaches home economics in the school and she says that she teaches child development and sex education in that course. Through the progression of the interview, I found out this course on "child development' is reserved for the "tech-track" students in the school; these courses, according to Caroline, are made up of "lower class black kids." She said she approaches the discussion of sex education from an abstinence perspective. But she recognizes that many students have sex and wants them to be protected. When asked if she has ever observed sexual harassment, she said she has "never witnessed a single episode." However, she responded to the question regarding the use of adverse sexual labels as "those words are used A LOT.

When I hear it, I just address it with them and explain to them that that is an ugly term, in my generation it was an ugly term and you don't call your people that."

On the sexuality of her students, she reiterated some of the same perceptions of race found in many of the other white teachers' accounts.

> I teach mostly the lower class black kids, hearing them talk is what I am basing this on, I think the upper class white kids are sexually active and I think a lot of the black kids are sexually active and it is probably across the board, but I think the black kids don't mind anybody knowing they are sexually active, whereas the upper class white kids tend to keep it a little quieter. When the black kids get pregnant, they have the babies; white kids get it taken care of.

This hypersexualized view of black students is especially problematic emerging from the teacher designated to teach "home economics" including sex education. Further, Caroline's disconnect of sexual harassment from the use of name-calling is equally problematic.

Rhonda: They Are Just More Open

Rhonda is a middle class, white woman teaching in a rural high school.

Rhonda was asked how sex, desire, and romance was represented in culture, she offered,

> I would say it basically depends on the economic status, really and truly and the principles and morals of that particular area. Love is of course, supposed to be the ultimate of all fruits of our being and the rest of it is just secondary. It is different for girls; they are always the more romantic. It is a fantasy thing for them, for guys it is the macho thing. Love for girls would be commitment; love for boys would be sex...

> Girls today will allow the guys to see their personal stuff, you know like their monthly stuff, what I call 'girly things', I would NEVER, I would have been too embarrassed. These girls today will openly talk about being pregnant or knowing somebody who is pregnant, it used to be you didn't talk about that.

Rhonda said she believes that most of her students are sexually active based on what she overhears in class. She showed a great deal of concern over the way girls are dressing, and in her response too there was a great deal of racial bias.

> Well to me, your blacks are probably more open with it. There are more black pregnant girls than there are white pregnant girls, but that doesn't necessarily mean there is more activity from one or the other. I think they [whites] are just apt to have abortions or [blacks may be] less careful maybe. White are less open, even though they

tend to talk about more than when I was in school, and the black girls seem to have done a bigger jump in that process because when I was in school, and I went to school with black girls, *but they tend to be more apt to have sex and be open with it and* usually evidence of it is that they are pregnant.

Her further responses indicate a perception of race/class and a negative perception of black family.

Basically, I just feel like that with the predominant amount of our black students' parents being on welfare or disability or something of that sort, some kind of government aid, that it is encouraged for them to have children to bring in more money. I have actually had black students make those comments, so it is not just a perception.

Judy: If You Won't Give It to Him, Why Are You Showing It to Him

Judy is a middle aged, white woman who grew up in a "very strict Baptist background." She said her background influences how she views sexuality and believes that sex should not exist outside of a married man and woman. On how she sees her adolescent students' sexuality, she offered:

A lot of it is affected by fashion and right now fashion is low cut everything, but I am just absolutely amazed at how girls are coming to school dressed and they are more and more well developed. There is no privacy. I tell them, "why if you wouldn't give it to him, why are you showing it to him?" I don't understand why you want to show off that part of your body to people that you don't want to give it to. I mean you are advertising to people – "here it is, come and get it!" I am blunt because I want them to think about the message their clothes are sending.

Judy did not mention addressing the aggressive attitudes of males students. Her views show a thinly veiled hostility toward the girls, and a sense of incredulousness over how they dress. She freely connects these views to her Southern Baptist upbringing and proffers, "I was taught that sex came after marriage, and only bad girls were sexually active, those girls that did sleep around ... and it was known were sluts. Now it seems like you only get that reputation if you have multiple partners."

Judy too revealed a distinction in the way in which she perceived black and white students within her school.

I have had a lot of girls tell me, especially from the black community, they won't date, because if a boy buys them supper, then they are expected to have sex with them as a payment. I see a great shrinking in that culture of people willing to speak out against sexual activity outside of marriage.

The absence of statements about masculinity, places the whole weight of responsibility squarely on the shoulders of the young girls.

Rachel: If They Wear Panties

Rachel was a young, white teacher teaching in a rural high school. Rachel said that a lot of the kids talk to her very openly as she is young, and her classroom is located near the counselor's office. Rachel teaches gifted courses, and in this predominantly black school, her classes are only comprised of 3% African American students.

When asked how she sees girls/boys representing their sexual desires, Rachel said, "Boys always do that hitting thing. They pick on, hitting, kinda flirting thing. Girls are more gentle, softer, and they are more verbal I think." When Rachel was asked if she had ever witnessed sexual harassment, she said,

> Yeah on minimal levels. I have never had a case where a student was really, really being harassed, though it is hard to draw the line. There have been cases where I have had a couple of students who would just do things to a student, but in their view they weren't harassing, they were giving compliments, but *when a girl is given a compliment from a boy and they don't like it, sometimes they can take that as harassment, you know things like, 'oh yeah, I'd like to get a hold of that."*

Rachel seems unaware of the impact of these attitudes in the environment on the climate for young girls. Rachel said the use of the terms 'whore, hoe, slut and bitch' are rampant. However, she did make the distinction of saying that "lower class girls are typically more often referred to as hoes and sluts."

Rachel said there is a difference between black and white students regarding sexuality:

> Our black community, it is first of all, we are a very low socioeconomic area. Very rural. The majority of our black students are free lunch. I see within that community, just a global acceptance of open sexuality, you will see it in the way they dress, they are the ones who always wear low cut shirts, they wear tight shirts, the ones that always ride up, you can see their panties – if they have them on – it is completely accepted for them to become pregnant as teens, their culture buys into that whole family unit raising a child, it is very accepted and again, prevalent, I guess for us to have many pregnant black teens in school. As opposed to when I first started teaching, we didn't have a lot of pregnant girls, but pretty much if they were [pregnant] they were black, but now you do see some pregnant white girls, but I think as a community, that community certainly accepts it more often and that whole group of kids is blatantly sexual. Within the black community there are very few sub-

cultures. There is a little group of good girls and good boys too, the ones who have intact family units, you know mother and father.

Rachel dismisses the impact of a hostile environment on the lives of the young girls in her school, since, as she sees it, the black community is "blatantly sexual." There are clear connections between her views and the Mayberry morality we are attributing to the teachers in our study. The presumption is that a traditional, white, two parent home would create a more acceptable set of mores. But, the poor, black, single-parent homes of their students are letting students run rampant and creating "blatantly sexual" communities.

We have included this large section quoting directly from the interview transcripts, even when many of the views are very similar to demonstrate the point that the participants in our study present views that are not isolated and unique. Rather, the participants in our study show a consistency that indicates broad acceptance of their views rather than anomalous perspectives. The overarching view is that Hop-Hop and BET (black culture) has invaded the mainstream (white culture) and has spread morally repugnant behaviors. Teen pregnancy, single-mothers, and sexual promiscuity are perceived to be aspects of black culture that have moved in to the white community.

Adolescents in schools today, especially in the southern landscape, clearly face pervasive and deeply seated views whereby teachers buy into Mayberry morality. This traditional and conservative view contributes to and exacerbates the sexual double standard. Males are largely left alone, unchallenged in their derision of women and young girls. Meanwhile, the largely female (and largely white) teaching force holds the next generation of females responsible and finds them guilty of moral decadence.

Conclusion

Educators and other school personnel can and should play a vital role in helping to reconstruct an empowering and libratory discourse of emergent female sexuality for all young women (Liston & Rahimi, 2005), one that is free from the violence of sexual harassment, potential abuse, and oppressive conceptualizations. Young women and young men need spaces to examine the contemporary struggles in their lives. As we acknowledge that young adolescents face a different context than one in which we (and many teachers) developed, we must seek to meet them in their space. We must recognize the "sexual terrorism" (Sheffield, 2007) adolescent girls experience by not knowing which of their behaviors will lead to ostracism and/or sexual violence against them. We should push for sexuality curricula which directly addresses the contradictions in girls' lives. As educators we must recognize the consequences for failing to provide access to a progressive sexuality education. We must acknowledge the consequences of gendered harassment, the limitations of a heteronormative agenda including pressing all students to conform to heterosexual and traditional gender roles, and the prevalence of sexual violence that adolescents experience frequently on school grounds (Meyer, 2008; Stein, 2007). We must address teachers' ideologies regarding issues of race, class, and sexuality with more fervor in teacher education programs. We must engage in discourse in teacher education surrounding issues of youth culture and sexuality more thoroughly and limit discourse on sexuality education to courses on diversity only (as we suspect many programs do).

Developing a contemporary, democratic sexuality education requires an honest examination of dominant cultural representation of students, particularly depictions of poor students and students of color. By acknowledging personal bias and examining marginalization, a first step towards resolving the systematic victimization of students can be taken. In teacher education programs, future teachers must be given opportunities to confront and challenge controlling of sexuality throughout their courses of study. As teacher education programs deliver messages of diversity and differentiated instruction for all students, sexuality education must also be addressed in courses throughout their training. Professional development highlighting the serious nature of gendered harassment must be offered to future and practicing educators. The pervasiveness of harassment of young girls in schools, on the streets, in their homes and via the internet (Barak, 2007) must be acknowledged and fought against. The eradication of gendered harassment must be a priority for school personnel. As educators examine the literature on school violence, we must not frame this as a discussion absent of the prevalence of sexual violence and sexual harassment, but we must be mindful of the reality of the existence of these phenomena on school grounds. Lastly, we need more research that examines the existence of sexuality education on school grounds and in teacher education programs in order to develop a more progressive education for the healthy development of our students.

References

American Association of University Women. 2001. *Hostile hallways: bullying, teasing, and sexual harassment in schools.* Washington, D.C.

Barak, A. 2007. Sexual harassment on the internet. *In Gender violence: Interdisciplinary perspectives*, 2nd ed., L. O'Toole, J. Schiffman, and M. Kiter Edwards (Eds.), pp. 181–193. New York University Press: New York.

Carlson, D., & Roseboro, D., Eds. 2011. *The sexuality curriculum and youth culture*. Peter Lang: New York.

Cavanagh, S. 2006. Spinsters, schoolmarms, and queers: Female teacher gender and sexuality in medicine and psychoanalytic theory and history. *Discourse: Studies in the Cultural Politics of Education*, 27(4) 421–440.

Collins, P.H. 2007. Pornography and black women's bodies. In *Gender violence: Interdisciplinary perspectives*, 2nd ed., ed. L. O'Toole, J. Schiffman, and M. Kiter Edwards, (Eds.) pp. 395–399. New York University Press: New York.

Duncan, N. 1999. *Sexual bullying: Gender conflict and pupil conflict in secondary schools*. Routledge: New York.

Epstein, D., and Johnson, R. 1998. *Schooling sexualities*. Open University Press: Buckingham. UK.

Fine, M. 1988. Sexuality, schooling and adolescent females. The missing discourse of desire. *Harvard Educational Review*, 58: 29–54.

Fine, M., & McClelland, S. 2006. Sexuality education and desire: Still missing after all these years. *Harvard Educational Review*, 76(3): 297–338.

hooks, bell. 1981. Ain't I a Woman: Black women and Feminism. South End Press: Boston, MA.

Kent, T. 2007. The confluence of race and gender in women's sexual harassment experiences, In *Gender violence: Interdisciplinary perspectives*, 2nd ed., L. O'Toole, J. Schiffman, and M. Kiter Edwards, (Eds.) pp. 72–180. New York University Press: New York.

Liston, D., & Rahimi-Moore, R. 2005. A disputation of a bad reputation. The impact of adverse sexual labels on the lives of five southern women. In *Geographies of girlhood: Identities in-between*, P. Bettis and N. Adams, (Eds.) pp. 211–230. Lawrence Erlbaum Associates. Mahwah, NJ.

McClintock, A. 1995. *Imperial leather: Race, gender, and sexuality in the colonial context*. Routledge New York.

McKenna, J.J. 2000. Cultural influences on infant and childhood sleep biology, and the science that studies it: Toward a more inclusive paradigm. In: Sleep and breathing in children: a developmental approach. pp. 101–106. G. M. Loughlin, J.L. Carroll & C.L. Marcus (Eds.) Marcel: Dekker, New York.

Meyer, E.J. 2008. Gendered harassment in secondary schools: Understanding teachers' (non) interventions. *Gender and Education*, 20(6): 555–570.

Morin, K. 2009. Vaccination nation: A bioethical feminist inquiry into the political, social, and ethical controversy surrounding the human papillomavirus vaccine (Doctoral Dissertation). Retrieved from Georgia Southern University Database. (Accession Number, N/A).

Orenstein, P. 2000. *Flux: Women on sex, work, love, kids and life in a half-changed world.* Doubleday: New York.

Phillips, L. 2000. *Flirting with danger: Young women's reflections on sexuality and domination.* New York University Press: New York.

Pratt, M.L. 1992. Imperial eyes: Travel writing and transculturation. Routledge: London.

Rahimi, R., & Liston, D. 2009. What does she expect when she dresses like that? Teacher interpretation of adolescent female sexuality, Educational Studies, 45(6), 512–533. Routledge: New York.

Regnerus, M. 2007. *Forbidden fruit: Sex and religion in the lives of American teenagers.* Oxford University Press: New York.

Sheffield, C. 2007. Sexual terrorism. In *Gender violence: Interdisciplinary perspectives*, 2nd ed., L. O'Toole, J. Schiffman, and M. Kiter Edwards, (Eds.) pp. 110–128. New York University Press: New York.

Siegel, D. 2007. *Sisterhood, interrupted: From radical women to girls gone wild.* Palgrave Macmillan: Hampshire, England.

Stein, N. 2007. Locating a secret problem: Sexual violence in elementary and secondary schools. In *Gender violence: Interdisciplinary perspectives*, 2nd ed., L. O'Toole, J. Schiffman, and M. Kiter Edwards (Eds.) pp. 323–332. New York University Press: New York.

Tanenbaum, L. 2000. *Slut: Growing up female with a bad reputation.* Harper Collins Publishers: New York.

Tolman, D.L.1991. Adolescent girls, women, and sexuality: Discerning dilemmas of desire. In *Women, girls, and psychotherapy: Reframing resistance*, C. Gilligan, A.G. Rogers, and D. Tolman, 55–70. Harrington Park Press: New York.

Tolman, D.L., Spencer, R., Reynoso-Rosen, M., & Porche, M. 2003. Sowing the seeds of violence in heterosexual relationships: Early adolescents narrate compulsory heterosexuality. *Journal of Social Issues*, 59(1) 159–178.

Weiler, J.D. 2000. *Codes and contradictions: Race, gender identity, and schooling.* State University of New York Press: Albany.

West, C. 2008. Mammy, Jezebel, Sapphire, and their Homegirls: Developing an oppositional gaze toward the images of black women. In *Lectures on the psychology of women*, J. Chrisler, C. Golden, and P. Rozee, (Eds.) pp. 289–299. McGraw Hill: Upper Saddle River, NJ.

Wolf, Naomi. 1997. *Promiscuities: The secret struggle for womanhood.* Random House: New York.

Chapter 6: Pervasive Vulnerabilities, Hidden in Plain Sight

"Sexual entitlement particularly for females, barely exists in the formal agenda of public schooling on sexuality (or it is) tagged with reminders and consequences - physical, moral, reproductive, and or financial." (Fine, 1988, p. 33)

"Young women are under pressure to construct their material bodies into a particular model of femininity which is both inscribed on the surface of their bodies, through such skills as dress, make-up, and dietary regimes, and disembodied in the sense of detachment from their sensuality and alienation from their material bodie." (Holland et al. 1994, p. 24)

Rooted in Sexism

The literature on sexual harassment reveals that there has been a shift in focus from the more pervasive and everyday sexism and harassment of women and girls to less frequent, but more sensational harassment based on sexual orientation and bullying. We contend, along with others, such as Stein (2003), this focus on "bullying" has led to a muted discussion of the sexual harassment of young women. We have noted how feminism had its heyday in 60s and 70s and sexual harassment policies in schools were developed as a result of this activism in the 80s and 90s. That important movement and the establishment of policies has been critical in addressing sexual harassment and at least giving consideration to safer academic and workplace environments for women. However, as we have demonstrated throughout this book, the social, academic, and vocational landscape for young women is still hostile. Sexism still is deeply in place and presents itself in a variety of ways, including sexual harassment and assault. Yet, the conversation centering on *sexual* harassment has been less prominent as the current discourse surrounding bullying has become more popular in examination. We fully acknowledge that bullying exists, is extremely problematic, and is a threat to the safety of children. We wish to simply resurrect the discussion of sexual harassment as a gendered phenomenon, and in so doing situate the phenomenon of bullying within the context of sexism as we believe that the sexist ideologies that exist in school serve to promote much of the aggression that takes place within school walls.

Our book is, in part, a response to discourse on bullying that leaves out discussion of sexual harassment, and is an attempt to bring the focus back to the more pervasive and everyday occurrences impacting the lives of girls and women, as well as boys and men. We hope this book illuminates the contemporary context in which sexual harassment occurs, through a variety of important perspectives. The triangulation of data presented in this book provides a telling portrait of the extent to which harassment exists as well as the extent to which it is denied, or hidden in plain sight.

We see sexism as forming the basis for both sexual harassment of young women (ways women are continuously subjected to harassment and objectification), and the basis for harassment based on sexual orientation and bullying. Therefore, we seek to bring attention back to the roots of harassment as steeped in sexist society. We wish to move attention back to the continuous harassment and objectification of women and girls since we see sexism as the lynchpin for all forms of sexual harassment.

Bridging Perspectives: Sexual Harassment Is Pervasive and Continual

The participants' account presented throughout this book detail the pervasiveness of harassment as it exists within the culture of contemporary middle and high schools. Although many initially claim never to have seen it or experienced it, all of our participants relate numerous incidents of sexual harassment marking their experiences in schools. In Chapter 2, the women reflecting back on their high school experiences of the 80s and 90s, discussed the frequency with which they were harassed, called misogynistic names (for a variety of reasons), and abused. As we flashed forward twenty years to the women of today, newly finishing high school, it appears very little has changed. The young female participants remarked that name calling was 'common,' they experienced harassment 'everyday,' and many of the participants articulated even more serious claims of abuse and violence, very reminiscent of the women's accounts from Chapter 2. Despite achievements that feminists can claim, it is clear that there is still a great deal of work remaining to be done to address sexism. Young women today are growing up with a culture that condones physical 'assaults' against them, with young men openly groping them in hallways, classrooms, dance floors, busses, and nearly everywhere they go. Consider nearly all of the participants in Chapters 3, 4 and 5, articulated the practice of grabbing girls' buttocks as 'common.' From the young women and men in the study, this practice was described generally in different manners. We found that the girls described the incidents with levels of disdain, while the male participants continually viewed the practice of touching girls as merely "kidding around." Additionally, the teachers involved in this study offered another layer of contempt, primarily for the girls. But in many of the teachers' comments, there was a larger contempt for their African American students revealed in their inter-pretations of the physical assaults. Consider the girls' perspectives:

(1) "Boys would touch them [young women] on the bus, and since they were on the football team, and were winning, they [teachers] would overlook it." (Cassandra)

(2) "Some students would run around smacking girls on the butts and the girls would be OK with it and they defend themselves and every-thing." (Morgie)

(3) "After the bell rang and stuff, I would see a dude walk by and hit a girl on the behind and something like that, but all she would be is just 'stop it' or 'don't do that.'"(Miranda)

(4) "The majority of it I see goes on in school. Just you know, boys touching girls on their butts and all that stuff; it is so common." (Dominique)

(5) "Girls would just be walking through the hallway and guys would just slap them on their ass, things like that... you see that all of the time." (Raven)

Of course, as the young women shared with us, they do not escape this outside of school either, consider the participants' accounts of other social settings:

(1) "You can go out to a club and guys just come behind you and put their genitals on you, like it is accepted, they don't think there is anything wrong with it...." (Tricia)

(2) "It is common for boys to feel like they can touch you, ... they will get to the point where if I wear a skirt, even if I am wearing leggings or not, they will start trying to pull it up, while I am trying to pull it down, then I will stop dancing with them and walk off." (Morgie)

(3) "Outside of school, I would see guys trying to feel up on the girl and if they were wearing a skirt or a dress, they would try to feel up their skirt or dress." (Ariel)

Yet, recall when the males give their accounts of the grabbing, touching of girls there is suggestion that this practice is 'not serious.' The boys seem to hold a rather 'laissez-faire' attitude regarding the harassment of young women overall.

(1) "Like, you might get offended by a guy coming and grabbing your butt, but me, it is like, football, ... when you are on the football field, I mean, it is subjective in my opinion." (Wayne)

(2) "Girls being touched on the butt wasn't in a negative way, just like joking around. I would see that like twice a day." (James)

(3) "Girls got their butts slapped a lot; it wasn't like any big thing." (Elijah)

(4) "I would see boys like saying let me take you out, you need to go out with me' and the girls were kinda like trying to get away and they got kinda cornered almost, there was some of that, but nothing real serious." (Joseph)

(5) "Like if a guy grabbed a girl's butt, no teacher intervened. But if it got like serious where she was like yelling or they were yelling, then the teacher intervened. Only if things got serious." (Ian)

(6) Most of my friends are female, and their butts have been grabbed, slapped; we have been at parties before and they have been like grinded on and like, I mean it is just common." (Sam)

(7) "I have seen it happen numerous times on the street... has become the standard. If a girl looks at a guy and smiles, they might think a girl is cute, so they will try to walk up to them and grab their butt, or try to grab her side or hold her." (Ryan)

Yet, despite the 'common' incidences of this that the students report, teachers in this study suggested that they rarely witnessed behavior. Teachers frequently contradict their own statements indicating that they don't see any sexual harassment in their classrooms and yet "boys do that a lot." When they do recognize the existence of these behaviors, their responses appear to indicate a level of blame on behalf of the girls and a level of acceptance regarding this behavior on behalf of the male students. They attest:

(1) "...putting their hands on girls... and what I mean is like around the shoulder and such, and they will try to do that to you as a teacher too... and I think that is just a way to show dominance, and I don't allow it, neither do other teachers. But those boys do that a lot, and they do it to girls and the girls usually let them." (Jane)

(2) "You know you can look at the halls, just look at the way they are treating each other in the halls." (Melissa)

(3) "As far as the little boys, they start hitting on the little girls, so therefore you know that little boy, doing like the caveman scene, I hit you, you run or whatever." (Louise)

(4) Boys always do that hitting thing. They pick on, hitting, kinda flirting thing. Girls are more gentle, softer, and they are more verbal I think." (Rachel)

Also interwoven in the teachers' accounts, as we elaborated on in Chapter 5, is the degree to which racial bias contributes to their interpretations. "They cannot quit touching each other and I see that more with the black group, with the kids in my classroom or whatever, they are just touchy feely all of the time. I have a student that is probably six months pregnant now, and I would have put money on it that would have happened sooner" (Sonja).

Further troubling, with each of these assaults, young women are left to fend for themselves as it appears they have very little recourse. As the young women and men in these studies tell us, 'writing kids up' as the common response for sexual harassment does little to nothing as a deterrent for the behavior. Since girls recognize the failure of the school to offer any real solution, the onus for dealing with the harassment rests almost entirely on them. Consider the following recollections from the young women and men in our study regarding faculty/staff reactions:

(1) "The school personnel didn't want to hear it." (Joanne)

(2) "Teachers didn't really get involved in that stuff, because it was more done outside in the classroom.... But they heard it, the teachers knew everything.... The teacher looked at the students differently too." (Kia)

(3) "Some teachers, they wouldn't mind it, ... but some teachers would actually write up for it. It definitely happened in the hallway, just because some teachers, they knew around certain teachers it wouldn't matter." (Morgie)

(4) "I think some teachers saw it and I believe some teachers would say something like they would just give them the little evil eye and that stare or they would be like, 'ok you guys need to cut that out' and that was it." (Ariel)

(5) "It was always a joking matter, but you could tell they [the girls] didn't like it. But I don't think anyone ever went to anybody and said anything." (Wayne)

(6) "I know school personnel have heard it. A lot of times they will come in and say 'you need to watch your mouth or you will get written up.' Occasionally they gave the blind eye because it was simply just friendly banter." (Steven)

(7) "Nowadays writing somebody up, doesn't really scare them, it doesn't do anything. It is like sitting somebody in a corner; it doesn't do anything…. I think teachers get lazy. I think because they hear it so much and they aren't going to be like 'hey don't say that.' (Sam)

Given that the students perceive that very little is done to address harassment in school, the behavior is perpetuated and girls have to resolve themselves to dealing with the harassment on their own. As Miller (2008) points out, perhaps the safest recourse for girls is to walk away or even feign enjoyment, or 'flirt back' as the young men in this study suggest. Yet, here is the awful catch 22 young women find themselves in; doing *nothing* suggests to onlookers that she does in fact *enjoy* the harassment, which only serves to strengthen its pervasiveness. The young men **and** the young women in this study point out that many of the young women 'laugh off' instances of name calling and touching. Then, the participants seem to blame the young women for 'participating,' or interpret their 'laughing off the behavior' as flirtatiousness. We wonder how much is flirting and how much of it is merely coping.

"They would just walk by and they [other boys] would grab their butts or whatever and be done with it. The girls never expressed discomfort with it, so I don't know if you can call it sexual harassment. Some girls would flirt back." (Wayne)

Steven said that he witnessed boys hitting girls on their buttocks, but "*it wasn't a big deal because girls hit boys too.*" When asked about the existence of sexual harassment on his campus, Ian said that it was hard to determine if touching was harassment because "sometimes the girls acted like they liked it, they would laugh and smile so how do you know if that's harassment?"

The teachers also presumed that the girls were willing participants in "playful banter" rather than victims of harassment. Consider one of the teachers' comments, "But those boys do that a lot [touch girls], and they do it to girls and the girls usually **let them**" (Jane). Without any recourse, are girls left with much else? With teachers also viewing the young women's responses with disdain, girls are in particularly difficult positions. To some extent, a culture that fosters sexism creates environments such as schools, where young women fend for themselves and then are held in contempt for their response (or lack thereof). We can only imagine this is a very uncomfortable place for young women to find themselves and serves to create a hostile climate in which young women are forced to exist. Recall the women's accounts in Chapter 2 as many of them discussed the social isolation they experienced in high school and even after as a result of being labeled and ridiculed in school. While the girls in the more contemporary study may not have suffered harassment to the extent of the women from our previous study, it is clear that there is still a degree of social marginalization and ostracism that permeates the lives of young women.

In addition to contending with young men grabbing their buttocks, teachers giving them disapproving messages regarding their sexuality, and dealing with 'daily' misogynistic language, young women also must deal with potential harassment and abuse from adults on school grounds (Shakeshaft & Cohan, 2002; Timmerman, 2002; Winters, 2004). While a comparatively small number of such assaults actually take place, fear of assault exists as a constant threat within girls' lives as they navigate the culture of school. Consider the comments made regarding some of the harassing behaviors students perceived from school staff.

> "We had one male principal that when I got to my class, we always stood outside the hall and waited for the bell to ring, you could sit there and watch him and every time a girl would walk by he would...(Wayne made a gesture that the male principal would ogle the girls up and down). He was kind of a joke. When you walked by, guard your butt. It was really funny. We knew what he was doing and we knew it was wrong." (Wayne)

You may recall from Chapter 4 that Wayne mentioned that this caused girls to 'dodge that hall' to avoid interaction with this principal. Ryan recalled male teachers participating in the harassment of students. He recalled some of the male teachers looking at girls inappropriately and even recalled one of them asking a female student when she 'would be legal.'

Further complicating their lives is the harassment and abuse young women endure outside of school as well. While we chose to examine school primarily, it is extremely important to note that girls don't escape the possibility of violence in *any space* in their lives. School only serves as one cultural arena (albeit it an extremely important one in the lives of youth). Recall the number of women from Chapter 2 who were involved in abusive relationships, many at the hand of older men. Also, the younger women from Chapter 3 provided examples of abuse and harassment experienced at the

hands of colleagues, peers and even family members. Girls begin to understand that they are to 'fear the world' almost from the time they are born, but
clearly adolescence and the onset of their sexuality and development of their
bodies, triggers messages to them that their worlds are unsafe and they must
monitor and guard everything they do: cross their legs, be careful because
they are pretty, help young men control their sin nature, don't tease young
men, bless their hearts, don't show them what you won't give them, don't
give it up before you're married or you will be damaged goods. All of these
statements were mentioned by our female participants as messages they remember permeating their lives as children and young women. These are familiar messages to most women. The women in Chapter 2 revealed similar
messages they received growing up decades earlier, including messages that
their sexual feelings were 'demonic' (Pepsi).

We argue that sexism drives these messages. Young men (particularly
heterosexual men) simply do not live with the same kind of fear. The messages of their youth celebrate their passage into sexual development. Their
sexual expression is welcomed; they are not proscribed by constant reminders to control their bodies and regulate their appearance and (hetero-)sexual
behavior (Fausto-Sterling, 2000; Younger, 2009). They do not worry about
harassment, "the gaze," or sexual violence in the same way in which young
women must. Young women are taught they must navigate the world with
caution and must exercise restraint themselves as not to *cause* young men's
aggression toward them. Much of this sexism exists, we argue, because of
the way in which sexism has been expressed through the culture of school.
Young men have very little understanding of the ways in which young
women experience their worlds. To many young men, as acknowledged by
the young men in this study, young women are still *passive recipients* of
sexuality. The young men we interviewed tended to view young women as
either 'good girls' (who desired to be with one man, wanted romantic love
for the sake of love, demonstrated resistance to sexuality, monitored and po-
liced her own body, and *demonstrated middle class vantage)* or 'others ("untouchables," hypersexualized temptresses and hos). Clearly, these 'other'
girls were more demonstrative in their sexual expression, dressed/behaved
more provocatively, did not represent a desire for the romantic ideal, and, as
we argue is coded throughout this book, did not exist within the middle class
white ideal. Underlying ALL of sexual harassment and bullying are sexist
assumptions. Chief among these is 'boys will be boys.' Violence against
women and against 'effeminate' males is not only tolerated, but is often condoned and encouraged. This has got to stop. We need to fully confront the
fact that the 'boys will be boys' attitude perpetuates a failure to hold males
responsible for their actions. As the young males we interviewed attest,

males who are not violent are perceived negatively by their peers and many in the general public. Simultaneously, 'good girls don't' punishes girls for their sexual autonomy. This punishment of girls' sexuality can be seen through what Michelle Fine and Sarah McClelland (2006) have called the 'missing discourse of desire.' We argue that part of eradicating sexual harassment is reconsidering the discourse on sexuality education to include one that recognizes the real desires of young women and does not serve to silence their experiences in sexuality curriculum.

As strongly as sexism exists in school, so do the tenets of classism and racism. Throughout this book, it is evident that hegemonic notions of class and race influence perceptions of sexuality. This can be seen from the variety of perspectives presented in this book. This is seriously problematic for a number of reasons. As many of our student participants recounted, there is a 'divide' between students with regard to class and race. As we note in the text, our participants who were in Advanced Placement courses, articulated disparaging views regarding 'general track' kids. We recognize this as code for poor, black students. In some instances, you may recall, students referred to the general track kids as "animals," "highly sexual," mentioning that "those kids" received sexual education, but the AP kids didn't really need it. In fact, when we interviewed the teachers, you may also recall, the students who were 'required' to take sexual education were 'vocational track' students. We argue that this structure of requiring sexual education (a sexual education that primarily serves as a risk discourse) is particularly aimed at young, poor women and in particular young, poor women of color, illuminating the sexist, racist, classist views that permeate contemporary school culture. Provided throughout participants' accounts were illuminations of the way in which class stereotypes serve to marginalize young women in schools.

(1) "I think lower class is more accepting of it, but they know it is sexual harassment but it is kinda like they care, but they really didn't." (Cassandra)

(2) "Back at my school, it was mostly perceived if they were not of the same class, they were dirty, so to speak, like the Indian caste system, there are untouchables; you just didn't go there. They didn't give them [girls from lower classes] the time of day. Just stay away that type of deal." (Wayne)

(3) "Some of the people that were a little bit different [in sexual orientation and social class as he revealed later in the interview] got picked on, but it wasn't anything ever real serious.... Our school is mainly upper middle

class, the people that didn't have a car or could not get around or like dressed different or something and didn't dress appropriate, didn't have the right style, people would kinda mess with them, but it was nothing ever real serious." (James)

The following highlight some of the teachers' perceptions of their students from lower economic classes.

(1) "It is accepted and they get that from their own culture. The whole idea about getting married, you know, they have very different ideas about that. They get benefits. Some of them have a lot of family pressure to get pregnant because it increases the family benefits. You are doing something to help the family if you get pregnant." (Jane)

(2) "Basically, I just feel like that with the predominant amount of our black students' parents being on welfare or disability or something of that sort, some kind of government aid, that it is encouraged for them to have children to bring in more money. I have actually had black students make those comments, so it is not just a perception." (Rhonda)

(3) "The majority of our black students are free lunch. I see within that community, just a global acceptance of open sexuality, you will see it in the way they dress, they are the ones who always wear low cut shirts, they wear tight shirts, the ones that always ride up, you can see their panties – if they have them on – it is completely accepted for them to become pregnant as teens, their culture buys into that whole family unit raising a child, it is very accepted and again, prevalent, I guess for us to have many pregnant black teens in school.As opposed to when I first started teaching, we didn't have a lot of pregnant girls, but pretty much if they were [pregnant] they were black, but now you do see some pregnant white girls, but I think as a community, that community certainly accepts it more often and that whole group of kids is blatantly sexual." (Rachel)

The teachers, for example throughout their responses in Chapter 5, made it clear that their own perceptions of race and class interfered with their understanding of the harassment of their students. The erroneous cultural image of 'the welfare mother' (Hill-Collins, 2009) seems to plague so many of their perceptions, causing them to fail to recognize the real issues of harassment and abuse that many young women face.

These perceptions that allow the establishment and maintenance of social structures within the schools actually ***condone*** and reinforce sexism and harassment. Attitude of 'boys will be boys' coupled with 'good girls don't' produces a social context in which sexism is the norm. Girls are always less than, while boys are excused and not held responsible. There seems to be in place an overall 'understanding' that girls should monitor themselves, their dress, their behavior, their actions, they should change halls to avoid harassers, avoid certain boys in class (which sometimes has meant skipping a class altogether), or drop out entirely, as many of the women from Chapter 2 attest to having done. (It should be noted that the young women we interviewed form Chapter 3 were college freshman, however, we suspect that there are a number of women who dropped out in more recent years in part due to the harassment they experienced; we have future plans to investigate their perspectives.)

When teachers fail to address harassment (as the students throughout this book reported); when schools fail to offer any significant *meaningful* sexual education (from almost everyone interviewed, their experience with sex ed was sparse and did not address the realities of their lives); when boys are allowed to touch young girls openly on school campuses (participants noted this as frequent occurrence on school grounds); when misogynistic, sexist language is permitted *daily* on school grounds (all participants noted this as an "accepted" part of the school day); *harassment is condoned and enforced* as part of the school culture. Having a policy written in a code of conduct document does not change the confirmation of sexism, harassment and violence.

Boys' sexual harassment of young women seems to be condoned as the mantra of 'boys will be boys'" gets reinforced over and over again. Their aggressive (hetero-)sexuality is encouraged. Of course, sexism is largely predicated on the establishment and refinement of hegemonic masculinity (Pascoe, 2007; Robinson, 2005; Banjoko, 2011) as we mention throughout this book. The harassment of young women is tolerated because it is an expected consequence of boys being boys. Recall the teachers' comments regarding boys not being able to control themselves because of the way in which the young women dressed. While there was a concern from the teachers, that if "girls get more aggressive, we teachers need to get more aggressive" (Sonja), there seems to be little concern about the sexual aggression of boys. We recognize that the perception of male aggression as 'normal' (Pascoe, 2007; Kenway & Fitzclarence, 1997) is deeply embedded within sexist culture. Of course, the establishment of hetero-masculinity also requires that males who challenge its existence are also ridiculed and harassed. In his work, *"Dude You're a Fag!": Masculinity and Sexuality in High School*, Pascoe points out that male culture 'requires' the use of homophobic slurs and degrading language to secure its own maintenance. Consider a quote from one of the teachers in our study, "the worst thing you can call a woman is a slut, the worst thing you can call a man is feminine" (Catherine). This quote captures the very misogynistic nature of our culture and cries out for feminist interpretation, but this conversation seems to also be circumvented in the larger discourse surrounding school bullying and violence. We would urge more research in the area of homophobic bullying with acknowledgement this too is predicated on the systematic establishment of *sexism*.

Vulnerabilities Hidden in Plain Sight

We assert that sexual harassment is *always* present; perhaps this is why it is often not acknowledged. As we noted above, and supported throughout this book by the participants in our studies, harassment is highly prevalent. Through the accounts provided by all of the participants in these studies (females, males, and adult teachers) it is obvious that *no one* is addressing the issue. Girls are not certain how to respond; boys laugh it off completely; and teachers seem to sit back in judgment; yet simultaneously most denying ever seeing harassment.

We must first acknowledge that harassment still exists before we can fully address it. We hope this book will help enlighten readers on the issues still facing girls in schools and the pervasiveness of sexism rampant on school grounds.

Sexual harassment creates a hostile environment for young women and certainly has implications for school climate and the well being of all students. Sexism and its ugly tenets serve to remind young women that there are impediments to their full development. As we noted, girls' sexual development continues to be couched in the 'good girl' discourse, despite the sexualization of young women in media (Durham, 2007). Recall what happened to so many of the women from Chapter 2 as a result of being given an adverse sexual label. They failed to engage in school activities, dropped out of school entirely, developed abusive relationships, struggled with poor self concepts, turned to drugs, became depressed, and many of them had reached their thirties without ever developing a healthy sense of sexual development. Further, many of the women in that study engaged in risky sexual behavior; for example, not carrying condoms, for risk of being labeled. We argue that the young women we interviewed who recently finished high school, while appearing to have fared better, are also struggling with many of the same issues. We also argue that the young homosexual men in our study too have had to navigate school within the sexist context and certainly did not escape the impact of being ridiculed and harassed. They discussed attempts of suicide, feeling isolated and depressed, and giving consideration to leaving school (again, they too were college freshman, so the stories of those students who dropped out were not part of this study).

We argue that sexism is detrimental to heterosexual males as well. Just as racism negatively impacts whites, too, sexism negatively impacts males – at least psychologically, they become dominators and oppressors. Recall the male participants describing 'pressure' they feel to harass women and be sexually assertive.

(1) "I think we do it to flirt or either, I think we did it more in front of the guys to just like, show off, like 'look I am slapping her butt,' like just to show off, just to say he did it." (Elijah)

(2) "I do think if you are a dude and you want to go ask out somebody and you are under the age of 40, you probably have to make the first move, otherwise you are a raging pu**y and your buddies will continue to berate you and they are **allowed** to berate you." (Mike)

(3) "Guys play it up when they are with their friends and have to behave a certain way, like a group mentality. But separately, you see the real deal." (Ian)

(4) "Honestly, male posturing is something that is really expected of them, so they are expected to treat women as if they are objects or something to be degraded." (David)

Countering Sexism in School Culture

As we conclude this book, we think it is important to note that there is hope, concern for social justice requires we view the world as promising. We see there are some concrete ways in which we can continue to work to eradicate sexism (and classism and racism) within the schools. In this section, we would like to offer suggestions for addressing harassment and countering the overarching ideology of sexism that seems to plague the culture of schools. We recognize this is no easy task, but we would like to contribute to work to end the pervasive harassment of young women and men.

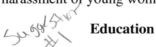

Education

From our perspective, the most important approach involved in the eradication of harassment is education. We are speaking about two levels of education. First, school personnel themselves must be better educated and trained to deal with issues surrounding gender and sexuality. We note just from course offerings in our own Colleges of Education, that diversity courses offered to undergraduates do not spend enough time devoted to issues of sexuality and sexual education. We recognize the importance of teacher training (and administer training, counselor training, coach training, etc.) in understanding sexual harassment and its consequences. While we want to hold teachers accountable for sexist, racist and classist views, we also recognize that in some cases harassment is not addressed because teachers *don't know how* to address it. Therefore, sexual harassment must be more thoroughly examined in teacher and school administrator training programs. But this training needs to go beyond identifying sexism. The interconnections between sexist assumptions and racism, classism and heterosexism must be made explicit in this training for school personnel.

Further, understanding the law behind sexual harassment, examining important legal cases and their consequences is an important part of the examination of how sexism impacts school culture. However, much more importantly, pre-service school personnel must have opportunities to explore notions of sexism in a more general context. Coming to understand sexual harassment as part and parcel of sexism is vital. Additionally, this conceptualization of sexual harassment needs to incorporate understanding that girls will employ coping strategies that make them look complicit (laughing it off); that boys will feel pressure to conform to aggressive displays of sexuality (especially in front of other boys); and that teacher failure to take appropriate action (beyond threats to write them up) will be perceived as condoning the harassing actions.

Studies such as the ones contained in this book should be explored and the 'boys will be boys' notion jettisoned. Teachers should have exposure to the stories of young men and women from a variety of contexts to uncover how youth culture understands harassment and how they navigate school within that context. This would need to include the stories of those who were less successful with that navigation as well. We contend that as teacher educators, we should do a better job of developing and encouraging teacher candidates' sensitivity to issues of harassment. School personnel (pre- and in-service) need more exposure to case studies involving female and male students at the hands of a sexist culture, as we have argued in earlier chapters of this book. Madson and Shoda (2002) developed a series of lesson plans designed for 6th grade teachers involving fictionalized case studies in order to help them learn to identify sexual harassment. The involvement with activities such as these is important for both pre-service and in-service school personnel.

More examination of the experiences of homosexual youth need to be infused in our teacher education programs as well as in service professional development courses to further illuminate the way in which harassment and abuse exists within schools. We urge teacher education programs to develop systematic infusion of curriculum into their programs that address harassment explicitly, and we encourage research which examines the extent to which this is taking place in teacher training programs across the nation. Of course, as we mention 'teacher education' programs, we recognize that it is imperative that all personnel involved in schools be educated regarding harassment, its impact, its contemporary forms, and the ideological assumptions that create it. An examination of school administrators' curriculum as well as curriculum designed for school counselors is an important piece of eradicating harassment within schools. Bradenburg (1997) points out this examination can be done through exploring community attitudes, gender bias psychological determinants, case studies, ethical/legal issues involving harassment and/or gender issues. Bradenburg also points out that we encourage teacher candidates and other school personnel to pay attention to materials used to make sure they don't reinforce sexist ideology.

School personnel (pre-service and in service) should fully explore stereotypes they have regarding class and race as well. The intersectionality of various forms of oppression has been amply documented throughout the research literature emerging from Critical Race Theory (Hill-Collins, 2009; Delgado & Stefancic, 2000). As demonstrated repeatedly by the participants we interviewed in this research, biased views of race and class contribute to the culture of sexism and serve to silence the experiences of so many young women and girls in our schools. Those adults who will be working with children and adolescents in schools must fully explore their own views and become exposed to the ways in which biased views are harmful to the healthy development of students. For example, as we found in this research, many teachers fail to recognize the sexual harassment of their African American female students. As the teachers in this study revealed their biased notions, holding to ideas like, 'that's just how they are,' allows teachers to fail to see girls were actually experiencing harassment at the hands of male students. We argue that exposing pre-service school personnel to sensitivity regarding these issues will help to eliminate the gross ignorance surrounding perceptions of the sexual harassment of women of color. Further, as the research in this book reveals, school personnel from both rural and urban settings can benefit from examining issues involving social class more in depth. The assumptions that were revealed throughout this text with regard to social class paint a disturbing picture of how particular students and families are marginalized with schools. We believe that in creating a more sensitive and unbiased school workforce, we can make strides in eradicating harassment. It is extremely important that the education and training on sexual harassment for school personnel not end as teachers enter the workforce.

Ongoing examination of harassment in schools is an important component to ending sexual harassment. This ongoing professional development, as Brandenburg (1997) points out, should be provided to *all* members of the school community, this would include anyone who works in the school building, including janitors, teachers, administrators, cafeteria works, coaches, nurses, and counselors. Providing such a whole scale education would ensure that the climate of harassment is addressed throughout the entire school, as we recognize and has been found in this research, harassment exists in all areas of the school building and its grounds, consider the participants accounts of harassment on school buses and in hallways. Adults, throughout the campus, on buses, and attending school related functions should be knowledgeable about information regarding the harassment of students if we wish to truly make a difference. Additionally, as part of the ongoing attention on eradicating sexual harassment, Brandenburg points out, surveys/focus groups should be developed to determine and monitor prevalence of sexual harassment. It is not enough to hear from the teachers. As we have discovered from this research, teachers often claim to not see harassment, yet students' accounts depict a very different story, with sexual harassment being 'common.' It is necessary that students' perspectives be identified and their perceptions of harassment be examined with school. Developing and administering surveys to students periodically would allow personnel to develop contemporary strategies for addressing harassment.

Secondly, with respect to education, we assert there is a need for a reconceptualization regarding approaches to sexuality and sexual education in the schools. As the participants in our study noted, there are very few meaningful experiences students have with sexual education in schools. Sexual education, according to most of our students, existed within the delivery of one or two courses in middle and or high school, and in many cases, students were only provided sexual education in a span of a week or two. The content, according to the young men and women, was largely an abstinence only message that did not reflect the realities of their lives. In other words, as popular media encourages adolescents to have sex and engage in sexually experimental behavior, schools and religious institutions are condemning them for this behavior. Sexual education which is proscriptive, and plagued with messages of consequences and punishment, fails to address the real issues that adolescents face, and as the participants in this book point out, is largely ineffectual and largely ignored by students. A sexuality curriculum which is inclusive (not just predicated on a heteronormative construct), balanced (we recognize that kids need information regarding contraception and disease), non-sexist (recognizes that young women also have desire that should not be viewed as deviant), and relevant (addressing contemporary issues that students face), is how we would like to see sexuality and sexual education contextualized.

We also argue that *all* students should be engaging in sexuality education; it should not be limited to 'vocational track' students, (in an effort to discourage their reproduction). All students need access to sexuality curriculum that addresses sexism, racism, classism and ableism directly.Finally, within the sexuality curriculum, there should be explicit education regarding sexual harassment, not from the punitive, 'we will write you up' position, but rather a sensitive, thoughtful presentation of harassment and its consequences for the harassed and those who witness it. We argue that young men need more opportunity to be exposed to the experiences of young women. Just as we argue pre-service and in service school personnel need more exposure to issues of harassment and the experiences of marginalized groups, so too do students. We would argue for a curriculum that allows for voices of those marginalized by race, class, gender, sexuality, and ability to be presented in the sexual education curriculum (Carlson & Roseboro, 2011). We contend that important to disrupting sexism and classism and racism is exposing it and that can be done through offering the experiences of those victimized by it to be examined. We as educators should work to develop more empathetic youth and we can do this by developing curriculum (in this case sexuality curriculum) that provides exposure to a variety of social experiences.

We also recognize that an important feature of sexuality education is an opportunity for students to examine, deconstruct, articulate, the various messages that bombard their daily lives. We further contend that students should have the opportunity within the important social, cultural venue of school to participate in critical media literacy (Keller & Share, 2009; Brown, 2000). We noted throughout this book the important influence that media has on students' lives; we recognize that the interaction with that media does not stop at the doors of the school, therefore, it is important that students have opportunities to critically examine and deconstruct meanings embedded within media. And in the context of sexuality education, critical media literacy is even more meaningful. There are so many pervading messages regarding sexuality that today's youth have mediate. As Johansson writes, "While boundaries, distinctions and moral norms are disintegrating in the media world, we can sometimes see in the everyday life that a repressive normative of sexuality has gained a foothold" (2007, p. 12). We argue that a sexuality curriculum that encourages student voice can help students mediate some of these conflicts they face. Consider the number of participants in all of our studies who mentioned the felt like they had no one to discuss these issues with.

We would argue that within the curriculum of sexuality education, students should have opportunities to *discuss* the portrayal of female sexuality/male sexuality, the pressures to *perform* gender and/or sexuality, issues such as Durham (2008) points out, such as the new "hooker-chic fashion" and media portrayal of young females. She argues, "Boys are in the relatively comfortable position of observing and evaluating without themselves being observed or evaluated. And girls are bombarded with the myth that semi-nudity constitutes girl power" (p. 80). We suggest that discourse, generated by students, concerning their mediation of media imagery is important for addressing how this imagery impacts their understanding of harassment and contributes to sexist attitudes.

School Practice

As we mentioned above, we recognize that addressing sexual harassment is a complex issue that involves layers of efforts. In the introduction to this book, we noted the development of sexual harassment policy has dated back to the 1980s. Most schools have in place an articulated policy regarding sexual harassment (Stein, 1995; Bradenburg, 1997). However, those policies, we would argue, have not been revisited often enough, and do not contain information addressing some of the more contemporary forms of sexual harassment such as cyber-sexual harassment that has presented itself in youth culture. Additionally, we argue, many in the schools (parents, teachers, and students) do not know about these policies, and implementation is spotty and inconsistent. As many of the student participants in our studies recalled, there were brief references made to the student code of conduct regarding sexual harassment, but outside of that, little discussion on it actually took place. Additionally, we argue that with teachers turning a blind eye to the harassment they witness in the building, the policy that is in place is being blatantly ignored and thus serves no real purpose. We urge schools to revisit their policies, reword them to match the contemporary forms of harassment, have them have a more prevalent placement within the school (not relegated to a blurb in a code of conduct manual), and have opportunities to discuss those policies and their implications with *all* school constituents.

Lastly, we believe that a very important piece of developing healthy school curricula and safe environments for all students free of harassment, ridicule and violence involves the extremely important role of guidance counselors. We are saddened by the current climate of schools which is so driven by test results, that the affective needs of students are largely ignored.

As the participants in our studies recounted, counselors within their buildings rarely addressed issues of social relevance, including the harassment of students. Consider the following comments from students:

(1) "I think that if there was more of an opportunity to talk to somebody to say this is what is going on. That would help." (Jocelyn)

(2) "I think (young women today) need sex education and a counselor. Like in my school, we did not have a counselor, so if you had a problem, you just had a problem, because some girls need someone outside the home to talk to and say, "OK, this is not right, this is right" and a counselor has first hand view cause they are in the schools." (Kia)

(3) "We had guidance counselors, but that was more for the education part, and they were crap too, they didn't help at all." (Sheila)

(4) "Education is a good idea; I don't think any of my peers have a good, clear understanding of what sexual harassment is." (Tricia)

(5) "Our counselors, for the most part, sucked. They lived in their little enclaves and you needed to do a bunch of passing and have a perfect dress code and do all sorts of crap if you wanted to get in to talk with them, so I figured the best way of dealing with the counselors was never, never speak to them. I was in the advanced kids program, we had our own special counselor, but she just mostly came in to go through and talk to us about college crap." (Mike)

We recognize that teachers are pressured to have students perform on standardized tests, and that it leaves them little time to address issues such as harassment with the school building. However, we are also very deeply saddened that the roles of school counselors have changed so dramatically that many counselors are now tasked with issues regarding testing, they too find themselves with no time to address emotional issues that plague students, such as harassment (Brown, Galassi, & Akos, 2009). We argue that it is imperative that a strong counseling program be part of each school program. Students need persons within the school that are trained to help them mediate the terrain of adolescence. Focus groups, peer counselors, biblio-therapy, critical literacy programs, all can be put in place in middle and high schools to address issues of relevance to students' lives, including harassment, violence and abuse. However, there must be personnel, such as counselors who can direct these programs. We believe programs, such as advisor-advisee, in which students have opportunities to engage in discussions surrounding issues faced by youth culture, will have tremendous impact on the overall culture of school. Otherwise, students will continue to harass and be harassed daily within school buildings with little opportunity to eradicate the sexist attitudes and behaviors on which this harassment is predicated.

Finally, we offer that in order to fully address sexism and its consequence, sexual harassment in schools, much more research is needed. We suggest more research is needed making the connections between harassment and bullying based on sexual orientation directly to *sexism*. (This was not a direct focus of our work in this book, but certainly the threads of this connection are here, and have emerged from our study.) We believe that the practice of harassment as a consequence of sexism should be explored in all aspects of women's lives. In their educational experience from primary grades through higher education institutions, in their social lives, in their dating relationships, familial and religious interactions, as well as their vocational experiences, women experience harassment, therefore, it is important to continue to examine the forms harassment takes to reinvigorate the discourse on harassment and sexism.

While the findings in this book indicate that sexism and sexual harassment continues to plague young women (and men) in contemporary schools, we do believe that there are ways that this harassment can be addressed. A more relevant education, including directly addressing sexism, racism, classism, and ableism, for students and the adults in their lives, a more comprehensive and thoughtful approach to addressing sexual harassment in schools, and providing adults within the school building working to explicitly meet the affective needs of students provides opportunities to truly make progress in eradicating the pervasive vulnerabilities of young women.

References

Banjoko, A. (2011). Adolescent African American Males and Hegemonic Aggressive Masculinity. In D. Carlson & D. Roseboro (Eds.) *The Sexuality Curriculum and Youth Culture.* Peter Lang: New York. Pp. 136–148.

Brandenburg, J. (1997). *Confronting Sexual Harassment: What Schools and Colleges Can Do.* Teachers College Press: New York.

Brown, D., Galassi, J., & Akos, D.. (2004) School Counselors' Perceptions of the Impact of High Stakes Testing. *ASCA: Professional School Counselor,* 8(1), 31–39.

Brown, J. (2000). Adolescents' Sexual Media Diets. *Journal of Adolescent Health,* 27(2), 35–40.

Delgado, R., & Stefancic, J., Eds. (2000). *Critical Race Theory: The Cutting Edge*. Temple University Press: Philadelphia.

Durham, M.G., (2008). *The Lolita Effect: Media Sexualization of Young Girls and What We Can Do about It*. Overlook Hardcover. Woodstock, New York.

Fausto-Sterling, A. (2000). *Sexing the Body: Gender Politics and the Construction of Sexuality*. Basic Books: New York.

Fine, M., & McClelland, S. (2006). Sexuality Education and Desire: Still Missing after All These Years. *Harvard Educational Review*, 76(3), 297–338.

Hill-Collins, P. (2009). Mammies, Matriarchs, and Other Controlling Images. In P. Hill-Collins (Ed.) *Black Feminist Thought: Knowledge, Consciousness, and the Politics of Empowerment*: Routlege: New York.

Johannson, T. (2007). *The Transformation of Sexuality: Gender & Identity in Contemporary Youth Culture*. Ashgate Publishing: Burlington, VT.

Keller, D., & Share, J. (2009). Critical Media Literacy Is Not an Option. *Learning Inquiry*, 1(1), 59–69.

Kenway, J., & Fitzclarence, L. (1997). Masculinity, Violence, and Schooling: Challenging 'Poisonous Pedagogies'. *Gender and Education*, 9(1), 117–134.

Madson, L., & Shoda, J. (2002). Identifying Sexual Harassment: A Classroom Activity. *Teaching of Psychology*, 29(4), 304–307.

Miller, J. (2008). *Getting Played: African American Girls, Urban Inequality, and Gendered Violence*. New York University Press: New York.

Pascoe, C.J. (2007). *Dude! You're a Fag: Masculinity and Sexuality in High School*. University of California Press: Berkeley.

Robinson, K. (2005). Reinforcing Hegemonic Masculinities through Sexual Harassment: Issues of Identity, Power and Popularity in Secondary Schools. *Gender and Education*, 17(1), 19–37.

Shakeshaft, C., & Cohen, A. (1995). Sexual Abuse of Students by School Personnel. *Phi Delta Kappan*, 76(7), 513–520.

Stein, N. (2003). Bullying or Sexual Harassment? The Missing Discourse of Rights in an Era of Zero Tolerance. *Arizona Law Review*, 45, 783–799.

Timmerman, G. (2002). A Comparison between Unwanted Sexual Behavior by Teachers and by Peers in Secondary Schools. *Journal of Youth & Adolescence,* 31(5), 397. Retrieved from http://search.ebscohost.com/login.aspx?direct=true&db=a9h&AN=6923155&site=ehost-live.

Winters, J., Clift, R., & Maloney, A. (2004). Adult-Student Sexual Harassment in British Columbia High Schools. *Journal of Emotional Abuse*, 4(3/4), 177–196.

Younger, B. (2009). *Learning Curves: Body Image and Female Sexuality in Young Adult* Literature. Scarecrow Press: Lanham, MD.

Appendix A

Participants/Contextualization

Participant	Interview Set	Sex /Age	Race/ Sex Orientation	Findings	Other
Tonya	Adult Women	F/27	White/ Heterosexual	Rape and Abuse Domestic Violence Social isolation Rejected by family Christian Upbringing	
Pepsi	Adult Women	F/35	Black/ Heterosexual	Prostitution Dropped Out of HS Christian Upbringing Sex Abuse as child	
Tammy	Adult Women	F/34	Black/ Heterosexual	Christian Upbringing Domestic Violence	
Shayanne	Adult Women	F/25	Hispanic/ Bisexual	Catholic Dropped out of HS Difficulty conforming to white ideals of beauty Social isolation	
Deanne	Adult Women	F/27	White/ Heterosexual	Double Standard, girls don't carry condoms	
Camille	Adult Women	F/26	Black/ Heterosexual	Christian Upbringing Romantic narrative Lack of discussion of female desire Abuse, Sexual abuse as child Social isolation	

Participant	Interview Set	Sex /Age	Race/ Sex Orientation	Findings	Other
Jocelyn	Adult Women	F/ 25	White/ Heterosexual	Christian Up-bringing Domestic violence Social Isolation	
Joanne	Adult Women	F/30	Black/ Heterosexual	Dropped out of HS Athletes immune to punishment Domestic violence	
Kathryn	Adult Women	F/25	White/ Heterosexual	Christian Up-bringing Demonstrates that any girl could be labeled	
Lee	Adult Women	F/27	Jewish/ Heterosexual	Labeled by hanging out with the wrong crowd/ metal heads Social isolation	
Heather	Adult Women	F/32	White/ Heterosexual	Sexual double standard Social isolation	
Kesha	Adult Women	F/25	Black/ Heterosexual	Dropped out of HS Domestic Violence	
Kia	Young Women	F/18-20	Black/ Heterosexual	Pervasiveness of SH Pregnancy increases harassment Dress sexy but don't appear sexual Lack of ineffective teacher response Counselors focus on tests Sex ed provided in lower tracks	

Participant	Interview Set	Sex /Age	Race/ Sex Orientation	Findings	Other
Sheila	Young Women	F/18-20	Black-white mixed/ Heterosexual	Romantic narrative Pervasiveness of SH Sexual double standard Sexual abuse, grandfather Sex ed is for general track Counselors don't help	
Tricia	Young Women	F/18-20	Black /Heterosexual	Pervasiveness of SH Ineffective teacher response Sexual double standard Dress/act sexy but don't appear sexual	
Kasey	Young Women	F/18-20	White/ Heterosexual	Pervasiveness of SH Dress/act sexy but don't appear sexual Dressed like a boy to avoid appearing sexual Romantic narrative Missing discourse of desire	
Colleen	Young Women	F/18-20	White/ Heterosexual	Pervasiveness of SH Lack of ineffective teacher response Dress/act sexy but don't appear sexual	

Participant	Interview Set	Sex /Age	Race/ Sex Orientation	Findings	Other
Cassandra	Young Women	F/18-20	Black/ Heterosexual	Lower SES Pervasiveness of SH Lack of ineffective teacher response Athletes immune to punishment "Just keep walking", response	
Kelsie	Young Women	F/18-20	White/ Heterosexual	Pervasiveness of SH Gatekeeper role Sexual Double Standard Missing discourse of desire	
Morgie	Young Women	F/18-20	Biracial/ Heterosexual	Pervasiveness of SH SH by Adults at school Lack of /ineffective teacher response Lack of sex ed in school	
Miranda	Young Women	F/18-20	White/ Heterosexual	Pervasiveness of SH Lack of ineffective teacher response Even gang rape blamed on girl, males not responsible	
Ariel	Young Women	F/18-20	Black/ Heterosexual	Pervasiveness of SH Lack of ineffective teacher response Missing discourse of desire	

Participant	Interview Set	Sex /Age	Race/ Sex Orientation	Findings	Other
Dominique	Young Women	F/18-20	Black/ Heterosexual	Pervasiveness of SH Lack of /ineffective teacher response Laugh it off, ignore it	
Raven	Young Women	F/18-20	White/ Heterosexual	Sexual double standard Lack of /ineffective teacher response Romantic Narrative Sexual abuse by older cousin	
Wayne	Young Men	M/19-20	White/ Heterosexual	Subjectivity of SH Fear of reprisal AP kids don't need Sex ed Lack of /ineffective teacher response Male principals and teachers participate in SH Joking around Pervasiveness of SH Race and class difference in SH, "untouchables" "over-sexed"	Christian
Steven	Young Men	M/19-20	White/ Heterosexual	Subjectivity of SH Race and class difference in SH, "untouchables" "over-sexed" Pervasiveness of SH Lack of /ineffective teacher response Joking around Sex orientation harassment No formal sex ed in school	Christian

Participant	Interview Set	Sex /Age	Race/ Sex Orientation	Findings	Other
James	Young Men	M/19-20	White/ Heterosexual	Girls as gatekeepers Pervasiveness of SH Class difference in SH, "untouch-ables" "over-sexed" "fair game" "Aber-crombie" Sex orientation harassment	
Elijah	Young Men	M/19-20	Black/ Het-erosexual	Missing Dis-course of desire Sexual double standard Fear of reprisal Pervasiveness of SH Joking around Lack of /ineffective teacher response Seeking male approval Establishing male dominance	Christian?
Ben	Young Men	M/19-20	Asian/ Heterosexual	Subjectivity of SH Pervasiveness of SH Class/Track dif-ference in SH	
Joseph	Young Men	M/19-20	White/ Heterosexual	Subjectivity of SH Sexual double standard Girls as gatekeepers Pervasiveness of SH Lack/ineffective teacher response Joking around Sex orientation harassment	Christian

Participant	Interview Set	Sex /Age	Race/ Sex Orientation	Findings	Other
Shawn	Young Men	M/19-20	White/ Heterosexual	Not much sex ed in school Didn't see harassment Lots of butt grabbing Joking around Sex orientation harassment	
Mike	Young Men	M/19-20	White/ No response	Fear of reprisal Seeking male approval Establishing male dominance Peer pressure on males to be sexual Race and Class difference in SH, "untouchables" "over-sexed" "fair game" Lack/ineffective teacher response Pervasiveness of SH (grope fest in hallways)	
Ian	Young Men	M/19-20	White/ Homosexual	Tied SH to hegemonic masculinity Peer pressure on males to be sexual Subjectivity of SH Girls laugh it off Lack/ineffective teacher response Sex orientation harassment Race and class differences	

Participant	Interview Set	Sex /Age	Race/ Sex Orientation	Findings	Other
Sam	Young Men	M/19-20	Black/ Bisexual	Pervasiveness of SH Definition focused on physical violence Lack/ineffective teacher response	
Ryan	Young Men	M/19-20	White/ Homosexual	Pervasiveness of SH Joking around Grabbing butts has become standard Male teachers participated in SH of young girls Sex orientation harassment Lack/ineffective teacher response	
Christopher	Young Men	M/19-20	Hispanic/ Homosexual	Compliments Joking around Pervasiveness of SH Lack/ineffective teacher response Part of the culture	
David	Young Men	M/19-20	White/ Homosexual	Seeking male approval Establishing male dominance Pervasiveness of SH Sex orientation harassment	
Catherine	Teachers	F/1yr	White, Heterosexual	Women can have autonomous desire Sexual name calling frequent SH same % girls as boys BET emphasizes being sexy	Largely black school

Participant	Interview Set	Sex /Age	Race/ Sex Orientation	Findings	Other
Jane	Teachers	F/50s	White, Heterosexual	Poverty, welfare, single-parent families BET is culprit Students who aren't like her Girls as gatekeepers Girls responsible for boys behaviors Sex orientation harassment, remove boy	Urban school setting
Ali	Teachers	F/50s	White, Heterosexual	(Black, poor) teaches it's ok to get pregnant Whole family being undermined	Urban school setting
Melissa	Teachers	F/50s	White, heterosexual	Girls dress too provocative Girls to blame Self proclaimed conservative views	Urban school setting
Louise	Teachers	F/40s	Black, Heterosexual	Guarding reputation very important for girls Boys will be boys	Urban school setting
Sonja	Teachers	F/30s	White, Heterosexual	Boys will be boys Boys can't control themselves when girls dress sexy Girls' sexual aggression should be countered with aggression from school	Rural school setting
Dana	Teachers	F/30s	White, Heterosexual	Concern for bi-sexuality as corrupting girls	Rural school setting

Participant	Interview Set	Sex /Age	Race/ Sex Orientation	Findings	Other
Caroline	Teachers	F/40s	White, Heterosexual	Black kids more overtly sexual	Rural school setting
Rhonda	Teachers	F/50s	White, Heterosexual	Black kids blatantly sexual Depiction of welfare families	Rural school setting
Judy	Teachers	F/50s	White, Heterosexual	Blame girls dress on male reactions Boys will be boys	Rural school setting
Rachel	Teachers	F/20s	White, Heterosexual	Black kids blatantly sexual Welfare families	Rural school setting